What Do Presbyterians Believe?

The Westminster Confession: Yesterday and Today

GORDON H. CLARK

With an Introduction by
John R. Richardson, D.D.

Presbyterian and Reformed Publishing Company
Phillipsburg, New Jersey

Copyright © 1956, 1965
Presbyterian and Reformed Publishing Company

All rights reserved. No part of this book may be reproduced in any form or by any
means, except for brief quotations for the purpose of review, comment, or scholarship,
without written permission from the publisher, Presbyterian and Reformed Publishing
Company, Box 817, Phillipsburg, New Jersey 08865.

Printed in the United States of America

ISBN: 0-87552-140-1

Library of Congress Catalog Card Number: 65-27481

PREFACE TO THE REVISED EDITION

The Westminster Confession, along with the Shorter and Larger Catechisms, has served as the doctrinal standard of all Presbyterian bodies since 1650. There are about eight Presbyterian denominations in this country at the present time. This very spring, May 1965, an event of major significance in church history occurred: the United Presbyterian Church in the United States of America, the largest of these eight denominations, by a five to one vote, took the initial step in a process to repudiate the Confession and substitute for it a new creed of vastly different content.

Whereas the Westminster Confession is based entirely on the Scripture, and in its first chapter and elsewhere asserts the infallibility of the Word of God, no such allegiance to the Bible is found in the new creed. Of course the United Presbyterian Church in the United States of America has for thirty years disregarded the authority of the Bible in its practice. In 1924 some 1300 of its ministers signed and circulated the Auburn Affirmation, a document that denied the infallibility of Scripture and asserted that the Virgin Birth, the miracles of Christ, his Atonement, and Resurrection were unessential. Regardless of what a minister believed or disbelieved on these matters, his good standing was not to be called in question and he was to be received with all confidence and fellowship. By 1936 the signers of the Auburn Affirmation showed that they had captured the church by reorganizing Princeton Seminary and placing one of the signers on its governing board, by electing one of their number Moderator of the General Assembly and, what was decisive, by excommunicating those ministers who had insisted on maintaining the Westminster standards in practice. Thus ministers who rejected the Scripture and all it contains were given authority, while men who believed the Bible and all it contains were ejected as disturbers of the peace. Since that day the Westminster Confession has been a dead letter in that denomination, and now the process to drop it officially has begun.

What then does the new creed teach? Well, obviously it does not teach the Virgin Birth, the Atonement, or the Resurrection. Indeed there is virtually nothing retained from the Westminster Confession. Predestination, original sin, total depravity, the mediatorial work of

Christ, effectual calling, irresistible grace, the perseverance of the saints, the return of our Lord, the reality of hell and even the hope of heaven are all missing.

What doctrinal standards then, does the new creed erect and impose? The answer is none. In the action of the General Assembly of 1965 no doctrinal commitment is envisaged at all. This is taken care of in the formula of subscription. In fact, the Westminster Confession could have been completely rejected without changing a word of it and without substituting anything. What the minister accepts is defined by the terms of his subscription. The Reformed Church in France has a fairly good creed, in many details similar to the Westminster Confession. But the ministers subscribe to it only as a statement of what the church used to believe. The minister does not say he himself believes it, nor does he engage to hold the church to its theology. Similarly the subscription now proposed, and in its first offical test accepted by a five to one vote, does not commit the minister to any definite theological position, not even to the vague meaningless phraseology of the new creed itself.

What then DO Presbyterians believe? Well, if the present proposal passes all the legal steps of the procedure, it can be said that the United Presbyterian Church in the United States of America will not believe anything. Just nothing at all.

But if it is asked, What do PRESBYTERIANS believe, the answer will always be, the Bible and its most excellent summary, the Westminster Confession.

The origin of this study is described in the Preface to the first edition, published under title, *What Presbyterians Believe,* in 1956. This revision includes the text of the Westminster Confession and too many other changes to be mentioned here.

Study groups are advised, requested, entreated, beseeched, implored, begged, and urged to read the Confession and to study the references in the Bible before, during, and after their discussion of this commentary.

G.H.C.

September 1965

It is hard to believe, though it is quite true, that the above was written a full twenty years ago. *Tempus fugits* at a remarkable rate.

That makes it reasonable to add just a couple of short paragraphs on these past twenty years.

First, the accusation that the ordinands from 1936 to 1967 committed perjury in their ordination vows finally got under the skin of the higher officials. Their action, adopted by the General Assembly of 1967, removed the Westminster Confession, along with some other creeds to keep it company, to a dusty shelf of bygone standards. From then on no candidate for the ministry was required to accept the Confession as "the system of doctrine contained in the Holy Scriptures."

In the eighties, to reply to some muted criticism, the General Assembly declared its belief in the resurrection of Christ. An amendment had been offered, changing the phrase to "the bodily resurrection of Christ." This amendment was decisively defeated. About the same time a minister publicly denied the deity of Christ. No remedial action was ever taken. How can any situation be more clearcut?

G.H.C.

PREFACE

During the winter of 1954-1955 there appeared in *The Southern Presbyterian Journal* a series of articles on the Westminster Confession. They were so well received that it was decided to republish them in book form.

However, the original articles, since they were intended to be altogether popular, made no pretense of covering the whole Confession in the manner of a commentary. It has been thought wise therefore to add a second section to each chapter so that the book might serve the purposes of study classes and discussion groups. Even so, it is still not a formal commentary.

There have been times in the history of God's people, for example, in the days of Jeremiah, when refreshing grace and widespread revival were not to be expected: the time was one of chastisement. If this twentieth century is of a similar nature, individual Christians here and there can find comfort and strength in a study of God's Word. But if God has decreed happier days for us and if we may expect a world-shaking and genuine spiritual awakening, then it is the author's belief that a zeal for souls, however necessary, is not the sufficient condition. Have there not been devout saints in every age, numerous enough to carry on a revival? Twelve such persons are plenty. What distinguishes the arid ages from the period of the Reformation, when nations were moved as they had not been since Paul preached in Ephesus, Corinth, and Rome, is the latter's fullness of knowledge of God's Word. To echo an early Reformation thought, when the ploughman and the garage attendant know the Bible as well as the theologian does, and know it better than some contemporary theologians, then the desired awakening shall have already occurred. To such an end this book is dedicated as a minor means.

G.H.C.

CONTENTS

INTRODUCTION

The Westminster Assembly convened in Westminster Abbey in London on July 1, 1643. This body engaged in honest and thoughtful activity for five years, six months, and twenty-two days. Thoroughness is conspicuous in all of its work. Church historians agree that this was one of the most learned bodies ever assembled on this earth for the formulation and promulgation of Christian truth. The personnel of this body was composed of the intellectual cream of the British Isles. Every member was carefully selected on the basis of learning and intellectual gifts.

This group of divines was characterized also by deep and genuine spirituality. These men were spiritual giants. For the full period of their labors it was their custom to set aside one entire day of each month for prayer and fasting. The men who composed this assembly were, therefore, prepared intellectually and spiritually for their task.

In our day of renewed interest in Biblical theology it is well to remember that the primary rule these servants of Christ laid down for themselves, to guide in all their discussions, was: "What any man undertakes to prove as necessary, he shall make good out of Scripture." Every member was required to take the following vow, and it was read to all of the members every Monday morning: "I do seriously promise and vow, in the presence of Almighty God, that in this Assembly whereof I am a member, I will maintain nothing in point of doctrine but what I believe to be most agreeable to the Word of God; nor in point of discipline, but what may make most for God's glory and the peace and good of His church."

Present in this body of men were some of the most brilliant of contemporary philosophers, but they permitted not one iota of human philosophy to influence their creedal statements. Their sole objective was to think Biblically and to express the mind of Scripture. The success of this undertaking is evidenced in the fact that although better than three centuries have passed since the publication of this work, the Confession of Faith has needed no significant change during all this time.

Richard Baxter, a contemporary of the Westminster divines, wrote in his autobiography an evaluation of this assembly. He affirmed: "The Divines there congregated were men of eminent learning, godliness, ministerial abilities, and fidelity; and being not worthy to be one of them myself, I may the more speak the truth, even in the face of malice and envy, that, as far as I am able to judge by the information of all history of that time, and by any other evidence left us, the Christian world, since the days of the apostles, had never a Synod of more excellent divines (taking one thing with another), than this and the Synod of Dort." Dean Stanley of the Anglican church declared that of all Protestant Confessions the Westminster Confession exhibits "far more depth of theological insight than any other."

Fair-minded scholars must concede that the goal that the Westminster Assembly kept before it of giving "to the accepted Bible system of truth a complete, impregnable statement, to serve as a bulwark against error, as a basis of ecclesiastical fellowship and cooperation, and as a safe and effectual instrument for the religious instruction of the people of God and their children," has been attained in a marvelous way. Judged by any sensible standard the Westminster Assembly ranks among the greatest of the ecclesiastical assemblies or councils in the entire history of Christianity.

During the past three decades many Presbyterians have ignored or failed to appreciate the wealth of Christian truth found in the Westminster Confession of Faith, the official creed of Presbyterianism. The result is, the Calvinistic system means little to them. This neglect of our inheritance has proved expensive to our Church. It is a source of weakness. Many who wear the label "Presbyterian" are destitute of knowledge and respect for this classical creedal statement of the Church.

About a year ago Dr. Gordon H. Clark, a front-line philosopher and a brilliant theologian, published in *The Southern Presbyterian Journal* a series of articles on the Confession of Faith. These studies were characterized by remarkable originality and lucidity. The spirit of his articles was affirmative and constructive. His purpose at all times has been to explain, and not explain away, the difficult portions of the Christian message. Each chapter presents a wealth of penetrating insights.

One of the presuppositions of the Confession of Faith was that the way to organize a group of ideas consistently is to put them in a systematic form. In this book Dr. Clark has taken the finest theological concepts expressed in systematic form in the Confession of Faith, and shown to us their relevance to the Church in the instruction of twentieth century Christians. It is obvious to every mature reader of this volume that in Dr. Clark's thinking there can be no real conflict between true philosophy and the revealed truth. The author demonstrates that the Christian's beliefs are not opposed to logic and Christians must employ it in their teaching. He avoids the snares of both rationalism and irrationalism.

We find in this volume the answers to the questions that thoughtful people are asking inside the church. There is a system of doctrine taught in the Bible, and Calvinism is this true system. This system provides the answers we need. This book is a real boon to all who are engaged in the teaching function of Christianity. It is adapted to high school groups, young adults, and older adults, who face daily the anti-Christian paganism in the modern world.

It is my conviction that our Church for a long time has been desiring a practical book of this kind on the Confession of Faith. I predict that thoughtful pastors and sessions will use extensively this work for group study. If Presbyterians are to be "workmen that needeth not to be ashamed," this book should be earnestly promoted in all Presbyterian circles.

Our church members seek guidance in matters pertaining to the Christian faith and life attitudes. This book shows the bewildered person of today where his salvation lies. Here we see that our salvation lies in placing ourselves under the sovereign and gracious rule of Christ, and not in the cheap schemes of auto-salvation so popular today. Dr. Clark has succeeded in making our Calvinistic heritage understandable to thoughtful minds, and in convincing us that no other theological school has yet been able to present to us a better system for our acceptance than the one we have in the Westminster Confession of Faith.

JOHN R. RICHARDSON, D.D.
Pastor of Westminster Presbyterian Church
Atlanta, Georgia

April 1, 1956

CONCERNING CREEDS

If you were asked what you believed, what would you say? Perhaps you already have had a conversation with a friend who asked you this question. What did you say? Do you think you made an adequate reply? Could you now write out a statement of your faith? Could you tell someone what he needs to know in order to be saved, to live a Christian life, to grow into a mature Christian? Then there is something more difficult. Could you compose a document to serve as a platform for an entire denomination? Before studying this book, maybe you should first write your own creed. You could at least begin by repeating a few phrases of the Apostles' Creed, couldn't you?

On a certain occasion I gave a series of theological lectures for the congregation of a brother minister. After the service one evening when most of the people had gone home, a woman and the pastor remained for conversation. Going beyond the limits of the lecture I continued by arguing that the phrase, "He descended into hell," might well be omitted from the Apostles' Creed. True, I had no conscientious reason for not using it, for Christ did indeed suffer the pains of hell for our redemption. But because of the real danger of fanciful interpretations of I Peter 3:19, I thought the omission might be wise. The woman resisted this line of argument with a determination that at first puzzled me. I finally came to understand when she very politely undertook to give me a gentle rebuke. When a group of the most learned and devout Christian scholars, she said, give careful consideration to the formulation of a Creed, it borders on rashness to attempt alterations.

The woman's statement is highly commendable, particularly in the present century when creeds are held in little honor. But unfortunately this woman did not know that the Apostles' Creed was not the result of learned discussions, as was the Nicene Creed, and that from the earliest times to the present it has been recited in

1

different forms. On this point the woman was unfortunately ignorant.

To most people such ignorance will appear to be a matter of little importance. It will not cause the woman to lead an evil life; there is little danger that she will come to believe in purgatory; and even if she entertains fanciful interpretations of I Peter 3:19, what harm will it do?

Now it must be granted that the illustration gives a rather minor instance of ignorance. It is hard to imagine any great harm resulting from the lack of this one piece of information. On the other hand, do we not all admit that in general ignorance is undesirable? And is it not possible that the lack of several pieces of information, even if each by itself is minor, could result in a moderate amount of harm?

In the early years of the Christian church, several men of exemplary devotion wrote out statements of what they believed. In addition to the Apostles' Creed, which like Topsy just growed, creeds were written by Ignatius of Antioch (A.D. 107), Irenaeus (A.D. 180), Tertullian (A.D. 200), Cyprian of Carthage (A.D. 250), Novatian of Rome (A.D. 250), and several others.

Let us choose another illustration. Not long after the conversation with that woman, I was studying the relation of the church to the state. It is an important problem. Now, of course, I am not as other men, or even as this ignorant woman; I study twice in the week, and give attention to all the books I possess; and this I have done from my youth up. But when I read *Aaron's Rod Blossoming* by George Gillespie, and some other works by that remarkable young man, I could only lower my eyes from heaven to earth, smite on my breast, and cry, God be merciful to me an ignoramus.

All these creeds were very short, running from less than one hundred to about two hundred words. Ignatius briefly mentioned the Davidic ancestry of Christ, his virgin birth, his crucifixion, resurrection, and ascension, and that is about all. Irenaeus also mentioned God's creation of the world and Christ's second advent. Cyprian, however, was extremely brief. He wrote simply, "I believe in God the Father, in his Son Christ, in the Holy Ghost. I

2

believe in the forgiveness of sins and eternal life through the holy Church."

These short creeds no doubt express deep Christian devotion. But can they serve as the official position for a large church? Are two hundred words adequate for a summary of what the Bible teaches? Suppose a minister never preached on any subject other than those mentioned in these creeds: would the congregation be well instructed? It would seem not. These short creeds say nothing about the Trinity, nothing about the Person of Christ, nothing about the plan of salvation. Therefore as time went on, the leaders of the Church saw the necessity of writing more adequate statements of faith. Thus in A.D. 325 the Nicene Creed was adopted and in A.D. 451 the Creed of Chalcedon.

Soon thereafter, for various reasons, the universal church fell into the abyss of Romish ignorance and superstition. The Bible was forgotten for a thousand years. But like the stock market, church history has its peaks as well as its depressions. In the sixteenth century there came a great discovery of the truth of God.

At an astounding rate new knowledge of the divine revelation was discovered by the leaders and taught to the populace. The culmination of those times of refreshing is enshrined in the Westminster Confession. But since then there has been a fairly steady process of forgetting. What in that day was a compendium for children, the Shorter Catechism, is today more than ample for a seminary graduate requesting ordination of presbytery. In that day when an attempt was made to reintroduce Romish superstitions unto the church service, a plain parishioner, Mrs. Jenny Geddes, threw her stool at the minister, with appropriate remarks. Is there any twentieth century Jenny Geddes ready to throw her stool at some prominent neo-orthodox moderator? Does our present day Mrs. Geddes know what neo-orthodoxy is? For that matter, does she know what orthodoxy is?

From the time of the apostles to the present moment, there has been no revival of true religion remotely approaching the Protestant Reformation in power and scope. Why? What differentiated that century from the others? The conspicuous difference between that age and all others is the amount of Biblical information possessed by the Reformers. Even in the Middle Ages there must have been, and in modern times too there undoubtedly are, men of zeal, humility, and devotion. But the Reformers knew the Scripture in great detail and understood its implications. They took great pains to teach exactly what God had revealed. They could well repeat the words of the apostle, "I have not shunned to declare unto you all the counsel of God." Would not a rediscovery of this truth today produce results similar to those of the Reformation? And what survey of Biblical teaching is a better guide than the Westminster Confession?

Today many church leaders consider creeds as obstacles to ecumenical union. It would please such men to hand over the discussions of creedal differences to those impractical fuddy-duddies, the theologians, while they themselves made the important organizational arrangements by which the right people would get the prominent positions.

There are other more humble people who sincerely believe that the adoption of a creed is an act of ecclesiastical presumption. Therefore several denominations have no creed. They insist on believing nothing. Then there are others who regard creeds, not exactly as presumptious, but as unnecessary. This would be the attitude of those who, though their zeal is unquestioned, find creeds, and Paul's epistles, intellectually heavy.

An evangelist I once heard seems to be an instance of both these latter types. In his appeal to the unsaved he said that first they must repent, then they must have faith in Christ, and finally they must be born again. Since his denomination has no creed, no rule of his church forbids him to preach in this way. But had he been a Presbyterian, he would have been sailing under false colors, for I take it that no intelligent and honest Presbyterian would preach that faith and repentance precede regeneration.

However, it is to be feared that not all Presbyterians are both intelligent and honest. There are those who regard the Westminster Confession as a meaningless form to which lip service is paid at ordination. In the United Presbyterian Church in the U.S.A. (before 1958, the Presbyterian Church in the U.S.A.) on several occasions candidates for the ministry, when examined by presbytery, have doubted or denied the virgin birth, the resurrection, the existence of Satan and hell—not to mention effectual calling and the perseverance of saints—and yet the presbytery voted to ordain them, and they professed in words their adherence to the Confession they had just contradicted.

No one compels a young man to become a Presbyterian minister. It is a voluntary choice. Therefore honesty seems to require that he be loyal to the flag he has chosen; or rather that he choose a flag to which he can be conscientiously loyal. If he does not believe the Confession, why should he solemnly affirm that he does? Similarly, if an older minister changes his views and comes to disagree with his ordination vows, no one compels him to remain in the denomination. Rather honesty compels him to find a church with which he agrees. How can God be expected to bless perjury and hypocrisy in the pulpit?

The Westminster Confession was never intended to be either an empty form or an obstacle to church union. With the other Reformed creeds, the Thirty-nine Articles, the Heidelberg Catechism, the Canons of the Synod of Dort, it was a statement of what all the ministers earnestly believed and faithfully preached. These creeds were bonds of union, not causes of discord. Discord comes when men of opposing views subscribe to the same verbal formula. But the creeds were never intended to hide differences behind a veil of meaningless words. On the contrary, the year before St. Bartholomew's massacre Bishop Jewel of the Anglican church wrote to Peter Martyr on the continent, "As to matters of doctrine we do not differ from you by a nail's breadth."

This hearty agreement, not only among the delegates to the Westminster Assembly, but with the other faithful ministers in Britain and their brethren on the continent, contrasts sharply with the discord in the contemporary ecumenical movement. Modern ministers cannot agree on anything except the desirability of a gigantic organization.

It was otherwise in the sixteenth century. When the Reformers attempted to sweep away the immorality, the idolatry, and the superstition of the Roman church, their task was to discover precisely what the Bible taught. The creeds they wrote are their summaries of the main Biblical themes. And the culmination of this effort, benefiting by over a century of cooperative study, is the greatest of all the creeds, the Westminster Confession.

The creed then is a statement of what the church must teach. It is the flag the church flies. It states the purpose for which the church exists. Lip service to the creed is dishonest. Diminishing its message is unfaithfulness. Scripture says more than the creed says, and this more must be preached too; but the creed summarizes the most important Biblical teachings, and these must receive the emphasis.

The Bible is the Word of God, who cannot lie. When his truth is vigorously and fully proclaimed, we may expect his blessing upon it.

More recently some attempts have been made to honor the creeds. These attempts mention the amount of labor expended in the writing of them. Their authors are recognized as having been sincere and capable. The documents themselves are said to be worth studying. Yet this apparent deference to the creeds is somewhat equivocal. Though the authors were sincere and capable, they are said to have been so blinded by sixteenth century ideas that they only dimly saw the kernel of truth and then enshrined the little they saw in a forbidding husk.

A modern scholar puts it as follows. "Doctrines," he says, "are not faith; they are statements of faith in propositional form."

One should immediately note that this remark applies not only to the creeds, but to the Bible as well, for after all, the Bible is written in sentences too.

The scholar continues with an illustration. "Faith has often been compared to a journey, or a pilgrimage. Doctrine may then be compared to a map. No one would suppose he had reached his destination merely because he had located it on the map, or traced the route that leads to it."[1]

This illustration is singularly misleading. Obviously a doctrine or a set of doctrines is not our ultimate destination, heaven. But it does not follow that doctrine is merely a map. If an illustration

1. George S. Hendry, *The Westminster Confession for Today*, p. 13; John Knox Press.

6

be needed, let us say that doctrine is the road itself. Here we can apply the words of Luke to the effect that doctrine, i.e., the propositions Luke wrote, is "a declaration of those things which are most surely believed among us."

In fact, this illustration of doctrine as a map is so inept that even when corrected so as to make doctrine the road, it remains misleading. After we arrive at a destination we not only throw away the map, we also have ceased using the road. But in heaven we shall continue to believe these doctrines. We shall continue to praise God by them and for them. They shall remain our precious possession forever.

If, now, you wished to do more than compose a short personal confession, if you wished to produce a document that would be useful in meeting many of the problems the Church faces, if you wished to preserve and propagate the gospel in the face of the world's antagonism, you would have to decide upon some logical, systematic arrangement. Ignatius followed the chronology of Christ's life. Irenaeus also adopted a chronological form. He began with creation and went on to Christ's return. But as this is insufficient, a better arrangement must be found.

How would you solve this problem? Would you argue that since God is the origin and source of all things, a creed should begin with a statement of who and what God is? If all things follow God, should not God be our starting point? Surely this sounds logical.

However, this argument overlooks one vital point: Where do we get our information about God? This question has been answered in different ways. These different ways have resulted in different opinions on the nature of God. If we must learn about God from Plato, or from Bultmann, we shall not have the same idea as if we had accepted information from Mohammed or Mary Baker Eddy. No doubt all or most men have some idea of God, but since these ideas differ, and differ widely, we would like to know whom we may trust.

Where and what is the source of reliable, accurate, full, and true information about God?

Therefore, the authors of the Westminster Confession did not put the doctrine of God in their first chapter. They put it in the second chapter. Chapter one has to do with our source of knowledge.

Chapter I.

OF THE HOLY SCRIPTURES.

Section I.—Although the light of nature, and the works of creation and providence, do so far manifest the goodness, wisdom, and power of God, as to leave men inexcusable;[1] yet they are not sufficient to give that knowledge of God, and of his will, which is necessary unto salvation;[2] therefore it pleased the Lord, at sundry times, and in divers manners, to reveal himself, and to declare that his will unto his Church;[3] and afterward, for the better preserving and propagating of the truth, and for the more sure establishment and comfort of the Church against the corruption of the flesh, and the malice of Satan and of the world, to commit the same wholly unto writing;[4] which maketh the Holy Scripture to be most necessary;[5] those former ways of God's revealing his will unto his people now ceased.[6]

1. Rom. ii. 14,15 ; i. 19,20,32 ; Ps. xix. 1-3 ; Rom. i. 21 ; ii. 2.—1. Cor. i. 21 ; ii. 13,14.—3. Hebrews i. 1.—4. Prov. xxii. 19-21 ; Luke i. 3,4 ; Rom. xv. 4 ; Matt. iv. 4,7,10 ; Isa. viii. 19,20. 5. 2 Tim. iii. 15 ; 2 Pet. i. 19.—6. Hebrews i. 1,2.

This first section of the Westminster Confession asserts that the light of nature gives us some knowledge of God. What does the Confession mean by "the light of nature"? Does it mean common sense? Does it mean that experience imprints the idea of God on the minds of all men? Does it mean that the existence of God can be rigorously demonstrated from an observation of natural phenomena, as the theorems of geometry are rigorously demonstrated from the axioms?

For example, in the accompanying diagram it can be rigorously demonstrated that angle one equals angle three. The proof is: angle one plus angle two equals a straight line, or 180 degrees; angle two and angle three equal a straight line also, since both line AB and line CD are straight lines; therefore by subtracting angle two from 180

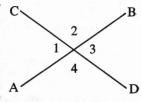

degrees, we get either angle one or angle three. They are therefore equal. The proof of the Pythagorean theorem is much more complicated, but every step is just as certain, every step is just as necessary. There is no escaping the conclusion. It has been completely demonstrated.

Thomas Aquinas, the great philosopher of the Roman Catholic church, believed not only that he had constructed a foolproof demonstration of God's existence, but also that the apostle in Romans 1:20 had guaranteed such a proof. On the other hand, David Hume, whom no church has canonized, argued that all such proofs are fallacies. Now, the psalmist said, "The heavens declare the glory of God." What does this imply? If it implies a formal cosmological proof, could we legitimately infer that anyone who is intellectually incapable of learning geometry, and who therefore could not follow the much more intricate cosmological argument, is not responsible for his sins? Knowledge is the basis of responsibility, and such a man does not know! Or, may we say that even if God's existence cannot be so demonstrated, and even if all of Hume's objections to these arguments are sound, still the truth of Christianity remains unaffected? Is it not possible that the knowledge of God is innate? May we not have been born with an intuition of God, and with this *a priori* equipment we see the glory of God upon the heavens? In this way we would not be forced to the peculiar position that the Apostle Paul was giving his advance approval to the Aristotelian intricacies of Thomas Aquinas.

This discussion as to the possibility of demonstrating the existence of God did not end with Thomas Aquinas or David Hume. Karl Barth today denies all natural knowledge of God. One of the proof-texts the Confession uses is Romans 1:19,20, which says,

> Because that which may be known of God is manifest in them; for God hath shewed it unto them.
> For the invisible things of him from the creation of the world are clearly seen, being understood by the things that are made, even his eternal power and Godhead; so that they are without excuse.

But Karl Barth insists that Paul is speaking only of Gentiles to whom he gave a knowledge of God by his preaching. Barth

10

denies that the Chinese and the Indians, prior to hearing the Gospel, could have any knowledge of God, either innate or derived from nature. This is a most unusual interpretation of Romans, and seems to be as erroneous as the idea that Paul was giving advance approval to St. Thomas.

Perhaps it would be better to understand the situation in terms of innate or *a priori* ideas. In the act of creation God implanted in man a knowledge of His existence. Romans 1:32 and 2:15 seem to indicate that God also implanted some knowledge of morality. We are born with this knowledge; it is not manufactured out of sensory experience. With the aid of this innate knowledge we may confidently sing:

> O Lord my God, when I in awesome wonder
> Consider all the worlds thy hands have made
> I see the stars, I hear the rolling thunder,
> Thy power throughout the universe displayed.
> Then sings my soul, my Savior God to thee,
> How great Thou art, how great Thou art.[1]

Within the limits of this first stanza, within the limits of the first chapter of Romans, and within the limits of ordinary observation of the universe, God should not be called Savior. The hymn writer, however, from his prior personal position as a Christian, may be permitted to use the name proleptically.

The Confession on the other hand, from its systematic construction, immediately makes it clear that any knowledge of God's great power displayed in creation is insufficient for salvation.

Even innate knowledge of morality gives no information how or even whether sin may be forgiven. "Therefore it pleased the Lord, at sundry times and in divers manners, to reveal himself, and to declare his will unto the Church."

Section II.—Under the name of Holy Scripture, or the word of God written, are now contained all the books of the Old and New Testaments, which are these:

---

1. Copyright 1955. Manna Music, Inc., Hollywood, California 90028. Used by permission.

11

OF THE OLD TESTAMENT

Genesis	I Kings	Ecclesiastes	Amos
Exodus	II Kings	The Song of	Obadiah
Leviticus	I Chronicles	Solomon	Jonah
Numbers	II Chronicles	Isaiah	Micah
Deuteronomy	Ezra	Jeremiah	Nahum
Joshua	Nehemiah	Lamentations	Habakkuk
Judges	Esther	Ezekiel	Zephaniah
Ruth	Job	Daniel	Haggai
I Samuel	Psalms	Hosea	Zechariah
II Samuel	Proverbs	Joel	Malachi

OF THE NEW TESTAMENT

Matthew	I Corinthians	I Timothy	I Peter
Mark	II Corinthians	II Timothy	II Peter
Luke	Galatians	Titus	I John
John	Ephesians	Philemon	II John
Acts of the	Philippians	Epistle to the	III John
Apostles	Colossians	Hebrews	Jude
Epistle to the	I Thessalonians	Epistle of James	The Revelation
Romans	II Thessalonians		

All which are given by inspiration of God to be the rule of faith and life.[7]
Section III.—The books commonly called Apocrypha, not being of divine inspiration, are no part of the canon of the Scripture, and therefore are of no authority in the Church of God, nor to be any otherwise approved or made use of than other human writings.[8]

7. Luke xiv. 29,31; Eph. ii. 20; Rev. xxii. 18,19; 2 Tim. iii. 16.—8. Luke xxiv. 27,44; Rom. iii. 2; 2 Pet. i. 21.

In section ii the Word of God is defined by listing the sixty-six books of the Bible, and section iii denies that the Apocrypha are canonical. Why? Have you heard a sermon recently that considered this point? What about the book of Enoch (though it is not in the Apocrypha)—it is quoted authoritatively in the New Testament, is it not? Or is it? Did Jude intentionally say "the seventh from Adam" for the express purpose of making clear that he was not depending on the book of Enoch that was written about 200 B.C.?

The question of the canon is very interesting. Jerome, who translated the Bible into Latin, did not accept the Apocrypha as canonical. But through the superstitious middle ages these books gained some approval. Yet the Roman church did not officially accept them until after the Protestant Reformation. The Reformers

12

accepted the Old Testament as the Jews originally had it. The Jews never had put the Apocrypha on a level with the Law and the Prophets. But in the council of Trent (session of April 8, 1546) the Romanists added these books to the Bible.

As it was then, so for us now, it is necessary to define the Word of God. Not only are the Romanists still with us, but other views are offered as substitutes for the Biblical position. Karl Barth, previously mentioned, has a chapter on *The Word of God in Its Three-Fold Form.*

For him the first form of the Word of God is the Sunday sermon. And it must be admitted that we do speak of a good sermon as the preaching of the Word of God. The second form for Barth is the Bible. This is a higher form because the Apostles, in spite of their mistakes, knew more than we do. Then there is a third and still higher form. But if anyone wants to puzzle out just what it is, he will have to read *Church Dogmatics* for himself. At any rate, we today, as well as the Reformers, need to know what various writers and various religions mean by the phrase the Word of God. There is no ambiguity in the Calvinistic position. The Word of God is the sixty-six books of the Bible.

Does it not now begin to appear that all the details of any writer's theology and all the practices of his religion depend on what he believes to be the source of information about God? If someone believes in the Atonement of Christ, or in Jupiter's thunder bolts, or purgatory, or reincarnation, or Allah, it is because he thinks he has some word from God.

Therefore section iv of the Confession states—though it might seem unnecessary to state it after defining the Word of God as the Bible—that:

> *Section IV.—The authority of the Holy Scripture, for which it ought to be believed and obeyed, dependeth not upon the testimony of any man or Church, but wholly upon God (who is truth itself), the author thereof; and, therefore, is to be received, because it is the word of God.*[9]
>
> *Section V.—We may be moved and induced by the testimony of the Church to an high and reverend esteem*

of the Holy Scripture,[10] and the heavenliness of the mat-
ter, the efficacy of the doctrine, the majesty of the style,
the consent of all the parts, the scope of the whole (which
is to give all glory to God), the full discovery it makes of
the only way of man's salvation, the many other incom-
parable excellences, and the entire perfection thereof, are
arguments whereby it doth abundantly evidence itself to
be the word of God; yet notwithstanding our full per-
suasion and assurance of the infallible truth and divine
authority thereof, is from the inward work of the Holy
Spirit, bearing witness by and with the word in our
hearts.[11]

9. 2 Pet. i. 19-21; 2 Tim. iii. 16; 1 John v. 9; 1 Thess. ii. 13.
10. 1 Tim. iii. 15.—11. 1 John ii. 20-27; John xvi. 13,14; 1 Cor. ii. 10-
12; Isa. lix. 21.

Some sections of the Confession may be hard to understand.
But there is no difficulty at all about the meaning of section iv.
The Bible, the Holy Scripture, is to be believed because it is the
Word of God.

Now when a Moslem says he does not believe the Bible, we
are not surprised. We hardly expect him to. Since, however, we
expect Christians to believe the Bible, especially Christian ministers, and, most of all, Presbyterian ministers, who have solemnly
subscribed to the Westminster Confession, we find it anomalous
when they deny the truth of the Bible.

Unfortunately we have had to become accustomed to attacks
on the Bible, coming, not from outside the church as in earlier
centuries, but from so-called Christian pulpits and publications.

The reason this is so serious is that if the Bible is not true, we
must find some other source of information about God. Bultmann
is far worse than Barth, and Tillich talks like an atheist, but even
Barth, the most conservative of the so-called neo-orthodox school,
says, "The prophets and apostles as such, even in their office, . . .
[were] actually guilty of error in their spoken and written word"
(*Church Dogmatics,* I 2, pp. 528-529).

But in order to maintain that the Bible is mistaken, not only
about some obscure dates, numbers, and names, but about points
of theology too, it is necessary to have some other source of information about God. If there is no other such source, how could
anyone know that the doctrine of the atonement, for example, is

wrong? If there is such a source, we should like to know what it is. By what criterion shall the Bible be judged? This question should be particularly embarrassing to Barth, for he wishes to hold that theology is an independent science without a foundation in philosophy, anthropology, natural science, or any other subject.

Before the time of neo-orthodoxy, modernism had incessantly attacked the truth of the Bible, and by the end of World War I had come to dominate Protestantism. Just before World War I a group of distinguished scholars, including James Orr, Benjamin B. Warfield, William G. Moorehead, E. Y. Mullins, and a score of others published twelve booklets called *The Fundamentals*. But to little avail. Protestantism was determined upon apostasy. In the early thirties, J. Gresham Machen, a scholar of world renown, tried to halt unbelief in the Presbyterian Church; but he was excommunicated for his loyalty to the Word of God—and excommunicated without being allowed the simple justice of presenting his defense in any of the three church courts through which his case was carried.

With the introduction of modernism into our churches in the nineteenth century and with the coming of neo-orthodoxy in the twentieth, an appearance of loyalty to the Bible and to the Confession has been attempted by emphasizing certain words in the standards, by failing to mention others, and by misinterpreting the whole. Thus unbelieving ministers made the double claims that they themselves accepted the Confession as originally intended, while the fundamentalists were inventing theories never before heard of.

Against the fundamentalists, who insisted on the inerrancy of the Bible, the modernists asserted that the Confession does not say that the Bible is inerrant. And today neo-orthodoxy loudly insists that the word of God is found in the Bible, perhaps only in the Bible, but that not everything in the Bible is true. These modernists could appeal to the Shorter Catechism, Question 2: "What rule hath God given to direct us how we may glorify and enjoy him? Answer: The word of God, which is contained in the Scriptures of the Old and New Testaments, is the only rule to direct us how we may glorify and enjoy him." Does it not say that the word of God is contained in the Scriptures? Somewhere, but not everywhere, between Genesis and Revelation, the word of God is to be found. This is their contention. But if now we wish to know whether or not this was the view of the Reformers, whether or not this is the position of the Presbyterian standards, and whether or not it is the teaching of the Scriptures themselves, which the standards summarize, we need only read other parts of the Confession. A few references follow, but quotations will not be multiplied because the reader should examine the Confession for himself:

Chapter I section i, said that at sundry times the Lord revealed his will to the prophets; afterwards, for the better preserving of the truth, it pleased the Lord to commit these revelations wholly unto writing. In this committal, may we ask, did it please the Lord to mix in some error with the truth he intended to preserve?

Section iv says that the authority for which the Scriptures should be believed depends wholly on God, who is truth itself and the author of the books; therefore the sixty-six books itemized in section ii are to be received because they are the Word of God. Here it is to be noted that the authority of God attaches to all the Scripture, not to a part only. Scripture has been defined as the sixty-six books, and God is declared to be the author of them all. God is truth itself, and the Scripture not merely contains but is the Word of God.

Section v even uses the word infallible. It says that our full assurance of the infallible truth and divine authority of these books is the work of the Holy Spirit. Can there be error in infallible truth? To the same end section ix teaches that the infallible rule of interpretation of Scripture is the Scripture itself.

Can it now be maintained that the Presbyterian standards admit the existence of error, of mistakes, of false teaching in the Bible? And if not, what can be thought of Presbyterian ministers who do not believe in the full truthfulness of the Scriptures? Though they may believe that the Word of God is to be found somewhere in the Bible, and perhaps only in the Bible, yet what can their ordination vows have meant to them, if they reject the very basis on which all the remainder of the Confession rests?

Somewhere along the line a modernist or perhaps someone to whom you are presenting the Gospel, will reply, "You assert that the Bible is the Word of God. I understand your assertion. There is no vagueness or ambiguity in your claim. But I don't believe it. How do you prove that the Bible is God-given information? Can you demonstrate your position?" This challenge brings us to section v, reproduced a few pages back.

It also returns us to the notion of proof or demonstration. If, while we are trying to win a man to Christ, he asks us to prove that the Bible is true, what sort of "proof" does he have in mind? And what sort of "proof" are we able to give?

Presumably it will not be geometrical demonstration. Nor can it be strictly historical. Consider. There may be, say, a thousand historical assertions in the Bible. Fortunately, many of these that the modernists said were false, are now known to be true. For example, the modernists asserted that the Hittite nation never existed. Today the museums have more Hittite books than they have time to translate. The modernists said that Moses could not have written the Pentateuch, because writing had not yet been invented in his day. Well, writing existed over a thousand years before the time of Moses. Still, the fact that the Bible is correct on these points does not "prove" that it is without error. Obviously there are many historical assertions in the Bible that we cannot check and never will be able to check. Who could hope to corroborate the assertions that Eliezer asked Rebekah for a drink of water, and that Rebekah drew water for his camels also?

Nevertheless, to discomfit the critics, we may take full advantage of archaeology. It has shown clearly how very wrong the unbelievers have been.

Archaeology, of course, can contribute little or nothing toward proving that the doctrines, as distinct from the historical events, of the Bible are true. With respect to the doctrines shall we accept the assurances of our parents? Shall we submit to the judgment of the Church? Shall we be persuaded by the style and sublimity of the Scripture itself?

17

You or I might be induced to accept the Bible by the testimony of the Church; but a Moslem would not. You or I might consider the matter heavenly, but the humanists would call it pie in the sky. The literary style of some parts of the Bible is majestic, but Paul's epistles are not models of style. The consent or logical consistency of the whole is important; for if the Bible contradicted itself, we would know that some of it would be false. Personal testimony as to the saving efficacy of the doctrine impresses some people; but others point out that queer people believe queer things and find great satisfaction in their oddities.

How then may we know that the Bible is true? The Confession answers, "Our full persuasion and assurance of the infallible truth and divine authority [of the Scripture] is from the inward work of the Holy Spirit."

Faith is a gift or work of God. It is God who causes us to believe: "Blessed is the man whom thou choosest and causest to approach unto thee" (Psa. 65:4).

Logically the infallibility of the Bible is not a theorem to be deduced from some prior axiom. The infallibility of the Bible is the axiom from which the several doctrines are themselves deduced as theorems. Every religion and every philosophy must be based on some first principle. And since a first principle is first, it cannot be "proved" or "demonstrated" on the basis of anything prior. As the catechism question, quoted above, says, "The Word of God is the only rule to direct us how we may glorify Him."[1]

> Section VI.—The whole counsel of God, concerning all things necessary for his own glory, man's salvation, faith and life, is either expressly set down in Scripture, or by good and necessary consequence may be deduced from Scripture: unto which nothing at any time is to be added, whether by new revelations of the Spirit or traditions of men.[12] Nevertheless, we acknowledge the inward illumination of the Spirit of God to be necessary for the saving understanding of such things as are revealed in the word;[13] and that there are some circumstances concerning the worship of God and government of the Church, common to human actions and societies,

1. For a more detailed analysis of the logical position of the truth of the Bible, *Can I Trust My Bible*, Chapter One, How May I Know the Bible Is Inspired, Moody Press, 1963.

which are to be ordered by the light of nature and Christian prudence, according to the general rules of the word, which are always to be observed.[14]

12. 2 Tim. iii. 15-17; Gal. i. 8,9; 2 Thess. ii. 2.—13. John vi. 45; 1 Cor. ii. 9-12.—14. 1 Cor. xi. 13,14; 1 Cor. xiv. 26,40.

Section vi and the second catechism question assert that the whole counsel of God, so far as the spiritual needs of man are concerned, is contained in the Bible. In the Scripture God's revelation is complete. How is this? Don't we need additional information and guidance? What about the mystics, such as Swedenborg, George Fox and others who have claimed that God gave them additional revelations? What effect has this section on Romanism, which also adds to its religion many things not found in Scripture? Isn't it all right to add to Scripture, if we are careful not to subtract anything? Can you think of any passages in the Bible that refer to adding and substracting?

There was a man in one of our churches, who had been converted from Romanism. Perhaps not soundly converted. Perhaps admitted to membership carelessly. At any rate, he thought it was all right to pray to Mary, if we also prayed to Chirst.

Some churches and Christian colleges forbid people to attend the movies. One young lady, in describing her church to an uninformed inquirer, said that first of all they didn't believe in using lipstick. The inquirer politely kept silent, but privately thought he would be uninterested in what that church put in second place. Another example is an amazing advertizement in a religious paper. It reads: "Free Table Cloth. We have a beautiful, plastic, washable, waterproof table cloth, with the picture of the Lord's Supper in the middle of it in gold color. Send for it. Lay your hands on it and pray over it, that everyone who touches it will be saved, healed, or filled with the Spirit. Read Acts 19:1-6. This beautiful table cloth sells for $5.00. We will send it to you free and postpaid, if you will order the 12 books on page 6." Roman Catholics are not the only unscriptural, superstitious people. Even some fundamentalists have fallen from their first estate of original righteousness.

Though we are not to add to the Scripture—no sign of the cross, no bowing at the second phrase of the Apostles' Creed, no

19

holy days or saint's days, no kneeling at the Lord's Supper—nonetheless we are not restricted to the explicit words of Scripture. God is wisdom, and Christ is the Logos or Reason of God; we were created in his image, and are therefore required to accept conclusions deduced from Scripture "by good and necessary consequence."

Christ himself, in arguing against the Pharisees, frequently drew out the implications of the Old Testament. John 10:34-36 is such an argument. Another example of implication, though not from the words of the Old Testament, is found in John 8:42. Paul in Rom. 3:20 draws a conclusion from a series of Old Testament verses. There are many other examples; and, to use the language of college textbooks, we "leave as an exercise for the student" the discovery of several of them.

This process of implication, which characterizes the New Testament, must also be applied today. Really, the trouble is not the justification of logic. Who can deny that when Scripture says, all men are sinners, we must, because we are men, draw the conclusion that we are sinners? Or, when Jesus says, "Him that cometh to me I will in no wise cast out," and we add the minor premise, I come to Jesus, the logical, necessary, inescapable conclusion is, Jesus will not cast me out. No, the trouble is not the justification of logic. The trouble is that some people doubt logic.

The neo-orthodox Brunner says logic must be curbed. Barth, at least in his earlier writings, insisted on Paradox. Some other people assume an appearance of piety and talk about "our merely human logic," which is so different from God's higher thoughts and ways. In effect these people deny that we have been created in God's image. But aside from their denial of the doctrine of creation, we wonder how they can talk, argue, or preach at all. Do they tell us, "all have sinned, but any implication that this means you is mere human logic and is not to be trusted"?

Away with such illogicality! Let us pay no attention to these confused people, no matter how pious they seem. The Confession is right, clearly and obviously right, in accepting what "by good and necessary consequence may be deduced from Scripture."

Of course, the validity of logic does not guarantee our infallibility. We may make mistakes in inference, and, what is more frequent, we may misunderstand some portions of Scripture. Especially with regard to a *saving* understanding of Scripture, we need the illumination of the Spirit of God. One of the reasons is that a saving understanding goes beyond an ordinary understanding. The worst infidel can easily understand that the Bible means to say that David was King of Israel and that Christ was Messiah. But in order that this information may be saving information, a man must accept it as the Word of God.

When Saul of Tarsus was persecuting the Church, he understood perfectly well that Christ claimed to be Messiah. But this understanding of the meaning of the words did not save him. It caused him to persecute. Then one day the Spirit of God illumined his mind. We too need such illumination.

It need not and will not be so spectacular as Paul's; but it must be equally real.

Finally, section vi says that, although we are not to add to the Scripture, the circumstances surrounding a worship service which it has in common with all human societies, are left to the prudent choice of the people. Every human organization must meet at some definite place. The Scripture does not specify the place at all, for the Church is to go into all the world. Nor does Scripture specify the time, except that on the Lord's Day worship services must be held. But aside from such common circumstances, the essential nature of the worship, the activities which the Church does not have in common with a chess club or baseball team, the contents of what one may call the ritual or order of service is prescribed by God. These prescriptions, such as singing, prayer, and preaching, the Lord's Supper and Baptism, cannot be omitted from the regular church program. Nor may a chess game or genuflection be added.

Section VII.—All things in Scripture are not alike plain in themselves, nor alike clear unto all,[15] yet those things which are necessary to be known, believed and observed, for salvation, are so clearly propounded and opened in some place of Scripture or other, that not only the learned, but the unlearned, in a due use of the

21

ordinary means, may attain unto a sufficient understanding of them.[16]

Section VIII.—The Old Testament in Hebrew (which was the native language of the people of God of old), and the New Testament in Greek (which at the time of the writing of it was most generally known to the nations), being immediately inspired by God, and by his singular care and providence kept pure in all ages, are therefore authentical;[17] so as in all controversies of religion the Church is finally to appeal unto them.[18] But because these original tongues are not known to all the people of God, who have right unto and interest in the Scriptures, and are commanded, in the fear of God, to read and search them,[19] therefore they are to be translated into the vulgar language of every nation unto which they come,[20] that the word of God dwelling plentifully in all, they may worship him in an acceptable manner,[21] and, through patience and comfort of the Scriptures, may have hope.[22]

15. 2 Pet. iii. 16.—16. Ps. cxix. 105,130.—17. Matt. v. 18.—18.Isa. viii. 20; Acts xv 15; John v. 39,46.—19. John v. 39.—20. 1 Cor. xiv. 6,9,11, 12,24,27,28.—21. Col. iii. 16.—22. Rom. xv. 4.

That not all things in Scripture are alike plain in themselves or alike clear to everyone scarcely needs any explanation. For example, Paul in I Corinthians 8:4-8 argues that refraining from eating meat offered to idols does not make a man a better Christian, nor does eating make him worse. Very easy to understand. But then why does John in Revelation 2:20 condemn the people of Thyatira for eating things sacrificed unto idols? Not so easy to understand.

If a Sunday School class or other study group is using this book, it might be interesting to have each member indicate what in the Bible is particularly puzzling to him. What perplexes one person may seem easy to another. Of course, some parts of the Bible seem difficult to nearly everybody; e.g., the details of the visions in Revelation.

Nonetheless, the basic truths of salvation are so clearly expressed that fishermen and slaves, as well as members of the Sanhedrin, can by a due use of ordinary intelligence attain unto a sufficient understanding of them.

Scholarship and superior intelligence are to be prized. But the Bible was addressed to the populace at large—the working men and slaves as well as to kings and those in authority.

If you and I are so stupid as not to be able to understand the Bible, but need priests, bishops, and popes to tell us what it means, are we not also too stupid to understand what the priests say? If we cannot understand the First Epistle of Peter—and the Romanists claim that Peter was the first pope—how can we understand contemporary papal letters? Indeed, a reading of the papal encyclicals may convince us that it is easier to understand Peter and Paul.

Section viii is also directed against Romanism. Because the Bible was addressed to all men, it should be translated into the languages men know. To conduct a service in Latin is to prevent the people from understanding. And why Latin, anyway? If it were out of (mistaken) reverence for the original words of the prophets and apostles, the service should be in Greek and Hebrew, not Latin. In any case, such reverence would be mistaken because the Bible has a message intended to be understood.

> *Section IX.—The infallible rule of Scripture is the Scripture itself; and therefore, when there is a question about the true and full sense of any Scripture (which is not manifold, but one), it must be searched and known by other places that speak more clearly.*[23]
> *Section X.—The supreme Judge, by which all controversies of religion are to be determined and all decrees of councils, opinions of ancient writers, doctrines of men, and private spirits, are to be examined, and in whose sentence we are to rest, can be no other but the Holy Spirit speaking in the Scripture.*[24]

23. 2 Pet. i. 20,21; Acts xv. 15,16.—24. Matt. xxii. 29,31; Eph. ii. 20; Acts xxviii. 25.

It seems undeniable that when there are two or more Scripture passages on the same subject, we should compare them for the light they throw on each other. Students of Plato and Aristotle use this method. Why not use it with the Bible also?

There are some matters to which the Bible refers only once. One case seems to be I Corinthians 6:3, "We shall judge angels." Perhaps another is Galatians 3:19, "The Law . . . was ordained by angels." Precisely what these verses refer to is difficult, perhaps impossible to know, because no further explanation is given.

The Reformers made it a principle never to establish a doctrine on the basis of a single verse. On one occasion a Bible School teacher tried to convince me of something by quoting a verse. I objected that what he was saying was said only once in the Bible. With crushing confidence he replied, "How often must God say something to make it true?"

The gentleman was of course considerably confused. If we take his reply very literally, we shall point out that God does not have to say something, reveal something to us, even once to make it true. All his secret decrees are true, though none of them is revealed. But more to the point, the Bible School teacher did not understand what is necessary for laying down doctrinal statements. The question has nothing to do with how many times God must say something to make it true, but, rather how many times must God say something before we can understand it. And the answer to this question is, usually several times.

Section x is the culmination of Chapter I. At the beginning of this chapter the question was asked, How can we obtain a knowledge of God? In the history of theology three main answers have been given. The first is an individual's personal hunches. This is dignified by calling it the Spirit speaking in one's own mind. Do not confuse this with the illumination that the Spirit gives us when we study the Scripture. In this case the Spirit enables us to understand what is written. But what the Confession refers to as "private spirits" is the view that the Spirit supplies to some men information not contained in and often contradictory to the Bible. Examples are Swedenborg, Anne Hutchinson, and Mary Baker Eddy.

The second attempt to locate the source of information about God is the Romish theory that the Councils are infallible. Since 1870 the Romanists make the claim that the Pope is infallible. We shall see, in examining the doctrines of the Confession, that the Pope frequently contradicts the Bible; and he explicitly acknowledges and claims to add to it.

The third answer is that of the Protestant Reformation and the Bible itself. "The supreme Judge by which all controversies

24

of religion are to be determined . . . can be no other but the Holy Spirit speaking in the Scripture."

Unfortunately the visible churches that have descended from the Protestant Reformation, especially the larger and wealthier denominations, have to a considerable degree repudiated the Bible. Schleiermacher, Ritschl, and modernism substituted religious experience for the Word of God. The neo-orthodox also deny the truth of Bible and substitute something called an existential encounter. They fail to tell us how this experience determines the number of the sacraments, the mode of baptism, the principles of church government, or even the doctrine of the Atonement. Without such information controversies of religion can be settled only by majority vote, that is, by the whims or ambitions of ecclesiastical politicians. No wonder this age is being called the Post-Protestant era. No wonder there is talk of church union with Rome. Without information from God, men are left to their own devices.

In conclusion, those sufficiently interested will find it profitable to read Gaussen's *Theopneustia*. Granted that its first fifty pages are elementary and tedious, from Chapter II on it exhibits a powerful mass of material. And also, do not fail to consult B. B. Warfield's *Inspiration and Authority of the Bible*.

Chapter II.

OF GOD AND OF THE HOLY TRINITY.

Section I.—*There is but one only[1] living and true God,[2] who is infinite in being and perfection,[3] a most pure spirit,[4] invisible,[5] without body, parts,[6] or passions,[7] immutable,[8] immense,[9] eternal,[10] incomprehensible,[11] almighty,[12] most wise,[13] most holy,[14] most free,[15] most absolute,[16] working all things according to the counsel of his own immutable and most righteous will,[17] for his own glory;[18] most loving,[19] gracious, merciful, long-suffering, abundant in goodness and truth, forgiving iniquity, transgression and sin;[20] the rewarder of them that diligently seek him;[21] and withal most just and terrible in his judgments;[22] hating all sin,[23] and who will by no means clear the guilty.[24]*

Section II.—*God hath all life,[25] glory,[26] goodness,[27] blessedness,[28] in and of himself; and is alone in and unto himself all-sufficient, not standing in need of any creatures which he hath made,[29] not deriving any glory from them,[30] but only manifesting his own glory, in, by, unto and upon them: he is the alone fountain of all being, of whom, through whom and to whom, are all things;[31] and hath most sovereign dominion over them, to do by them, for them, or upon them, whatsoever himself pleaseth.[32] In his sight all things are open and manifest;[33] his knowledge is infinite, infallible and independent upon the creature,[34] so as nothing is to him contingent or uncertain.[35] He is most holy in all his counsels, in all his works and in all his commands.[36] To him is due from angels and men, and every other creature, whatsoever worship, service or obedience, he is pleased to require of them.[37]*

1. Deut. vi. 4; 1 Cor. viii. 4,6.—2. 1 Thess. i. 9; Jer. x. 10.—3. Job xi. 7-9; xxvi. 14.—4. John iv. 24.—5. 1 Tim. i. 17.—6. Deut. iv. 15,16; John iv. 24; Luke xxiv. 39.—7. Acts xiv. 11,15.—8. James i. 17; Mal. iii. 6.—9. 1 Kings viii. 27; Jer. xxiii. 23,24;—10. Ps. xc. 2; 1 Tim. i. 17. 11. Ps. cxlv. 3.—12. Gen. xvii. 1; Rev. iv. 8.—13. Rom. xvi. 27.—14. Isa. vi. 3; Rev. iv. 8.—15. Ps. cxv. 3.—16. Ex. iii. 14.—17. Eph. i. 11.—18. Prov. xvi. 4; Rom. xi. 36.—19. 1 John iv. 8,16.—20. Ex. xxxiv. 6,7.—21. Heb. xi. 6.—22. Neh. ix. 32,33.—23. Ps. v. 5,6.—24. Neh. i. 2,3; Ex. xxxiv. 7.—25. John v. 26.—26. Acts vii. 2.—27. Ps. cxix. 68.—28. 1 Tim. vi. 15; Rom. ix. 5.—29. Acts xvii. 24,25.—30 Job xxii. 2,3.—31. Rom. xi. 36.—32. Rev. iv. 11; 1 Tim. vi. 15; Dan. iv. 25,35.—33. Heb. iv. 13.—34. Rom. xi. 33,34; Ps. cxlvii. 5.—35. Acts xv. 18; Ezek. xi. 5.—36. Ps. cxlv. 17; Rom. vii. 12.—37. Rev. v. 12,14.

While most of the sections of the Confession are succinct, Chapter II sections i and ii give the appearance of being wordy and unarranged. No doubt the Bible says that God is "most loving, gracious, merciful, long-suffering," but why should each of these be mentioned in the Creed? Could not these four and several others be simply summarized under the word goodness? If these four and the remaining dozen are to be mentioned, why not also list various other designations? Should we not add that God is a Shepherd of his sheep, or, at least, a Father of his children. Should we not also state that God is a jealous God? Is there a reader who knows how many designations of God there are? I remember a Sunday School contest in which the pupils were to find and list the names and titles of Christ. These were easily more than a hundred. For a creedal statement how can one decide what to include and what to omit?

Perhaps nearly all could be omitted because in Christian circles there is so little dispute concerning this material that it may seem unimportant. It is not unimportant, however.

It is not unimportant because there have been and still are pagan religions that have different concepts of God. Not to mention the ancient paganism of Greece and Rome, Hinduism today denies just about all the items in these sections. Similarly the tribal religions of Africa have gods distinctly different from the God described here. Buddhism and Shintoism also do not acknowledge such a God. Besides these pagan religions, there are movements nearer home that reject the God of the Confession and the Bible. These movements have exercised a great influence on western civilization and have succeeded in doing considerable damage to our Christian churches.

Examples are the philosophies of Spinoza and Hegel, and their followers. The influence of Spinoza led to theories of mechanism, materialism, and naturalism. These views, offered as the conclusions of science, deny the existence of soul or spirit, and limit reality to physical bodies in motion. This type of philosophy regards religion as all superstition.

The Hegelians, on the other hand, seem to approve of religion. They talk about mind and spirit. They hold to a principle of reason and unity transcending the particular things of the visible world. But though their terminology seems to favor religious notions, the Hegelians and the Spinozists agree that nothing exists beyond the universe itself. Though Spinoza's followers dropped the term God, Spinoza himself used it. He frequently spoke of God; but for him God and nature were precisely the same thing. Hegel too speaks of God or the Absolute; but like Spinoza he means nothing else than the totality of things.

If the followers of Spinoza attacked Christianity from the outside, the Hegelians worked within the church. During the nineteenth century Hegelian theologians, though they made an outward profession of Christianity and had their names on church rolls, denied the personality of God. This resulted in Protestant modernism. Jesus was regarded only as an ethical example, a mere man; and God was a principle that neither addressed the prophets nor intervened in history. Modernism's God neither spoke nor acted. It cannot therefore be surprising that the *Christian Century* about thirty years ago asserted that the God of the fundamentalists and the God of the modernists were not the same God.

Both of these schools of philosophy, the materialistic as well as the idealistic, have profoundly influenced many Americans. If the Hegelian influence is dying out now in the sixties, the materialistic or naturalistic influence seems to be increasing, with the result that America is becoming or has become predominantly secular and anti-religious. Therefore these sections of the Confession, which may at first have seemed not worth setting down, take on an importance today that they did not have earlier in this country. Their material should be learned and preached with diligence.

Even aside from the challenge of secularism, these sections have an importance entirely within the area of Christian thought itself. Some new converts, who know little philosophy and little theology too, may not recognize the value of these sections.

A young Christian in the fervor of his recent conversion may occupy his mind with evangelism, the doctrine of the atonement, and perhaps with justification by faith. This is commendable. But older Christians find more time to meditate on God. The doctrine of God underlies all the others. Could therefore the spiritual age of a Christian be judged by whether he finds these sections dull or rich?

Other devout Christians beside the Westminster divines have been prolix on the attributes of God. Stephen Charnock, who felt the heavy, impuritan hand of Charles II after 1660, wrote a volume of over 1000 pages, *The Existence and Attributes of God.* Discourse III On God's Being a Spirit, with John 4:24 as a text, takes twenty-eight pages; but this is little in comparison with Discourse VIII On God's Knowledge: this fills ninety-one pages. Then follows another 109 pages On the Wisdom of God. You ask, What could he find to say? The question can be answered by reading the book.

But back to the Confession. If there is but one living and true God, are there any dead or false gods? What is meant by saying that God has no passions? Is the word passion used in its contemporary romantic sense, or does it have a broader meaning? Is an emotion a passion? If it is, shall we say that God has no emotions? Do we ordinarily consider it a compliment when we call a man emotional? Can we trust a person who has violent ups and downs? Is it not unwise to act on the spur of the moment? Would then an emotional God be dependable? How could God have emotions, if he is immutable?

But someone says, God is love, and love is an emotion, is it not? Well, is it? Or, better, is what we call love in God an emotion? For that matter, is our love for God an emotion? In common conversation we do not think it makes much sense to command one person to love another. We are inclined to think it unreasonable to demand that a man should get emotional about something that happens to please us but does not please him. Love cannot be commanded. Yet God commands our love. He issues an order: Thou shalt love the Lord thy God. Is this a command to become emotional? To have ups and downs, sudden surges and ebbings? Oh, No! someone replies. Our love should never ebb. But if it never ebbs, it cannot surge. Without a down, there can be no up. We agree, do we not, that our love for God should be steady. And we agree that God's love for us is unchangeable. Then is not such a mental activity or attitude better designated a volition than an emotion?

It is interesting to note that in modern psychology, not initiated by but vigorously advanced by Freudianism, the emotions are greatly emphasized. On the other hand there is little discussion of the will. The situation was different in the time of Calvin and before. Perhaps some people think that the medieval theologians were overly intellectual. No doubt they think the same of Calvin too, for he emphasized the will and paid little or no attention to the emotions.

Now, those who fear that people may become too intellectual—though as a college professor I see little danger—ought not to shy away from a very practical application of this discussion. In evangelism should the evangelist appeal to the emotions? Many do. Or, would it be better to appeal to the will? Which is it better to say to an audience: "Stir up your emotions," or, "Decide to make Christ your Lord"? The way in which these questions are answered throws light on whether God is emotional or immutable and dependable.

Consider Augustus Toplady. This great Anglican Calvinist, author of *Rock of Ages,* approves Bradwardine (*Complete Works,* pp. 106, 107, London 1869) who said, "God is not irascible and appeasable, liable to emotions of joy and sorrow, or in any respect passive. Later on p. 687 Toplady adds in his own words, "When love is predicated of God, we do not mean that he is possessed of it as a passion or affection. In us it is such |sometimes?|; but if, considered in that sense, it should be ascribed to the Deity, it would be utterly subversive of the simplicity, perfection, and independency of his being. Love, therefore, when attributed to him, signifies, (1) his eternal benevolence, i.e., his everlasting will, purpose, and determination to deliver, bless, and save his people." So Toplady.

Next, what is meant by saying that God is incomprehensible? Does it mean that the Bible is unintelligible? Does it mean that God's thoughts are absurd? Is his mind characterized by "Paradox"? Does incomprehensibility mean that God is irrational? Unknowable? Herbert Spencer, an English philosopher, knew a great deal about the unknowable, for he wrote several large volumes about it. Or, does incomprehensibility simply mean we do not know everything that God knows? Even Charnock's thick volume is not exhaustive.

Section one also describes God as "working all things according to the counsel of his own immutable and most righteous will." Is this so? Does God really work all things according to his will? Or are there just a few things he fails to manage? Can anyone resist or go contrary to the will of God? Chapter III will have more to say on this subject.

Then, next, what is the relation between God and morality? And immorality? Can a loving God be terrible in his judgments? Isn't God too good to punish anyone? Then too, preaching the justice and punishment of God might lead people to worship him through fear; and fear is an unworthy motive and a pathological condition, is it not? Wouldn't it be better not to believe in God at all than to do so through fear? Freudians know more about fear than God does, anyway!

Further, isn't the God of Christianity an oriental despot and petty tyrant? Morris Cohen and other contemporary writers assure us that this is so. And the Confession itself states that God has sovereign dominion over all men, to do by them, for them, or upon them, whatsoever himself pleaseth.. Isn't this terrible! Surely a God worthy of the name would have to respect the rights of man! But what does Romans 9:19ff. say?

Charnock wrote ninety-one pages on God's knowledge. Does God learn by looking into the future and seeing what is going to happen? Does he learn by looking at the present and seeing what is here now? Are any events contingent or uncertain in God's knowledge? Is there anything past, present, or future that God does not know? Section ii says, "In his sight all things are open and manifest; his knowledge is infinite, infallible, and independent upon [of] the creature, so as nothing is to him contingent or uncertain." If God knows that it will rain tomorrow, is it possible that no rain will fall? If God knows that you will be in church next Sunday morning, can you possibly avoid going? If God has predestinated you to salvation, can you possibly be lost? Again Chapter III will have more to say on this subject.

Section III.—In the unity of the Godhead there be three persons, of one substance, power and eternity; God the Father, God the Son, and God the Holy Ghost.[38] The Father is of none, neither begotten nor proceeding; the

31

*son is eternally begotten of the Father;[39] the Holy Ghost
eternally proceeding from the Father and the Son.[40]*

38. 1 John v. 7; Matt. iii. 16,17; xxviii. 19; 2 Cor. xiii. 14.—39. John
i. 14.18.—40. John xv. 26; Gal. iv. 6.

While sections i and ii describe a basic monotheism, which,
with many proof texts from the Old Testament, could largely and
perhaps altogether be accepted by a devout Jew, section iii has to
do with the Trinity.

This trinitarian third section is very short. In fact, those who
wish to rewrite the creeds would do better to consider expanding
here rather than contracting elsewhere. The doctrine of the Trinity
centers in the deity of Christ. The personality of the Spirit and the
relations among the Persons are included, but surely it is not incorrect to say that the deity of Christ forms the center.

Naturally the theologians who followed Hegel and denied the
personality of God also denied the deity of Christ. This denial
was somewhat obscured in the minds of the too naive and trusting
orthodox by the use (in English) of the term divinity instead of
deity. This latter term came into use near the beginning of the
twentieth century in order to dispel the smoke screen the modernists had laid down. Historically the phrase "divinity of Christ"
meant that Jesus was God. But the modernists used it in a novel
sense.

Controlled by a pantheistic construction of the immanence
of God, they could speak about a spark of divinity in every man.
On this basis they assured any suspicious questioner that they did
indeed believe in the divinity of Christ.

More recently the unbelievers have been using the phrase
"God was in Christ, reconciling the world unto himself." This is,
of course, a good Scriptural phrase; but when detached from its
context and given a non-biblical setting, it becomes a phrase that
can be said of any man. God is in every man, obviously he was in
Jesus too. Indeed, God was in Jesus to a greater degree and made
a larger use of this good man than is the case with other people;
but none of this pious phraseology means that Jesus is the second
Person of the Trinity.

On the whole, however, the controversies of this century in
American churches did not very explicitly or very publicly discuss

the Trinity as such. For example, in 1924 more than 1200 Presbyterian ministers, over their signatures, issued a document, the Auburn Affirmation, which denied the inerrancy of Scripture and asserted that the Virgin Birth, the Atonement, and the Resurrection were not essential parts of Christianity. Some of these men, I know for a fact, believed in the deity of Christ. And therefore it might seem that this latter doctrine was not called into question.

Nevertheless a religion in which Christ was not virgin born, did not suffer the penalty due us for sin, and did not rise from the dead, is such a distorted form of Christianity—or, better, is not a form of Christianity at all—that one can hardly believe that the doctrine of the Trinity has remained intact.

Another example is found in the hymn book of the Disciples' denomination. They have rewritten "Holy, Holy, Holy," so as to exclude all reference to "God in Three Persons, blessed Trinity." A defense that is offered for such disconcerting editing is that the doctrine of the Trinity is based more on pagan Greek philosophy than on the Scriptures. But such a defense can be credited only by those who are ignorant of the extensive Scriptural arguments in the writings of Athanasius. Some ignorance of Greek philosophy also helps.

By mid-century the attack on the Trinity took a different form. Instead of arguing against the doctrine, as an honest Unitarian might do, the new fashion is to declare loudly that the doctrine of the Trinity expresses a deep and abiding truth. Of course the words of the Confession cannot be taken literally, but they must be understood as symbolic. They are like a map, which is not the road itself.

This is the line taken by Reinhold Niebuhr in *Faith and History*. On page 165 he writes, "Trinitarian definitions are indeed embarrassing rationally [that is, they make no sense]; but they are necessary to embody what is known about the character of God as apprehended in faith's recognition of the revelation of divine mercy | and this makes less sense] . . . . [Theistic interpretations of the Trinity] acknowledge that the world we know points beyond itself to a creative ground."

This last phrase makes some sense. It apparently means that when we speak of the Godhead as consisting of three persons, of whom Jesus is the second, we really mean nothing more than that the world requires a creative ground—whatever "creative ground" may mean.

Although the present temper of the churches with their doctrinal laxity and ecumenical obsession does not issue in explicit attacks on the Trinity, it would be a mistake to conclude that this doctrine more than others enjoys uniform acceptance. Whether the Virgin Birth is rejected as an impossible biological miracle, or whether creeds are eviscerated by making them symbolic, pointers, or myths, the very nature of the Godhead is called into question.

An attack against a citadel is not always frontal. Sometimes the outer defenses are first put out of commission, one by one; sometimes the foundations are undermined; sometimes the supplies are cut off. This is not to suggest that all those who attack some doctrine or other intend to weaken their testimony to the deity of Christ. It does not even imply that all those who deny the Virgin Birth are conscious enemies of trinitarianism. The ecclesiastical situation is similar to the political, where many Americans have advocated this or that part of communistic propaganda without knowing its source and aims.

But put the question thus: If the Virgin Birth is not an historical event, and if the body of Christ did not come out of the tomb, and if the Scriptures are often in error, what hope is there of long maintaining the deity of Christ? Indeed, can one be said truly to believe in Christ if he denies these things? The New Testament does not present us with a mere name, but with a real person who did things. Suppose one should say, I believe Napoleon was a real historical character who actually lived; but I reject the legendary accretions which say he put an end to the French revolution, became Emperor, fought Spain, Italy, Austria, invaded Russia, lost the battle of Waterloo, and was exiled on St. Helena. But of course, I firmly believe in Napoleon!

Is this any more silly than to say, I believe in Jesus Christ, but of course miracles are impossible and the story of the resurrection is a kerygmatic myth?

There is either one Christ or there is none. If Jesus was not the eternal Son of God, equal in power and glory with the Father, then let's have done with all talk about Christianity. Let us admit honestly that we are Unitarians, Jews, Buddhists, or humanists. But not Christians. For the historical Jesus said, Upon this rock, of the deity of Christ, I will build my Church. Some other organization may call itself a church, but it is not his.

CHAPTER III.

OF GOD'S ETERNAL DECREE

Section I.—God from all eternity did, by the most wise and holy counsel of his own will, freely and unchangeably ordain whatsoever comes to pass:[1] yet so as thereby neither is God the author of sin,[2] nor is violence offered to the will of the creatures, nor is the liberty or contingency of second causes taken away, but rather established.[3]

Section II.—Although God knows whatsoever may or can come to pass upon all supposed conditions,[4] yet hath he not decreed anything because he foresaw it as future, or as that which would come to pass upon such conditions.[5]

1. Eph. i. 11; Rom. xi. 33; Heb. vi. 17; Rom. ix. 15,18.—2. James i 13,17; 1 John i. 5.—3. Acts ii. 23; Matt. xvii. 12; Acts iv. 27,28; John xix. 11; Prov. xvi. 33.—4. Acts xv. 18; 1 Sam. xxiii. 11,12; Matt. xi. 21,23.—5. Rom. ix. 11,13,16,18.

The Protestant Reformation, the greatest religious awakening since the days of the Apostles, was characterized by a zeal to understand God's Word. Not only were its obvious teachings emphasized, e.g., the sufficiency of Christ's work for our salvation and the uselessness of purgatory and penance, but also its deeper doctrines, e.g., predestination, were carefully examined.

However, two or three centuries later, after the love of many had waxed cold, and when unbelief came in like a flood, the discouraged and fragmented faithful became Fundamentalists and were content to defend a few vital doctrines. Sometimes they even said that Christians ought not to go too deeply into the Scriptures. It is presumptious, useless, and worst of all, divisive.

Such an attitude is not commended in the Scriptures themselves, nor was it the practice of the Reformers and Westminster divines. The Bible says that all Scripture is profitable for doctrine, not just some. And the Reformers did not draw back from the difficult passages on predestination, foreordination, and God's eternal decrees. Really, these passages are not difficult to understand, though many people find them difficult to believe. But if they are God's words, then we should study, believe, and preach them.

The Westminster Confession, summarizing the Bible, asserts in Chapter III that God from all eternity did ordain whatsoever comes to pass. Obviously, if God is omnipotent, if nothing can thwart his will, and if he decided to make a world, then all his creatures and all their actions must be according to his plan.

This is easy to understand; but many people find it difficult to believe that God planned to have sin in the world. Does Chapter III of the Confession mean that God commits sin? And even in the case of a man's doing something good, does it mean that God makes the man do the good act while the man willed to do something evil? These questions have perplexed many minds, but the first question is, What does the Bible say? If the Bible talks about foreordination, we have no right to avoid it and keep silent.

Summarizing the Scriptures, the Confession says here that God is not the author of sin; that is, God does nothing sinful. Even those Christians who are not Calvinists must admit that God in some sense is the cause of sin, for he is the sole ultimate cause of everything. But God does not commit the sinful act, nor does he approve of it and reward it. Perhaps this illustration is faulty, as most illustrations are, but consider that God is the cause of my writing this book. Who could deny that God is the first or ultimate cause, since it was he who created mankind? But although God is the cause of this chapter, he is not its author. It would be much better, if he were.

The Scripture references show clearly that God controls the wills of men. During Absalom's rebellion against David, Hushai gave poor advice but Ahithophel gave good advice to Absalom. Absalom, however, "and all the men of Israel said, the counsel of Hushai the Archite is better than the counsel of Ahithophel. For the Lord had appointed [ordained] to defeat the good counsel of Ahithophel, to the intent that the Lord might bring evil upon Absalom" (II Sam. 17:14). It is clear then that God, in his purpose to bring evil upon Absalom, so controlled the wills of Absalom and his men that they chose Hushai's poor advice instead of Ahithopel's good advice. By controlling the wills of these evil men,

37

God established the throne of David, from whom the Messiah descended.

This does not mean that violence was done to the will of the creatures. It was not as if the men wanted to adopt Ahithophel's plan and were forced to follow Hushai against their desires. Their psychological processes issued in a desire to follow Hushai's plan. But it must be noted that God established psychological processes just as truly as he established physical processes.

This ties in with the next phrase, "nor is the liberty or contingency of second causes taken away, but rather established."

In the case of Absalom the secondary causes were the psychological processes. The decision the men of Israel made was not made in opposition to those processes, nor even without them. God has established such processes for the purpose of accomplishing his will. He does not arrange things or control history apart from secondary causes.

To mention other examples, God decreed to bring the children of Israel out of Egypt; but they had to do the walking themselves. God decreed that Solomon should build the temple; but Solomon had to collect the materials. God does not decree the end apart from the means. He decrees that the end shall be accomplished by means of the means.

Further discussion on these matters may be found in *The Cause of God and Truth*, by John Gill (an eighteenth century Baptist), published by the Sovereign Grace Book Club. See particularly pp. 183-198. Also, *Religion, Reason, and Revelation*, by the present author, Chapter V; published by the Presbyterian and Reformed Publishing Company, 1961.

The importance of section ii becomes much clearer when later the idea of grace alone is examined. Here, in a general way, it is necessary only to understand that God does not obtain his knowledge by watching how the world goes on. Not only is it unnecessary, or, better, impossible, that God should have to wait to find out what happens; but God's knowledge does not depend on his looking into the future to see what will happen. Quite the reverse. God did not decree that David would defeat Absalom because he knew ahead of time that David would do this. Rather, David did this because God had decreed it.

In human society men often change their plans. Sometimes they change their minds voluntarily; sometimes accidents prevent the carrying out of their plans. Obviously therefore the human situation does not parallel the divine situation. But if we attempt to make allowances, we might ask, "Do I decide to use the Queen's Pawn opening in a chess tournament because somehow I can predict that that is what will happen; or am I able to predict that I shall use this opening because I have decided to?" The answer is obvious, is it not?

> *Section III.—By the decree of God, for the manifestation of his glory, some men and angels[6] are predestinated unto everlasting life, and others foreordained to everlasting death.[7]*
>
> *Section IV.—These angels and men, thus predestinated and foreordained, are particularly and unchangeably designed, and their number is so certain and definite, that it cannot be either increased or diminished.[8]*
>
> *Section V.—Those of mankind that are predestinated unto life, God, before the foundation of the world was laid, according to his eternal and immutable purpose, and the secret counsel and good pleasure of his will, hath chosen in Christ unto everlasting glory,[9] out of his mere free grace and love, without any foresight of faith or good works, or perseverance in either of them, or any other thing in the creature, as conditions, or causes moving him thereunto;[10] and all to the praise of his glorious grace.[11]*

6. 1 Tim. v. 21; Matt. xxv. 41.—7. Rom. ix. 22,23; Eph. i. 5,6; Prov. xvi. 4.—8. 2 Tim. ii. 12; John xiii. 18.—9. Eph. i. 4,9,11; Rom. viii, 30; 2 Tim. i. 9; 1 Thess. v. 9.—10. Rom. ix. 11,13,16; Eph. i. 4,9.—11. Eph. i. 6,12

Section iii is the one that anti-Calvinists abominate. They may not object too much to the idea that God predestinates some men to everlasting life; although the more Arminian they are, the more they prefer salvation to spring from man's will, rather than God's will. But what irritates them without measure is the idea that God has foreordained other men to everlasting death. Indeed a popular notion in this twentieth century is that there is no hell at all, and everybody is saved. God is too good to punish anybody, whether or not he believes in Christ, and whether or not he has committed great crimes. Hitler and Stalin seem to inherit the same felicity as the Apostle John.

Now, the first thing to do is to see what Scripture says. Make a list of all the verses that bear on the topic. Do they or do they not say that God foreordains some people to everlasting death? Three verses are given in the references. Can you find three more?

Some of Calvin's detractors, following John Wesley, attempt to give the impression that Calvin himself felt a revulsion from the notion of reprobation, and therefore probably did not sincerely believe it, or at least had serious doubts about it. They say he referred to the idea as a "horrible decree." This charge against Calvin's integrity is at best explained on the basis of an ignorance of Latin. True, in Latin Calvin referred to reprobation as a *decretum horrible*; but in Latin *horrible* does not mean horrible. It means awe-inspiring. Cicero (*Oratio pro Quinct.*) says, "It is an awful (*horrible*) undertaking to plead a cause in which life and death are concerned, more awful still, to be the first opener of such a cause." Lucan writes, *Arboribus suus horror inest*; that is to say, "There is something awe-inspiring in a grove of trees." And a post-reformation writer refers to Scaliger in this manner, *Cujus nomen sine horrore et religione commemorare non possum*; to wit, "The very mention of his name strikes a sort of religious awe upon my mind." Calvin therefore was saying that the decree of reprobation was one that inspired awe in the presence of God.

Calvin's words are, "I inquire again how it came to pass that the fall of Adam, independent of any remedy, should involve so many nations with their infant children in eternal death, but because such was the will of God. Their [those who object to divine decrees] tongues, so loquacious on every other point, must here be struck dumb. It is an awful decree, I confess; but no man can deny that God foreknew the future final fate of man before he created him, and that he did foreknow it because it was appointed by his own decree" (*Institutes*, III xxiii, 7).

Section iv asserts that the number of the saved and the number of the lost is so certain and definite that it cannot be either increased or diminished. The additional Scripture references are hardly necessary to support this statement. Since God is omniscient and therefore knows exactly who will be received into heaven, any change in their number would require ignorance in God. Since also God is immutable, and since he decides whom he will save, any alteration of the number would imply that God had changed his mind. This is impossible. Hence the number of the saved is fixed and unalterable.

Section v teaches that those whom God predestinates to salvation, he chose in Christ. This is in keeping with the principle that God determines the means as well as the end. God did not choose to save some people in just any way; he chose to save them by the work of Christ. Recently some of the neo-orthodox, in addition to their theory of universal salvation, have asserted that original Protestantism separated divine election from Christ, and that they, the neo-orthodox, are the first to discover this doctrine. Evidently the neo-orthodox have not read this section of the Confession.

Subsidiary ideas in this section—free grace, without foresight of faith or good works, and perseverance—will be discussed in later chapters.

But there is one idea that is not subsidiary. Section v says that all the details mentioned are arranged so as to display God's glorious grace. The Shorter Catechism begins by declaring that man's chief purpose in life is to glorify God. Answer seven stresses that God foreordains everything for his own glory.

Chiefly we see God's glory in the provisions for salvation: predestination and free grace. We do indeed see God's glory in the stars and hear it in the rolling thunder,

> But in the grace that rescued man
> His brightest form of glory shines;
> Here on the cross, 'tis fairest drawn
> In precious blood and crimson lines.

Section VI.—As God hath appointed the elect unto glory, so hath he, by the eternal and most free purpose of his will, foreordained all the means thereunto.[12] Wherefore they who are elected being fallen in Adam, are redeemed by Christ;[13] are effectually called unto faith in Christ by his Spirit working in due season; are justified, adopted, sanctified,[14] and kept by his power through faith unto salvation.[15] Neither are any other redeemed

41

*by Christ, effectually called, justified, adopted, sanctified
and saved, but the elect only.[16]*

*Section VII.—The rest of mankind, God was
pleased, according to the unsearchable counsel of his own
will, whereby he extendeth or withholdeth mercy as he
pleaseth, for the glory of his sovereign power over his
creatures, to pass by, and to ordain them to dishonour
and wrath for their sin, to the praise of his glorious
justice.[17]*

12. 1 Pet. i. 2; Eph. i. 4,5; ii. 10; 2 Thess. ii. 13.—13. 1 Thess. v. 9,10;
Tit. ii. 14.—14. Rom. viii. 30; Eph. i. 5; 2 Thess. ii. 13.—15. 1 Pet. i. 5.
—16. John xvii. 9; Rom. xiii. 28; John vi. 64,65; viii. 47; x. 26;
1 John ii. 19.—17. Matt. xi. 25,26; Rom. ix. 17,18,21,22; 2 Tim. ii. 19,
20; Jude 4; 1 Pet. ii. 8.

Perhaps sections vi and vii do not add much to what pre-
ceded, except by way of detail. Examination of the Scripture
references will reinforce and elaborate the ideas of the previous
sections. Once again it is said that God's purpose is eternal, his
decree is not subject to any external compulsion, and includes all
means as well as the final end. This is true both with respect to
the saved and to the lost. All is done for the glory of his sovereign
power.

In the United States too little has been heard recently about
the sovereignty of God. In England there is an association called
the Sovereign Grace Union. Cooperating with it to some degree
there is in this country the Sovereign Grace Book Club, previously
referred to. And there is a group of Baptist ministers loosely as-
sociated under the name of Sovereign Grace Baptists. No doubt
Presbyterians, those who are Presbyterians not just in name but
in reality, believe in sovereign grace too. But would it not be
better if we dusted off our Confession, used it as a guide in our
Bible study, and then proclaimed the message with heavenly enthusiasm?

It is a message the world needs, for if God is not sovereign,
the world is in a hopeless jam.

*Section VIII.—The doctrine of this high mystery
of predestination is to be handled with special prudence
and care,[18] that men attending the will of God revealed
in his word, and yielding obedience thereunto, may, from
the certainty of their effectual vocation, be assured of
their eternal election.[19] So shall this doctrine afford*

42

matter of praise, reverence and admiration of God,[20] and of humility, diligence and abundant consolation, to all that sincerely obey the gospel.[21]

18. Rom. ix. 20 ; xi. 33 ; Deut. xxix. 29.—19. 2 Pet. i. 10.—20. Eph. i. 6 ;
Rom. xi. 33.—21. Rom. xi. 5,6,20 ; 2 Pet. i. 10 ; Rom. viii. 33 ; Luke x. 20.

The last section of this chapter says that the doctrine of predestination is to be handled with special prudence and care. But many ministers think that it is not to be handled at all. They may be willing to preach the Deity of Christ and his Atonement on the cross, but not God's eternal decree on which the Atonement is based.

One summer a big tent was set up in Indianapolis, and over a ten-week period various evangelists spoke. I heard one of them blast all the contents of this chapter in loud emphatic tones. At the end of this five-minute harangue he concluded by assuring the audience that of course he believed what the Bible said about predestination. But he certainly gave no indication of what he thought the Bible said.

There is also the case of the Bible professor in a so-called Christian college, who told me, "Even if you believe in predestination, don't let anyone know you do." He constantly told his students never to study the subject nor mention it in their preaching. One student who held his teacher in high respect was shocked to find that the Bulgarian laborers with whom he worked in Chicago were extremely interested in the forbidden subject. But if predestination is not to be mentioned, God must have made an embarrassing blunder in revealing it to us.

Professor George S. Hendry[1] has something interesting to say relative to the Confession's advice in section eight about handling "this high mystery of predestination . . . with special prudence and care." Professor Hendry writes, "No reader who compares the statement of doctrine in the Confession with the Biblical passages . . . can fail to notice a profound difference in tone between them. . . . Ephesians 1:3-14 and Romans 8:29-30 . . . breathe an air of exultant joy; both exemplify what has been called 'truth that sings.' The chapter in the Confession, by contrast, breathes an air of dread and doom, and it ends with the

1. *The Westminster Confession for Today,* pp. 51, 52.

43

advice to handle the subject with extreme caution. There is no suggestion of caution in Ephesians 1 and Romans 8; there, if ever, the apostle is letting himself go."

Now, it may be that Professor Hendry has a point here. Not only is there no suggestion of caution in Paul; but also there was more enthusiasm in the preaching of the Reformers than in the contemporary preachers who, as Hendry notes, so often pass over the doctrine in complete silence. For example, Jerome Zanchius, in his *Absolute Predestination* (republished by the Sovereign Grace Book Club), may be said to "let himself go" with enthusiasm. If church members in large numbers should read this classic, it would be like life from the dead. It was Augustus Toplady who translated Zanchius' book. Toplady too was enthusiastic, and his other writings would also inspire moribund congregations.

Yet Dr. Hendry may have exaggerated the "air of dread and doom" which he says pervades the Confession. The advice is not "to handle the subject with extreme caution," as he says, but it is to use "special prudence and care." Clearly the latter phrase has less dread and doom about it than the former. Furthermore, the advice is given in order that "men attending the will of God revealed in his word . . . may, from the certainty of their effectual calling, be assured of their eternal election." Then the Confession immediately adds, "So shall this doctrine afford matter of praise, reverence . . . and abundant consolation to all that sincerely obey the gospel." There is no doom and dread here. Even if a formal statement specifically prepared as the official standard of a church or churches is not so exuberant as Paul, Zanchius, or Toplady, when they let themselves go, yet the careful creedal language still speaks of praise and abundant consolation.

The reason Dr. Hendry disparages the Confession is not that he wishes this doctrine to be preached with enthusiasm. Dr. Hendry casts aspersions of doom on the Confession because he does not believe the doctrine. He does not want the Reformed doctrine of predestination preached at all. He wants a different doctrine preached.

The Reformed doctrine, he tells us, "is no longer held by the Presbyterian Churches in the form in which it is set forth in this chapter." The original doctrine is a "forbidding husk" that hides

44

some different truth. What this other truth is, Dr. Hendry does not very clearly say; but he gives certain reasons for rejecting the Presbyterian position.

The first reason is a very confused bit of exegesis. Romans 9:19-23, he says, stresses God's grace. This grace was extended to the Gentiles and it will also persevere to the final salvation of Israel. But from the fact that such is the main theme, it does not follow, as Hendry would have it, that the Reformed doctrine of predestination is not supported in the course of the argument. He insists that the phrase "vessels of wrath fitted to destruction" does not indicate by whom those vessels were so fitted. He fails to observe, however, that the context explicitly refers to only one divine Potter and that no other can possibly be imagined.

Further confusion is produced by comparing the Romans reference to the Potter who has power over the clay, of the same lump, to make one vessel unto honor and another unto dishonor—note the sole agency of God throughout—with Jeremiah 18:4, where a potter clumsily mars a vessel, squeezes it into a lump again, and makes another vessel. The argument seems to require the conclusion that all the vessels God makes will be vessels unto honor, though Hendry on a later page avoids a profession of universalism by what seems to be an argument based on ignorance.

At any rate the words in Jeremiah do not require us to extrude predestination from Romans. The wording and the meaning of Romans is too clear. Verses 13, 18, 19, 22 can be misunderstood only by means of the greatest perversity. The illustration in Jeremiah, although it overlaps the subject in Romans, is incomplete, and like the parables of Christ is not applicable in every detail to the reality. The Scripture teaches that God is both omnipotent and omniscient; but Jeremiah's potter makes mistakes. One wonders whether Dr. Hendry intends to imply that God also makes mistakes. In the paragraph he suggests that the doctrine of predestination pictures God as a petty official, operating mechanically, bound by red tape. Of course, the Confession does no such thing. But in opposition to the Confession Dr. Hendry thinks of God as "free to modify his action from day to day according to the reaction of those with whom he is dealing." Now, if this phrase does not simply mean that God foreordained David

45

to be anointed King on one day and that he foreordained another day as the day of Christ's crucifixion—this of course would be in accord with the Confession and is therefore not what Dr. Hendry means—then what else can the phrase mean other than that God has to alter his plans from day to day because of human reactions that God cannot anticipate?

Professor Hendry also gives other reasons for rejecting the Confession. One has to do with the relation between eternity and time. Without tracing the intricacies of the argument, it is doubtless inadequate to report that I find in it misstatements of fact plus a dash of nonsense. But that the author opposes the doctrine of the Church, the Confession, the Reformation, and the Bible is beyond question. He says, "The fault of Augustine, later aggravated by Calvin, was that he traced the sovereignty of grace to the sovereignty of an inscrutable will, which was then absolutized [whatever that means] and made the basis of a *double* predestination" (p. 55). This, I say, is nonsense, for what else can grace be but an act of will?

Nor, to continue with Hendry's following sentences, does the fact that God's decree is not fully revealed to us, but that there are many events foreordained which we do not yet know, imply, as Hendry plainly suggests, that assurance of salvation is impossible. If God has revealed to us information sufficient to produce assurance, his non-disclosure of other matters does not negate these promises.

Since Dr. Hendry is Professor of Systematic Theology in Princeton Theological Seminary, one is inclined to trust his assertion that his Church does not accept the doctrine of the Confession. His position in that prominent seminary clearly indicates that his views are not merely tolerated but widely approved in that denomination. Now, in the Machen controversy thirty to forty years ago, those who denied the Virgin Birth, the Atonement, and the Resurrection argued that these were not essential to "the system of doctrine contained in the Confession." And since their ordination vows required only their acceptance of "the system," they were free to reject the Virgin Birth and the Resurrection. But if anything at all is essential to the system, it is the doctrine of the Divine Decree. This doctrine very particularly constitutes Presbyterianism, Calvinism, or the Reformed Faith. It follows therefore that the United Presbyterian Church in the United States of America is not a Presbyterian Church. Indeed, without the Virgin Birth, the Atonement, the Resurrection, and the Divine Decree, one wonders what sort of a church it can possibly be.

Somehow it must be made clear to ministers who profess to believe God's Word that a refusal to preach that Word is sinful. Earlier we criticized and rightly condemned the modernist hymnbook where the doctrine of the Trinity had been edited out of "Holy, Holy, Holy." But is this any worse than editing predestination out of the Bible?

Aside from the fact that God has commanded his servants to preach all his revelation, one great reason for preaching on the eternal decree is that a knowledge of sovereignty, election, and predestination is necessary in order to understand many other doctrines.

How else can we understand the perseverance of the saints?

And assurance of salvation, far from being inconsistent with divine sovereignty, is impossible without the doctrine of election. If God has not from all eternity decided to preserve me in grace, do I have any spiritual power in myself to persevere to the end? And if I have such power, would not salvation be achieved through my own efforts and by my own merits, rather than by God's grace.

This doctrine of the eternal decree underlies not only the doctrine of the perseverance of the saints, but also that of effectual calling, the necessity and nature of regeneration, the gifts of saving faith, and in short the whole gospel.

For the whole Gospel is not just a few disjointed truths. It is an ordered and logical system. Each part bears on each other part. This is what is meant in Chapter I, section v, where it says we may be induced to a reverend esteem of the Scripture by the consent, the logical consistency, of all the parts.

Given the sovereignty of God, his omnipotence and omniscience, predestination follows by logic alone. Given the creation of the world by an Almighty Creator, it necessarily follows that history must accord with the eternal decree. Or, if a person believes that men are dead in sin and that God can give them eternal security, he ought to recognize that this is possible only through the irresistible grace of foreordination. But the Lord has not left us to our own logical resources. Not everyone is quick to see implications. Therefore predestination is explicitly asserted in many passages throughout the Bible. The exegesis is on the whole so easy that even he who skims the surface may understand.

Therefore we should not regard the eternal decree as a doctrine hard to understand. Indeed it is very easy to understand. That is why it provokes such instant animosity in those who prefer sinful rebellion against God.

But for us who are very glad and thankful that God controls the world, this doctrine affords matter of praise, reverence, and admiration of God, and abundant consolation to all that sincerely obey the Gospel.

CHAPTER IV.

OF CREATION.

*Section I.—It pleased God the Father, Son and Holy
Ghost,[1] for the manifestation of the glory of his eternal
power, wisdom and goodness,[2] in the beginning, to create,
or make of nothing, the world, and all things therein,
whether visible or invisible, in the space of six days, and
all very good.[3]*

1. Heb. i. 2; John i. 2,3; Gen. i. 2; Job xxvi. 13; xxxiii. 4.—2. Rom. i.
20; Jer. x. 12; Ps civ. 24; xxxiii. 5,6.—3 Gen. i. 1, to end; Heb. xi. 3;
Col. i. 16; Acts xvii. 24.

Although the main subject of this chapter is the creation of
the world, and in section ii the creation of man in the world, it
is stated at the beginning that the purpose of creation is the manifestation of God's power, wisdom, and goodness. This in effect
is a repetition from Chapter III, section iii, where the purpose of
predestination and reprobation was said to be the manifestation of
his glory. Before the details of creation are discussed, a little
more time should be spent on this purposeful character of God's
decrees and their execution.

God always acts for a purpose. He always has an end in
view. There is no blind chance in God's doings. Therefore the
means he uses to accomplish his plans can be understood only as
they are seen to aim at the end. If you see a friend hurrying in
a certain direction, doesn't your understanding of his action depend
on a knowledge of where he is going?

Many, in a sense most, passages in the Bible explain the
steps in God's plan. Christ's atonement for sin is the central part
of that plan; and the world had to be created in order that Christ
might die on Calvary. Had there been no world, there would have
been no hill Golgotha. So, by putting all the parts together, it
is possible to infer the purpose of the act of creation. But while
these hints and implications are abundant, there are few passages
that explicitly and in so many words connect the act of creation
with God's final and comprehensive purpose. Some people say
there is only one such passage. We shall therefore examine with

all the greater care that one passage. It is found in Ephesians 3:9-10.

The main exegetical problem of Ephesians 3:10 is the identification of the antecedent of the purpose clause: "in order that the manifold wisdom of God might now be made known, by means of the Church, to the principalities and powers in heavenly places, according to the eternal purpose which he purposed in Christ Jesus our Lord." Something happened in the preceding verses for the purpose of revealing God's wisdom. What was it that had this purpose?

There are three and apparently only three possible antecedents: (1) Paul was called to preach in order that, (2) The mystery was hid in order that, and (3) God created the world in order that.

First, I should like to eliminate from consideration the second of these possibilities. This interpretation would hold that God kept a certain secret hidden from the beginning of the world in order to reveal it in New Testament days. The only textual support for this exegesis, aside from the fact that the event of hiding is mentioned prior to the purpose clause, is the word *now*. By emphasizing the word *now*, one may say that the mystery or secret was kept hidden for the purpose of revealing it now. It is true that the emphatic position is given to the verb *might be made known*, and hence a contrast with the previous hiding is pointed out. The word *now*, however, is not particularly emphatic and cannot bear the burden of this exegesis. The burden is considerable, for while it is possible to hide something in order to make it known at a later date, it is more probable that the revelation is the purpose of Paul's preaching or of God's creation of the world. Hiding is a more or less negative idea, and it seems reasonable to expect some definite and outward event that has the purpose stated here.

Let us then consider the next possibility. The interpretation that Paul was called to preach in order that God's wisdom might be made known seems to fit in very well with the preceding context.

In verse 8 Paul had just referred to the grace God had given him for the purpose of preaching the gospel to the Gentiles. From

50

this point the long complicated sentence continues to the end of verse 13. Even further back, as early as verse 2, the idea of Paul's preaching had been introduced. Therefore no one can doubt that Paul's preaching is the main idea, or at least one of the main ideas, of this passage. Whether or not Paul's personal ministry recedes from its main position as the paragraph approaches its end, and what other subordinate ideas may be found in verses 9-11, must of course be determined by direct examination. But the idea of Paul's preaching is without doubt prominent.

We now ask the question whether or not the revelation of God's wisdom to powers in heaven is the purpose of Paul's preaching.

Charles Hodge thinks it is. Aside from his objections to other views, which we shall study presently, his positive argument is as follows: "The apostle is speaking of his conversion and call to the apostleship. To him was the grace given to preach the unsearchable riches of Christ, and teach all men the economy of redemption, 'in order that' through the Church might be made known the manifold wisdom of God. It is only thus that the connection of this verse with the main idea of the context is preserved. It is not the design of creation, but the design of the revelation of the mystery of redemption, of which he is here speaking (*Commentary, in loc.* p. 119).

For the moment the only objection to Hodge's exegesis is the seemingly peculiar notion that Paul's preaching on earth reveals God's wisdom to the powers in heaven. One would not be surprised if Paul's preaching on earth revealed God's wisdom to men. But Paul did not preach to angels, demons, or whomever these powers may be. Admittedly, Paul's preaching and the founding of the Church can be said to reveal God's wisdom to these powers, if we suppose that God directed their attention to what was going on. In this case Paul's preaching would have this purpose, but it would be a purpose one or two steps removed. Immediately it would seem more natural to connect Paul's preaching with its effects on men, rather than on angels or demons.

However, since no decisive grammatical reason can be advanced against this interpretation, it is presumably impossible to disprove it.

51

On the other hand, there is a third interpretation, also grammatically possible, one that seems to have weightier reasons in its favor, and which does not suffer under the objectons raised against it. Grammatically, in fact, this third interpretation is not merely equally good, but somewhat preferable.

When we say that God created the world for the purpose of displaying his manifold wisdom, we connect the purpose clause with the nearest antecedent. As anyone can see, the reference to Paul's preaching lies several clauses further back. The immediate antecedent is creation, and this position, we hold, is of some value in deciding the matter.

Since therefore the syntax is at least somewhat in its favor, the best procedure is to examine objections against so understanding it.

We turn again to Hodge for these objections. The view that God created the universe in order to display his manifold wisdom is, as Hodge says, the supralapsarian view. Against this interpretation Hodge urges four objections: (1) This passage is the only passage in Scripture adduced as directly asserting supralapsarianism, and supralapsarianism is foreign to to the New Testament. (2) Apart from doctrinal objections, this interpretation imposes an unnatural connection upon the clauses. The idea of creation is entirely subordinate and unessential: it could have been omitted without materially affecting the sense of the passage. (3) The theme of the passage concerns Paul's preaching; only by connecting the purpose clause with Paul's preaching can the unity of the context be preserved. (4) The word *now*, in contrast with the previous hiding, supports the reference to Paul's preaching. It was Paul's preaching that had *now* put an end to the secret's hiddenness. Such are Hodge's four objections.

Let us consider the last one first. Admittedly, it was Paul's preaching that founded the Church, and the founding of the Church made known God's wisdom to the powers in heaven. The supralapsarian interpretation does not deny that Paul's preaching played this important part in God's eternal plan. But even so, Paul's preaching was not the immediate cause of the revelation of God's wisdom. It was the existence of the Church that was the immediate cause. Yet grammar prevents us from saying that the

Church was founded in order that God's wisdom might be revealed. It is true that the Church was founded to reveal God's wisdom, but this is not what the verse says. Now, if several events had occurred, leading up to this revelation of God's wisdom, including the founding of the Church, Paul's preaching, and of course the death and resurrection of Christ which Paul preached, the word *now* in the verse cannot be used to single out Paul's preaching in contrast with other events mentioned in the passage. Hodge's fourth objection is therefore poor.

Next, the first objection: this is the only passage in Scripture adduced as directly asserting supralapsarianism, and supralapsarianism is foreign to the New Testament. The latter half of this objection is of course *a petitio principii*, i.e., Hodge begs the question. If this verse teaches supralapsarianism, then the doctrine is not foreign to the New Testament. We must first determine what the verse means; then we shall know what is in the New Testament and what perhaps is not.

To be sure, if this one verse were indeed the only verse in the Bible with supralapsarian overtones, we would be justified in entertaining some suspicion of the interpretation. Hodge does not say explicitly that this is the only verse; he says it is the only verse adduced as directly asserting supralapsarianism.

Well, really, even this verse does not directly assert the whole complex supralapsarian view. Very few verses in Scripture directly assert the whole of a major doctrine. Therefore we must recognize degrees of directness, partial and even fragmentary assertions of a doctrine. And with this recognition, regularly acknowledged in the development of any doctrine, it is evident that this verse does not stand alone in suspicious isolation.

Supralapsarianism, for all its insistence on a certain logical order among the divine decrees, is essentially, so it seems to us, the unobjectionable view that God controls the universe purposefully. God acts with a purpose. He has an end in view and sees the end from the beginning. Every verse in Scripture that in one way or another refers to God's manifold wisdom, every statement indicating that a prior event is for the purpose of causing a subsequent event, every mention of an eternal, all-embracing plan contributes to a teleological and therefore supralapsarian view of

God's control of history. In this light Ephesians 3:10 clearly does not stand alone.

The connection between supralapsarianism and the fact that God always acts purposefully depends on the observation that the logical order of any plan is the exact reverse of its temporal execution. The first step in any planning is the end to be achieved; then the means are decided upon, until last of all the first thing to be done is discovered. The execution in time reverses the order of planning. Thus creation, since it is first in history, must be logically last in the divine decrees. Every Biblical passage therefore that refers to God's wisdom also supports Ephesians 3:10.

Next comes objection number two. Hodge claimed that the supralapsarian interpretation of this verse imposes an unnatural connection upon the clauses. The idea of creation, he said, is entirely unessential and could have been omitted without materially affecting the sense of the passage.

Is it not evident that Hodge does not know how to handle the reference to creation? He claims that it is unessential, a chance and thoughtless remark that does not affect the sense of the passage. Such careless writing does not seem to me to be Paul's usual style.

For example, in Galatians 1:1, Paul says, "Paul, an apostle, not from men nor through a man, but by Jesus Christ and God the Father who raised him from the dead." Why now did Paul mention that God raised Jesus Christ? If it were a chance remark without logical connection with the sense of the passage, a remark intended only to speak of some aspect of God's glory, Paul could as well have said, God who created the universe.

But it is fairly clear that Paul had a conscious purpose in selecting the resurrection instead of the creation. He wanted to emphasize, against his detractors, that he had apostolic authority from Jesus Christ himself. And Jesus Christ was able to give him that authority because he was not dead, but had been raised up by God.

So, as Paul chose the idea of resurrection instead of creation in Galatians 1:1, he also chose creation instead of resurrection in Ephesians 3:9 because the idea of creation contributed some meaning to his thought. Certainly the supralapsarian or teleological interpretation of Ephesians 3:10 accommodates the idea of creation, and contrariwise an interpretation that can find no meaning in these words is a poorer interpretation.

The remaining objection is that only by making Paul's preaching the antecedent of the purpose clause can the unity of the context be preserved. The reverse seems to be the case. Not only does Hodge fail to account for the mention of creation, and thus diminish the unity, but further the stress on purpose, running from creation to the present unifies the passage in a most satisfactory manner.

The teleological understanding of God's working in fact enables us to combine all three of these interpretations, including the second which in itself has so very little in its favor, in a unified thought. Since God does everything for a purpose, and since whatever precedes in time has in a general way the purpose of preparing for what follows, we may say that God kept the secret hidden in order to reveal it now, and also that Paul preached the gospel in order to reveal it now. But if God had not created the world, there would have been no Paul to preach, no Church by which the revelation could be made, no heavenly powers on which to impress the idea of God's manifold wisdom. Only by connecting the purpose clause with the immediate antecedent concerning creation, can a unified sense be obtained from the passage as a whole.

Therefore, in conclusion, although the other interpretation is grammatically possible, the idea that God created the world for the purpose of revealing his wisdom makes much better sense.

After this special excursus on the purpose of creation, we finally come to creation itself. The main assertion is that God created all things of nothing, in the space of six days, and all very good. This Biblical world-view is called theism; it stands in opposition to pantheism and naturalism.

In the preceding chapter mention was made of the philosophies of Spinoza and Hegel. They were both forms of pantheism, a view that identifies God and nature. Awed by the splendor of the universe, these thinkers spoke in religious tones about the world as a whole. Unlike ancient and uncivilized peoples who worshiped the sun or moon, pantheists do not deify any single part of nature, but rather deify the whole. Spinoza regularly spoke of

Deus sive Natura, which can most accurately be translated, "God, that is to say, Nature."

Naturalism, so often contrasted with pantheism, declines to use religious language about the world. It prefers scientific terminology and is more obviously atheistic.

American humanism too, or at least an important segment of it, refuses to speak of God. With some honesty they point out that the term *God* regularly means a transcendent person; therefore to say *God* when talking about the universe is to confuse other people and perchance oneself as well. Those humanists may be a little more "religious" in their language than the scientific naturalists; but their philosophy is essentially the same.

Otherwise, theological humanists redefine God. For example, the Chicago professor, Henry Nelson Wieman, in one place defines God as an interaction between individuals, groups, and ages which promotes the greatest possible mutuality of good;[1] and in another place modifies the definition to equate God with those parts of the universe which enable us to achieve the greatest goods and avoid the greatest evils.

Therefore the difference between pantheism, which says all is God, and naturalism, which says nothing is God, and Wieman's definitional method of religious obfuscation, is merely a difference in literary style. They all deny that a Sovereign Spirit created the universe.

The doctrine of creation presents us with perplexities both philosophical and scientific. There are exegetical problems also. Critics like to accuse Christians of being unwilling to examine their faith, of refusing to face the facts, of fearing the results of investigation. That there are some such Christians is evident from the previous chapter. But they are Christians of little faith, and little logic too. The mere fact that you or I cannot satisfactorily answer a critic's objection is no evidence that the objection has no answer. Last century Christians could not satisfactorily answer the charge that the Bible had invented Hittites and that no such nation ever existed actually. That is one attack on the truth of the Scriptures that has been completely defeated in this century. Maybe we shall have to wait until we get to heaven to be able to answer some

---

1. Wieman, Macintosh and Otto, *Is There a God?* p. 13.

other attacks; but we must always remember that secular philosophies contain greater difficulties than Christianity does.

As for creation, science makes it almost impossible to believe that the world was created in 4004 B.C. But then, the Bible does not say that it was. Bishop Ussher said so, and good man though he was, he might have been mistaken on this point. The Christian position is that the Bible—and not the Bishop—is infallible. The chronology of the early Old Testament is exceedingly difficult to decipher, and when it comes to the creation of the world, there is no chronology given. Let us not insert one between the lines.

It was said that science makes it almost impossible to believe in the 4004 B.C. date. Some secular scientists might raise their supercilious eyebrows and declare with finality that science makes it totally impossible. Those who say so, however, must face this question upon pain of being charged with being afraid to face the facts. What evidence is there that the world was not created only last week? Yes, that is right, only last week, or even yesterday. Presumably either God created the world or it is the result of chance. It is hard to think of any other alternative. Now, if God created the world, might he not, since he is omnipotent, have created trees with rings in them, rocks with fossils in them, and human beings furnished with ready-made memories? In this case the world could be exactly as it is now and not have existed five minutes. But suppose there is no God and chance is the basis of the universe. The argument for chance has it that in an infinite time all possible arrangements of atoms takes place, and this is one of them. But if all possibilities are eventually realized, may not this world be the one in which the cosmos arranged itself this way yesterday? Scientists who neglect the statements of revelation have their logical difficulties too, worse difficulties than Christians have; and they do not face their difficulties nor solve their problems by trying to laugh them off.

But of course, creation can perplex us too. If God is immutable, how could he change from a state of inactivity to the act of creation? A little less difficult perhaps is the question why God did not create the world an hour sooner or an hour later. Another that is not often repeated is similar: why did God put the solar system or the entire universe right here rather than at some other place in the vast expanse of space? St. Augustine made a noble attempt to answer these questions.

Secular or pagan thought has regularly denied that the world had a first moment. Naturalism holds that the physical universe has always existed. With the present popularity of evolution, it is also denied that great changes take place suddenly. Recently, however, the eminent physicist, Professor George Gamow, in his book *The Birth and Death of the Sun*, said that "the elements were formed in not more than half an hour." This is interesting in that its admission of a sudden unique event contrasts with previous views of a slow, gradual, evolutionary uniformity; but it can hardly be said that Dr. Gamow has proved the truth of the Biblical account.

That the Bible is not a book on science is often given as an excuse for its many alleged mistakes. The assumption seems to be that science books do not make mistakes. But over the centuries scientific theories have come and gone. Even in the last half century physics has been almost completely altered. Professor Gamow has a new theory and his successor will have another. Of course, the Bible is not a science textbook, but when it mentions natural phenomena, it speaks the truth.

In order to undermine the doctrine of creation, destructive Biblical critics have proposed to translate Genesis 1:1, "When God began to make the heavens and the earth." This wording obscures the idea of a sudden act and a creation out of nothing. It should be noted, however, that the Hebrew verb, *bara*, in the form or "voice" used in Genesis 1:1, never refers to human productions. Even the other "voices" in which a human subject cuts down a tree or kills an enemy are extremely rare. Verbs of doing and making occur hundreds of times in the Old Testament, but this verb with a human subject occurs less than five times. Its characteristic use is to express divine production.

That God created out of nothing is seen negatively by the absence of any mention of a pre-existing matter, and positively by the all-embracing extent of the sphere of creation. God is said to have created all things: Nehemiah 9:6; Colossians 1:16; Revelation 4:11. The expressions are so universal that no possibility remains for anything uncreated.

58

Then there is the matter of the six creative days. Does the word *day* necessarily mean twenty-four hours? In English *day* most frequently means about twelve hours. We also say that there were no telephones in George Washington's day. Further, Genesis 2:4 seems to refer to all six days as one day. And again, can we speak of six days of creation when the first chapter of Genesis uses the verb create only three times? Bernard Ramm has written a very interesting book, *The Christian View of Science and the Scripture*. I cannot agree with some of the things he says, but it is worth reading.

The suspicion that the days of creation were not twenty-four hour days is not a recent attempt to harmonize modern science and the Bible. Perhaps some Christians whose faith has been shaken by naturalistic science have been so motivated. But our opponents, who are so quick to ridicule Bishop Ussher, usually fail to mention the fact that Augustine, the great theologian of the early fifth century, considered the six creative days to be six periods of time—and he was not motivated by nineteenth century science.

Section II.—After God had made all other creatures, he created man, male and female,[4] with reasonable and immortal souls,[5] endued with knowledge, righteousness and true holiness, after his own image,[6] having the law of God written in their hearts,[7] and power to fulfil it;[8] and yet under a possibility of transgressing, being left to the liberty of their own will, which was subject unto change.[9] Besides this law written in their hearts, they received a command not to eat of the tree of the knowledge of good and evil;[10] which while they kept, they were happy in their communion with God, and had dominion over the creatures.[11]

4. Gen. i. 27.—5. Gen. ii. 7 ; Eccles. xii. 7 ; Luke xxiii. 43 ; Matt. x. 28.—6. Gen. i 26 ; Col iii. 10 ; Eph. iv. 24.—7. Rom. ii. 14,15.—8. Eccles. vii. 29.—9. Gen. iii. 6 ; Eccl. vii. 29.—10. Gen. ii. 17 ; iii. 8-11,23.—11. i. 26,28.

The most important part of creation was the creation of man. The heavens and the earth, grand as they are, are, as it were, nothing but the stage setting for the actors in the Divine Comedy. The reason is that while nature displays the manifold wisdom of God, man bears God's own image. Dogs don't. I still love dogs, dachshunds and St. Bernards. But God gave man a reasonable or rational soul. Man can learn mathematics. Dogs can't. And I still love dogs, Doberman pinschers and Toy Manchesters.

Further, dogs, not to speak of trees and stones, cannot be righteous or holy. To them the Ten Commandments and the Biblical requirements for worship do not apply. But man was created with the law of God written in his heart.

Students of philosophy will be interested to note that the Bible and the Confession do not support the epistemological empiricism of John Locke and Aristotle. Those who are not students of philosophy can look up epistemology and empiricism in the dictionary, though it will not do them much good. At any rate the Bible denies that we are born with a blank mind and a morally neutral character. The image of God consists of certain innate ideas, at least the ideas of formal logic, and certain principles of morality.

Today, of course, men are born with a sinful character; but Adam was created with a positively righteous character. He did not have to learn by experience what was right and wrong. Even today, after the fall, the human mind begins with innate ideas. It is not true that all knowledge comes through experience.

The theory of innate ideas and the denial that man is born morally neutral, i.e., without any definite character one way or another, helps us to understand what is meant by "the liberty of their own will." In the Confession this phrase does not mean the freedom of the will as the Pelagians, Roman Catholics, and Arminians use it. But as a later chapter takes up this point, we shall postpone it for the present.

In brief, this is the doctrine of creation. Such was the skill of the Westminster divines that they were able to outline these marvelous themes in less than 150 words. In two short paragraphs they summarized the main burden of the Bible on this point. A Presbyterian ministry that fails to preach these Westminster doctrines would be unfaithful to its ordination vows; and any other ministry or any communicant member who neglects the Confession is thereby deprived of the best brief guidebook to an understanding of the Bible.

CHAPTER V.

OF PROVIDENCE.

Section I.—God, the great Creator of all things, doth uphold,[1] direct, dispose and govern all creatures, actions and things,[2] from the greatest even to the least,[3] by his most wise and holy providence,[4] according to his infallible foreknowledge,[5] and the free and immutable counsel of his own will,[6] to the praise of the glory of his wisdom, power, justice, goodness and mercy.[7]

1. Heb. i. 3.—2. Dan. iv. 34,35; Ps. cxxxv. 6. Acts xvii. 25,26,28; Job xxxviii., xxxix., xli.—3. Matt. x .29-31.—4. Prov. xv. 3; Ps. civ. 24; cxlv. 17.—Acts xv. 18; Ps. xciv. 8-11.—6. Eph. i. 11; Ps. xxxiii. 10,11.—7. Isa. lxiii. 14; Eph. iii. 10; Rom. ix. 17; Gen. xlv. 7; Ps. cxlv. 7.

The authors of the Westminster Confession compressed the doctrine of the Trinity into one section of five lines; but when they came to God's control over all his creatures and all their actions, they wrote two fairly lengthy chapters. The eight sections of Chapter III outline the Bible's teaching on predestination to life and foreordination to death, so that those who sincerely obey the gospel may praise God in humility and be assured of their eternal election from the certainty of their effectual calling. Chapter V differs in that predestination is more specific and providence is more general, and also in that it considers God's controlling power during the course of history rather than his eternal plan itself.

The devout scholars who made these chapters so long must have done so under the belief, a belief fully justified, that the Bible has a great deal to say about God's sovereignty and that it is all-important. Calvinism proportions its emphases to those of the Bible.

Not all Christians are Calvinists; some do not believe that "all things come to pass immutably and infallibly"; they wish to reserve some sphere in which man can be independent of God. It must not be supposed that these people are therefore lacking in sincerity and devotion or that they are outside the fold of Christ. But such is the clarity of the Bible in its teachings on God's sovereignty that Presbyterians cannot convince themselves that such people have a

sufficient understanding to discharge the responsibilities of an ecclesiastical office. They stand in need of further instruction. They
should study the proof texts cited by the Confession.

For example: "He doeth according to his will in the army of
heaven and among the inhabitants of the earth; and none can stay
his hand" (Dan. 4:35). "Whatsoever the Lord pleased, that did
he" (Ps. 135:6). "Being predestinated according to the purpose of
him who worketh all things after the counsel of his own will"
(Eph. 1:11). And many other verses.

Because the doctrines of predestination and providence are
sometimes misunderstood, the Calvinists, when they explain these
doctrines, regularly try to absolve them of the charge of fatalism.
Then too, because the words predestination, foreordination, and
election are indisputably in the Bible, the non-Calvinists also try
to rid the Bible of any appearance of fatalism. All of the latter and
some of the former succeed better in removing the predestination
than the fatalism.

There is a technical and there is a popular view of fatalism.
The more technical view, if the word is to be used at all, is that
of scientists and philosophers who deny that the universe has a
purpose. Natural processes seem not to be directed to any foreseen end. Such is the view of Spinoza, Bertrand Russell, and others.
Obviously this is exactly the opposite of the Biblical doctrine of
providence. God sees the end from the beginning and controls all
his creatures and all their actions so as to guarantee the planned
result. In this sense the Bible is not fatalistic.

A more popular view comes from Moslem countries. My
uncle once hired a chauffeur to drive him around a mountainous
part of Turkey. As the chauffeur kept up too fast a speed around
the sharp curves along the precipices, my uncle urged more caution. But the Turk replied that the date of their deaths was fated;
and if this was the day, caution would be of no use; whereas if
this was not the day, caution was unnecessary. The Turk was
clever, but not Calvinistic. The Bible teaches that all things are
certainly determined, but that God's providence (Chapter V, section ii) arranges events according to the nature of second causes,
either necessarily, freely, or contingently. God does not decree an
auto wreck apart from its causes; caution is the usual cause of
safety, and wrecks are caused by recklessness.

Superficially similar is another popular view to the effect that fatalism means that man should sit quietly by and do nothing to avert the tragedies which threaten him. Not very many people are tempted to believe such a theory. It is not much of a danger to Christianity. But if a few are so tempted, they can easily see that the Bible commands us to do various things. Adam was commanded to subdue nature to his needs. Abraham was commanded to leave his home. Christ, who was delivered up by the determinate counsel of God, went deliberately to his death. None of these sat idly by.

Now, no one denies that the Bible contains these commands and these actions. The Bible also teaches predestination and election. If a person is puzzled and thinks these two facts constitute an inconsistency, a puzzle or a paradox, he ought at least admit that the Bible so teaches. Therefore he ought to preach both and slight neither. Unfortunately his bewilderment is likely to reduce the force of his preaching.

But it is not necessary to remain bewildered. This is not to say that a man can become omniscient and solve all the problems with which he may be confronted. It does mean, however, that the Bible itself, all of which is profitable for doctrine, contains enough information to show that action and volition by man are not inconsistent with foreordination by God. God decreed the peculiar status of the Jews, and he decreed to bring it about by Abraham's journey to Palestine. God decreed that Joseph would be sold as a slave in Egypt in order to preserve the family from famine. God decreed the death of Christ from before the foundation of the world, and therefore Christ steadfastly set his face toward Jerusalem. It was by means of, not in spite of, these volitions and actions that God had determined to accomplish his purpose.

The Christian should always remember that God is the potter and man is the clay; of the same lump God can make a vessel of honor or a vessel of dishonor. The Christian should also remember that God works in us, of his own good pleasure, both to will and to do. So remembering, the Christian will be a Calvinist and will praise God that his servants at Westminster constructed our Confession as a standard against error and as a bulwark of truth.

*Section II.—Although, in relation to the foreknowl-
edge and decree of God, the first cause, all things come
to pass immutably and infallibly;[8] yet, by the same providence, he ordereth them to fall out according to the nature of second causes, either necessarily, freely or contingently.[9]*

*Section III.—God in his ordinary providence mak-
eth use of means,[10] yet is free to work without,[11]
above,[12] and against them,[13] at his pleasure.*

8. Acts ii. 23.—9. Gen. viii. 22; Jer. xxxi. 35; Ex. xxi. 13; Deut. xix.
5; 1 Kings xxii. 28,34; Isa. x. 6,7.—10. Acts xxvii. 31,44; Isa. lv. 10,11;
Hos. ii. 21,22.—11. Hos. i. 7; Matt. iv. 4; Job xxxiv. 10.—12. Rom. iv.
19-21.—13. 2 Kings vi 6; Dan. iii. 27.

Section ii first acknowledges that all events are predetermined.
The course of history has from all eternity been immutably and
infallibly fixed. But this does not deny the role of secondary
causation; and secondary causation seems to be either necessary,
free, or contingent. What do these three words refer to?

In theology and philosophy necessity has been regarded sometimes as mechanical causation and sometimes as logical implication. One may say that if a given force is applied to one end of a
lever, the other end will of necessity lift a certain weight. Or, one
may say that two premises necessarily imply a given conclusion.
Spinoza held that the world follows necessarily from God as conclusions follow from premises. More frequently philosophers have
defended mechanical necessity. Which does the Confession refer
to? Similarly, one would like to know the meaning of freely and
contingently.

What the Reformation theologians meant by these terms may
be fairly well surmised from a passage in Jerome Zanchius' book,
Absolute Predestination, The Will of God, Position 11. He writes:

"Position 11. In consequence of God's immutable will and infallible foreknowledge, whatever things come to pass, come to pass
necessarily, though with respect to second causes and us men,
many things are contingent, i.e., unexpected and seemingly accidental."

Thus the term contingent refers to man's way of looking at
events, or more explicitly to man's incomplete knowledge of how
the events were caused.

The Scripture references appended to this section of the Confession also provide some hints as to how these words should be

understood. They refer to the succession of seedtime and harvest, summer and winter, the sun as a light for the day and the moon by night. Presumably these things are examples of what is necessary; but the framers may not have meant that these things occur by the philosophic theory of mechanism. Other references point to accidental homicide, shooting an arrow at random, and the role of Assyria in carrying out God's purposes without knowing it. Are these free or are they contingent? Can we be sure that they are not necessary? Is the shooting an arrow, even at random, any less mechanical than the alteration of summer and winter? Theories of causation have varied greatly over the ages, but whatever our theory of secondary causation may be, the Scripture is clear that God ordains events in relation to each other, and not in the disjointed fashion that the Turkish chauffeur had in mind.

The strong recommendations frequently found on these pages may suggest to someone that the Confession itself is the very Word of God. Of course, this is not true. The Presbyterian Churches recognize the Bible alone as the Word of God and they explicitly refer to the Confession and Catechisms as subordinate standards of the church.

No claim is made that the Confession is infallible. Through the years different Presbyterian denominations have altered it in one way or another. Later we shall see one chapter that was substantially altered. And in other chapters there may be errors or at least infelicities in a few phrases.

Such may be the case here in section iii. The first idea is that God uses means to accomplish his purposes. This was said before and is incontestibly true. But is God free to work without, above, and against them?

One might reply that God can do all things: he is omnipotent. Quite true; but irrelevant. The first thing we must do is to determine what "without, above, and against" mean. Let us take these three terms in reverse order.

One of the proof texts to show that God can work against means refers to the miracle of the floating axe head. The other proof text concerns the safety of the three young Hebrews in Nebuchadnezzar's fiery furnace. Now, if the word *against* means nothing other than God's power to work miracles and thus to accomplish his aim in opposition to the usual processes of nature, it is clear that the Bible supports this word in the Confession.

What, then, is meant by working above means? Here again the one proof text has to do with the miraculous or at least very unusual birth of Isaac. Perhaps then above and against are synonymous.

Next we ask, does God ever work without means? Hosea 1:7 merely says that God will not save the Israelites by means of sword and battle. But there is no indication that God will not use some other means. Matthew 4:4, another proof text, says that man shall not live by bread alone, but by every Word of God. This surely does not teach that God works without means. In fact, it states what the means are. The third proof text is Job 34:10. How this verse got attached to this phrase in the Confession is a puzzle. It seems to be completely beside the point. And if so, the Confession just might be in error in using the word *without*.

Think a moment first, however. Does God ever accomplish his purpose without using some means or other? Perhaps in two of God's actions he uses no means. In creating the world from nothing, there were no means to use. Also in continuing to uphold in existence the universe in its entirety, there could be no means. But these two actions are not to be classed as "his ordinary providence"; and so we may continue to wonder whether this is a mistake in the Confession.

> *Section IV.—The almighty power, unsearchable wisdom and infinite goodness of God, so far manifest themselves in his providence, that it extendeth itself even to the first fall, and all other sins of angels and men,[14] and that not by a bare permission,[15] but such as hath joined with it a most wise and powerful bounding,[16] and otherwise ordering and governing of them, in a manifold dispensation, to his own holy ends;[17] yet so as the sinfulness thereof proceedeth only from the creature, and not from God; who being most holy and righteous, neither is nor can be the author or approver of sin.[18]*
>
> *Section V —The most wise, righteous and gracious God, doth oftentimes leave for a season his own children to manifold temptations and the corruption of their own hearts, to chastise them for their former sins, or to discover unto them the hidden strength of corruption and*

deceitfulness of their hearts, that they may be humbled;[19] *and to raise them to a more close and constant dependence for their support upon himself, and to make them more watchful against all future occasions of sin, and for sundry other just and holy ends.*[20]

Section VI.—As for those wicked and ungodly men whom God, as a righteous judge, for former sins doth blind and harden,[21] *from them he not only withholdeth his grace, whereby they might have been enlightened in their understandings and wrought upon in their hearts,*[22] *but sometimes also withdraweth the gifts which they had,*[23] *and exposeth them to such objects as their corruption makes occasion of sin,*[24] *and withal, gives them over to their own lusts, the temptations of the world and the power of Satan;*[25] *whereby it comes to pass that they harden themselves, even under those means which God useth for the softening of others.*[26]

Section VII.—As the providence of God doth, in general, reach to all creatures; so after a most special manner, it taketh care of his Church and disposeth all things to the good thereof.[27]

14. Rom. xi. 32-34; 2 Sam. xxiv. 1; 1 Chron. xxi. 1; 1 Kings xxii. 22, 23; 1 Chron. x. 4,13,14; 2 Sam. xvi. 10; Acts ii. 23; iv. 27,28.—15. Acts xiv. 16.—16. Ps. lxxvi. 10.; 2 Kings xix. 28.—17. Gen. i. 20; Isa. x. 6,7,12.—18. James i. 13,14,17; 1 John ii. 16; Ps. l. 21.—19. 2 Chron. xxxii. 25,26,31; 2 Sam. xxiv. 1.—20. 2 Cor. xii. 7-9; Ps. lxxiii.; lxxxvii. 1,10,12; Mark xiv. 66, to end; John xxi. 15,17.—21. Rom. i. 24,26,28; xi. 7,8.—22. Deut. xxix. 4.—23. Matt. xiii. 12; xxv. 29. —24 Deut. ii. 30; 2 Kings viii. 12,13.—25. Ps. lxxxi. 11,12; 2 Thess. ii. 10-12.—26. Ex. vii. 3; viii. 15,32; 2 Cor. ii. 15,16; Isa. viii. 14; 1 Pet. ii. 7,8; Isa. vi. 9,10; Acts xxviii. 26,27.—27. Amos ix. 8,9; Rom. viii. 28.

God's relation to the sinful acts of men, the stumbling block that so many people find in Chapter III, is considered again in section iv of Chapter V. The sphere of providence extends to the first sin of Adam and to all other sins of angels and men. God's relation to sin is not that of bare permission; in fact, as Calvin shows in his *Institutes*, II, iv, 3 and III, xxiii, 8, permission in the case of the Almighty has no specific meaning; the proof texts cited in the Confession and many other passages not cited amply support the creedal statement. God bounds, orders, and governs all sinful actions for his own holy purpose. How could it be otherwise? This does not mean, as the Confession makes plain, that God commits sin or that God approves sin. On the contrary God punishes sin. Many people think that this is paradoxical. But is it not clear, in the case of good deeds, that God does not himself do the good deed that his servant does? It was Abraham, not God, who left Ur to go to Canaan. Similarly it was Herod and Pilate with the Gentiles who crucified Christ. God approved Abraham's act and disapproved of Pilate's; but he foreordained both; and in particular it says that the crucifixion was determined before the world was. The Scripture is clear; but some people are recalcitrant.

Section v spells out the details of God's providence with reference to his children; section vi does the same with the children of disobedience. There is little to do but verify the fact that the Confessional statements simply summarize hundreds of Biblical passages. The last section, of one sentence, applies the same truth to the Church.

CHAPTER VI.

OF THE FALL OF MAN, OF SIN
AND OF THE PUNISHMENT THEREOF.

Section I.—Our first parents being seduced by the subtilty and temptation of Satan, sinned in eating the forbidden fruit.[1] This their sin God was pleased according to his wise and holy counsel to permit, having purposed to order it to his own glory.[2]

Section II.—By this sin they fell from their original righteousness and communion with God,[3] and so became dead in sin,[4] and wholly defiled in all the faculties and parts of soul and body.[5]

1. Gen. iii. 13 ; 2 Cor. xi. 3.—2. Rom. xi. 32.—3. Gen. iii. 6-8 ; Eccles. xii. 29. Rom. iii. 23.—4. Gen. ii. 17 ; Eph. ii. 1.—5. Tit. i. 15 ; Gen. vi. 5 ; Jer. xvii. 9 ; Rom. iii. 10-18.

In these times when religious periodicals are so full of politics and so empty of Biblical exposition, the ignorance of the people is so great that every doctrine of the Westminster Confession needs vigorous proclamation. As we look at the doctrine of sin in chapter VI, it is hard to avoid thinking that it needs even a more vigorous presentation than the others. This natural reaction may be exaggerated, but surely the chapter contains a wealth of material pertinent for our careless age.

Section i teaches that our first parents sinned by eating the forbidden fruit. Why did God test Adam by forbidding him to eat of a certain tree rather than by forbidding him to murder Eve? Some pious people would castigate such a question as frivolous and irreverent. But not at all; it is very serious, and, I believe, substantially instructive. Adam might have refrained from murdering Eve by reason of natural affection. Obedience in this case would not have come solely from a respect for God's authority. But had Adam refused to eat the forbidden fruit, sheer obedience to the divine command could have been the only motive. God set a test of obedience uncomplicated by extraneous considerations. Therefore Adam's sin was insubordination without extenuating circumstances.

69

It is important for many reasons to know precisely what sin is. We need to have this knowledge in order to be able to identify particular sins. Otherwise we could make no attempt to avoid them. Then, too, we need to know the nature of sin in order to assess the value of suggested cures. Can Christian Science cancel the effects of sin? Or Buddhism? Well, if such religions do not know what they are trying to combat, it is not likely they will have much success. Again, a knowledge of sin is essential in order correctly to evaluate its seriousness. Different religions, and even different groups of professing Christians, assign different degrees of seriousness to sin. To some sin seems trivial; to others it is moderately bad; Calvinists regard sin as fatal.

The reason for the Calvinistic position is that the Bible describes sin as an affront to the majesty of God. It is a violation of God's law. The Shorter Catechism says that sin is any want of conformity unto or transgression of the law of God. Apart from the law there can be no sin. The verse in John's first epistle says sin is lawlessness.

None of this is to be understood as tying sin solely to the Mosaic law. The Bible does not tell us of an age of conscience prior to and an age of grace subsequent to an age of law. Romans 5:13-14 reminds us that death, the penalty for sin, reigned from Adam to Moses, indicating that the law of God antedated the Mosaic law. Of course it did: God gave some commandments to Adam.

Similarly, our present age is not an age of grace subsequent to fifteen hundred years of law. This is indeed an age of grace; but it is also an age of law. If it were not an age of law, there would be no sin at all. Not only some Christians, but even all criminals would have achieved sinless perfection.

Toward the end of the first century and again at the Reformation there were some professing Christians who claimed that the Ten Commandments had been abrogated, and that therefore, being "free from the law" they were at liberty to indulge in all the vices they wanted to. This virulent form of antinomianism is not so prevalent in the visible Church today, but some of its doctrinal aberrations remain to becloud the gospel.

Now, as a matter of fact, the phrase "free from the law" (Rom. 6:7) should have been translated "justified from the law."

The meaning is that the redeemed sinner escapes the law's penalty through the death of Christ. It does not mean that he is free to ignore divine instructions and to live a criminal life.

The main point here, however, is that antinomians implicitly deny the existence of sin. Not only have all Christians attained sinless perfection, but everybody else has as well. On their theory sin is utterly impossible because where there is no law, there is no transgression. One cannot break a law that does not exist.

Fortunately this extreme form of antinomianism does not now much disturb the Church. But it is as necessary as ever to understand what sin is. This necessity can be seen in evangelistic activity. Before a man is willing to accept Christ as Savior, he must admit that he is a sinner in need of salvation. In spite of the vice, the juvenile delinquency, the college students' sex orgies, the violent crime and brutality, the riotous mobs, not to mention the big and little wars that characterize this century, few people admit that they need a Savior. Nearly everyone thinks that, even though not perfect, he is good enough to get to heaven. To these people the faithful evangelist must preach the law of God. He must tell them what sin is. To suppose that the law of God no longer applies in this age is to eviscerate evangelism. Sin is any want of conformity unto the law of God.

This first section also states that God, for his own glory as previously explained at length, was pleased to permit our first parents to disobey his command.

Most people would say that the word *permit* is a softer expression than the word *ordain*. Some would even say that permission half puts sin out of God's control. But we cannot permit anyone to suppose that Chapter VI contradicts Chapters III and IV. Not being infallible, the men at Westminster may have fallen into some slight inconsistency somewhere; but it can hardly be maintained that they anywhere contradicted the doctrine of the divine decree.

It is better to understand the word permit as merely a convenient linguistic expression. Indeed, permission as it is used in human affairs is inappropriate to the divine omnipotence and sovereignty. Of course, it is quite true to say that God permitted

Adam to sin; but if by this we intend to deny that God foreordained Adam's sin, we are quite mistaken. God foreordains whatsoever comes to pass.

For reasons such as this John Calvin wrote, "Here they [those who object to the divine decrees] recur to the distinction between will and permission, and insist that God permits the destruction of the impious, but does not will it. But what reason shall we assign for his permitting it, but because it is his will?" (*Institutes,* III, xxiii (8; cf. II, iv, 3). This is clearly a sufficient reply.

Now, next, Chapter IV had said that man was created righteous; the present chapter adds that our first parents sinned, and "by this sin they fell from their original righteousness, and communion with God, and so became dead in sin, and wholly defiled in all the faculties and parts of soul and body."

Roman Catholicism holds that man was not created positively righteous, but, rather, neutral; after his creation God gave him an extra gift of righteousness; and when Adam sinned, he lost the extra gift and fell back to the neutral state in which he was created. Thus man's present condition, according to Romanism, is not too bad. The Bible and the Confession say that man fell far below the estate in which he was created and is now wholly defiled in all his faculties and parts.

The modernists have a better opinion of themselves than even the Romanists have. If the race fell at all, it was an upward evolutionary fall; and man has been making rapid progress ever since. Herbert Spencer set the norm for much modernistic preaching in his prediction that the little evil remaining on earth would vanish in a short time. Books were written about moral man in an immoral society that needed only a good dose of socialism to become utopian. Ministers dilated on human perfectibility. And in the summer of 1914 a college president and Presbyterian elder had almost finished a book to prove there would be no more war. He had forgotten what Christ said. Now, forty years later, two world wars and the brutality of totalitarian governments have shaken the confidence of this type of muddleheadedness.

The neo-orthodox are now ready to admit that something is wrong with man. But do they agree with the Bible as to what this something is? Does their obscure mixture of a few Biblical phrases and a great deal of esoteric terminology mean that man is dead in sin, "utterly indisposed, disabled, and made opposite to all good, and wholly inclined to all evil"? One thing is clear: the neo-orthodox deny that the guilt of Adam's sin was imputed to his posterity. Adam was not our representative in his trial before God. Indeed, Adam is only an unhistorical myth. And yet these men have had the effrontery to claim that they, rather than we, preserve the position of the Reformers. Let them read the Confession.

We too should read the Confession. And we should preach it with vigor. Not only have Romanists, modernists, and the neo-orthodox departed from the teachings of the Bible, but there are also others, who in spite of professing to adhere to the Scripture, have diverged, sometimes widely, from the truth.

There was a Bible professor in a Christian college who taught that man was a sinner, man was in a bad way, man was sick in sin. Now salvation, so this Bible professor explained it, is like medicine in the drug store; and the sick man ought to drag himself to the store and get the medicine, and be cured. There was also a convinced Presbyterian on this faculty, who taught in accordance with the Westminster Confession. So evident to the students was the contrast between these two theologies that the president disconnected the Presbyterian from his post.

The Bible and the Confession teach that man is not just sick in sin; he is dead in sin; and salvation rather than being compared with medicine is compared with a resurrection.

> Section III.—They being the root of all mankind, the guilt of this sin was imputed,[6] and the same death in sin and corrupted nature conveyed to all their posterity, descending from them by ordinary generation.[7]
>
> Section IV.—From this original corruption, whereby we are utterly indisposed, disabled and made opposite to all good,[8] and wholly inclined to all evil,[9] do proceed all actual transgressions.[10]
>
> 6. Gen. i. 27,28; iii. 16,17; Acts xvii. 26; Rom. v. 12,15-19; 1 Cor. xv. 21,22,45,49.—7. Ps. li. 5; Gen. v. 3; Job xiv. 4; xv. 14.—8. Rom. v. 6; viii. 7; vii. Col. i. 21.—9. Gen. vi. 5; viii. 21; Rom. iii. 10-12.—10. James i. 14,15; Eph. ii. 2,3; Matt. xv. 19.

Section iii contains two main ideas: God imputes the guilt of Adam's first sin to all his posterity, Christ alone excepted; and, second, Adam's corrupt nature is conveyed to the same individuals.

First, Adam, when he disobeyed God's command, did not act for himself alone. He was the representative of his natural posterity. In this connection a careful study of Romans 5:12-21 should be made. Note that men are sinners because of the one act of the one man. You and I are not sinners because we commit sins, at least not in the first instance; but rather we are guilty because our representative sinned for us. Note especially how Romans 5 stresses the one act of the one man. God imputes Adam's guilt to us. Imputation is explicitly mentioned in Romans 5:13 and is implied throughout the section, especially in verse 19 which says, "by one man's disobedience many were made sinners."

But Romans 5 is not the only section of the New Testament where the idea of imputation is found. The previous chapter is full of it. Verses 6, 8, 11, 23, and 24 all contain the English word imputation, and verses 3, 4, 5, and 10 contain the same word in Greek. A concordance will show that the same word and the same idea is also found in II Timothy 4:16, II Cor. 5:19, Philemon 18, and elsewhere. Some of these references speak of the imputation of sin, some of the imputation of righteousness, some use the idea in relation to human obligations. But all exemplify the idea of imputation.

Critics have complained that the authors of the Confession, by reason of the intellectual climate of the seventeenth century, were prepossessed of exaggerated notions of law. Everything had to be expressed in precise legal terminology. With such a prepossession the authors failed to grasp the Biblical position clearly and therefore distorted it in this forbidding language. Now, aside from the unlikelihood that the seventeenth century was more legally minded than many or all other centuries, the plain truth of the matter is that the authors of the Confession found law and imputation all through the Bible. An honest exegete could not possibly miss it.

For some theologians imputation is merely a sort of bookkeeping that is unworthy of true religion. For others the idea of a representative whose guilt is imputed seems absolutely immoral. Dr. Hendry[1] asserts, "it is manifestly unreasonable that one individual should be saddled with the guilt of another for an act committed far away and long ago." But do those who complain

---

1. *Op. cit.*, p. 81.

that honest bookkeeping is unworthy of religion advocate dishonest bookkeeping? Do those who think that imputation is too legal prefer something illegal? And if the charge of immorality is made, let us ask what is immoral about representation?

In fact let us ask what is it to be immoral? Eating the forbidden fruit was immoral or sinful because God had forbidden it, and for no other reason. Is there any other reason why murder or adultery is wrong? Is it not God's commandments that set the distinction between right and wrong? There may be conflicting or extraneous motives in the human mind, both in cases of obedience and of disobedience, but what else beside God's command makes anything right or wrong? If God is sovereign, and if he has approved the principle of representation, then there is nothing immoral about representation and imputation.

In addition to the idea of imputation, section iii also tells us that the corruption and deterioration which came upon Adam as a result of his sin is transmitted to us by heredity. Here it is important to note a difference between Adam and ourselves. Adam first committed a voluntary transgression and as a result and punishment of it his nature became depraved. But in our case the depravity precedes the voluntary transgressions. We were not created righteous. We were born with a corrupt nature and from that nature our voluntary transgressions naturally follow.

This fact throws further light on the previous point of imputation. A corrupt nature is a kind of punishment. Because Adam sinned, God punished him with the corruption of his nature. Now, we are born already corrupt. That is to say, we are born in a state of punishment. But what is this punishment a punishment of? It cannot be a punishment for any of our voluntary transgressions; at birth we are not guilty of any evil action of our own, for we have as yet done nothing at all, either good or evil. Therefore the sin for which we are punished must be Adam's sin, the guilt of which has been imputed to us. Theologians, like Dr. Hendry, without imputation, cannot explain why we are born already corrupt. It is imputation that explains why we are born in a sinful condition.

Some theologians and some philosophers hold that we are born neutral. Aristotle taught that we have no moral character at birth; we are neither good nor bad. So too the English philosopher

Locke insisted that all our knowledge, including our moral principles, are derived from experience. The philosophy of the debate is intricate and out of place here. But as a slight indication that being born with a pre-formed character is not at all absurd, one may note that puppies and kittens arrive with a built-in antipathy. They do not learn it from experience; they are born that way. At any rate, however it may be with biology and philosophy, the Bible clearly says that we are born sinners.

Section iv states that this corruption pervades our whole nature. There is no part or function of man that is unaffected by sin. If anyone says that man's intellect is sinful, but his emotions are pure, he is mistaken. If anyone reverses the assertion, he is also mistaken. Man is totally depraved.

An illustration or two will make this clear. And since the subject is sin and depravity, the illustration will be in accord. Suppose several boys are shooting craps. One urchin rolls out the dice and they come seven. That's lucky. He picks them up and rolls them a second time. They come seven. That's remarkable. He picks them up and rolls them a third time—baby needs shoes—and they come seven. That's suspicious.

The other boys with the acumen of philosophers ponder over what uniform cause could be the explanation of the uniformity of the result. With a stroke of genius they conclude that the cause is inside the dice.

So it is with man's nature. If sin were a product of the slums, as some seem to think, why do the teen-agers from wealthy homes engage in vandalism? And why do wealthy adults attempt embezzlement or raid the public treasury? Or, if sin were a disease of the tropics, why are not the Canadians and Siberians perfect? Sin knows no geographical, sociological, or academic boundary. When all men everywhere do wrong, we must conclude, providing we have the philosophic insight of crap-shooting urchins, that the cause is inside the men. We are born inherently sinful.

Someone may be tempted to reply that the commission of a few sins, even by everybody, does not prove inherent and total depravity. Even desperate criminals do not commit murder every day, only on Saturday night. And respectable people do many more good deeds than bad deeds. Therefore, if a few bad deeds are evidence of an evil nature, the many good deeds are better evidence of a much stronger good nature.

This reply, however, misses the point. It is not a question of the proportion of a man's good deeds to his evil deeds. In a moment we shall discuss this proportion, but it is not the question at issue.

What then is the question? Simply this: Does human nature, of itself, tend toward innocence and favor with God, or does it not? Let this main question be clear: does man of himself tend toward innocence and favor with God, or does he not? Now, innocence requires, not just a few good deeds, not even many good deeds. Innocence requires no bad deeds, no not one. Proportion misses the point. Innocence requires perfection. Can we avoid admitting now that human nature tends toward evil? The cause is inside. We were born that way.

Let us try another illustration. Suppose for our summer vacation we take a trip to Europe. We could go by jet in six hours, but since we enjoy the water we take a slow freighter. Day after day the sun shines and we enjoy the breeze in a deck chair. But on the eleventh day a storm arises. A violent storm. And the plates of the ship loosen, drop off, and the ship sinks. As we bob up and down in our life preserver, we see for the last time, from the crest of a wave, the stern of our ship as it makes its final plunge. Then gulping down a mouthfull of sea water we sadly say, what a fine ship! It sailed so pleasantly for ten days. It sank only once. Its goodness was ten times its badness.

Such is the irrelevance of proportion. But as a matter of fact men's good days are not ten times as numerous as their evil days. The proportion is much worse. No doubt an unbeliever would refuse to recognize "Remember the Sabbath Day to keep it holy" as a divine command. He might not even recognize the sin of worshiping images—since so many are carried on instrument panels. But I think even an unbeliever, unless he is just being stubborn, would admit that God requires man to love him with all his heart, mind and strength. Now, let us ask ourselves, how much of the time do we obey that commandment? Do we obey ten days to one? If we are honest with ourselves, we shall have to confess that we do not obey any day. Even in our devotions extraneous thoughts intrude. We never love God with all our heart and mind and strength. The proportion is against us. Sin affects us all the time, totally. We were born that way.

That is why such a great salvation is necessary.

> *Section V.—This corruption of nature, during this life, doth remain in those that are regenerated,[11] and although it be through Christ pardoned and mortified, yet both itself, and all the motions thereof, are truly and properly sin.[12]*
>
> *Section VI.—Every sin, both original and natural, being a transgression of the righteous law of God, and contrary thereunto,[13] doth in its own nature, bring guilt upon the sinner,[14] whereby he is bound over to the wrath of God,[15] and curse of the law,[16] and so made subject to death,[17] with all miseries spiritual,[18] temporal,[19] and eternal.[20]*

11. 1 John i. 8,10; Rom. vii. 14,17,18,23; James iii. 2; Prov. xx. 9; Eccles. vii. 20.—12. Rom. vii. 5,7,8,25; Gal. v. 17.—13. 1 John iii. 4.— 14. Rom. ii. 15; iii. 9,19.—15. Eph. ii. 3.—16. Gal. iii. 10.—17. Rom. vi. 23.—18. Eph. iv. 18.—19. Rom. viii. 20; Lam. iii. 39.—20. Matt. xxv. 41; 2 Thess. i. 9.

The Confession will start to describe the great plan of salvation in the next chapter; but before leaving the doctrine of sin, it includes section v on the sinfulness of the regenerate person. The main point is that regeneration does not immediately eradicate sin. Indeed no matter how saintly a Christian may become, he never achieves sinless perfection in this life.

Some professing Christians profess that sinless perfection is possible, and some even profess to have attained it. Have you ever had contact with the holiness groups? Have you ever heard of the victorious life movement? Do you recall the phrase, *complete, instantaneous perfection?*

One book[1] that has been widely circulated through four editions teaches that "Growth in grace is neither . . . a washing . . . nor a cleansing process. . . . Growth in grace is a natural process . . . Sanctification is a supernatural and divine work . . . Entire sanctification is something experienced. . . . There is no gradual growing out of sin. . . . There are no degrees and progressive stages, but the work is complete at the first, and instantaneous as to time" (pp. 212-214).

---

1. Chester Wilkins, *A Handbook for Personal Soul-Winning;* Light and Hope Publications, 1950.

Now, one might at first think that anyone who claimed to be perfectly sinless must be an extremely hypocritical reprobate. As a matter of fact, this is not so. I knew a professor in a Christian college who claimed that he had not sinned for twenty-six years. This man was not an outrageous hypocrite. He was a rather saintly old gentleman, and compared with other church members he was really a very good man. But if we compare him or anyone else with Biblical standards, we must say something different.

The great objection to the holiness groups is their deficient opinion of the law of God. They are seriously mistaken as to the nature and definition of sin. Instead of defining sin by reference to the law of God, they are usually satisfied to distinguish right from wrong by local customs or to follow pious hunches. For example, when our daughter studied at a Bible institute in France, there were strict rules as to how the girls should put up their hair. Other silly details also loomed large.

Not only do the holiness people substitute social or ecclesiastical customs for the law of God, but they also make an unbiblical distinction between voluntary sin and something that is not quite sin. Mr. Wilkins speaks of "the difference between willful sins and transgressions against God and his law, and the likely mistake which one may make, which is of the head and not of the heart . . . God always looks at the motive of the heart and never holds us guilty when we make mistakes" (p. 214).

Now, in the first place the Bible nowhere contrasts the heart and the head. Nor does the Bible contrast sins and mistakes. And finally, Mr. Wilkins' words imply that it is possible to have entirely pure and unmixed motives. It would seem, on the contrary, that external conformity to law is more easily attained than inward purity of mind.

In opposition to the claim of instantaneous perfection, we must insist that voluntary transgression is not the only form of sin. Sin is any want of conformity to the law of God. This means that our inborn depravity is itself sin. Sin is as much a state or character as it is an act. And this source of voluntary transgressions seems to have escaped their notice.

The error of the "holiness" groups is similar to the Romanist and the modernist error in that it is a failure to recognize the exceeding sinfulness of sin. To them, sin seems rather superficial, and therefore it can be eradicated in this life. They sometimes restrict sin to "known sin." But if the aim of the Christian life is merely to avoid known sin, then the more ignorant of the law we are, the more righteous we would be.

Yet for all their sinless perfection, these are the people who hold that one can lose one's salvation and become unregenerate a second time. Can anyone imagine a perfection as imperfect as that? This shows that the Scriptural view of sin, so accurately summarized in the Confession, has far-reaching implications. Its force is seen in the nature of salvation, the perseverance of the saints, the varieties of free will, the imputation of Christ's righteousness, and in fact, throughout the whole system. Nor should we be satisfied with knowing only a part. We need the complete Confession.

Now, many of the phrases used by the holiness groups are Scriptural. For example, does I John 3:6,9 (whosoever is born of God doeth no sin) teach sinless perfection in this life? It looks so, doesn't it? But has John in these verses forgotten what he so shortly before said in I John 1:8 and 2:1? And if the verses first mentioned taught sinless perfection, what would be implied? They say, Whosoever is born of God doeth no sin. In this case, instead of just a few Christians attaining the state of perfection, all Christians would be sinless, wouldn't they? In other words, no one in whom a trace of sin remained could be a born-again Christian. Even the holiness groups might not relish this implication.

For conclusive evidence that the Bible does not teach sinless perfection in this life, one ought to read B. B. Warfield's *Perfectionism*. For an account of personal struggle against the corruption of our nature, one should read Bunyan's *Pilgrim's Progress* in its original form.

The final section of this chapter points out God's wrath upon sin. God is righteous and the penalty of any and every sin is death, both temporal and eternal. Jonathan Edwards has few descendants today. *Sinners in the Hands of an Angry God* is not a popular sermon title. Universalism is a welcome doctrine. Hell is only a swear word.

But who was it in the New Testament that spoke most about hell? Peter? Paul? John? No, it was not any one of these. Check a concordance and see. The preacher who most emphasized hell was Jesus Christ himself. It was Christ himself who most emphasized the seriousness of sin and who himself provided a commensurable salvation.

Chapter VII.

OF GOD'S COVENANT WITH MAN.

*Section I.—The distance between God and the crea-
ture is so great, that although reasonable creatures do
owe obedience unto him as their Creator, yet they could
never have any fruition of him as their blessedness and
reward, but by some voluntary condescension on God's
part, which he hath been pleased to express by way of
covenant.[1]*

*Section II.—The first covenant made with man was
a covenant of works,[2] wherein life was promised to
Adam, and in him to his posterity,[3] upon condition of
perfect and personal obedience.[4]*

1. Isa. xl. 13-17; Job ix. 32,33; 1 Sam. ii. 25; Ps. cxiii. 5,6; c. 2,3; Job
xxii. 2,3; xxxv. 7,8; Luke xvii. 10; Acts xvii. 24,25.—2. Gal. iii. 12.
—3. Rom. x. 5; v. 12-20.—4. Gen. ii. 17; Gal. iii. 10.

Since God is truth, and since Christ is the Logos, Wisdom,
or Reason of God, one naturally expects that the contents of revelation would form a system. This expectation is not disappointed.
The various doctrines of the Bible dovetail and fit into each other.
A later part explains more fully the implications of an earlier
part. For this reason a given chapter of the Westminster Confession is understood more clearly when it is compared with others.
Predestination and providence were closely related; the chapter on
the fall of man lays the foundation for the doctrine of the atonement, effectual calling, and sanctification.

In these cases the logical connection between two doctrines
is very obvious. The one is an implication or a presupposition of
the other. With the doctrine of the Covenant, however, the matter
is different. From the bare idea of a covenant, the terms of God's
covenant cannot be deduced, any more than from the fact that two
men have signed a business contract can its provisions be discovered. This does not mean the idea of a covenant is less, but
rather more pervasive; for the following chapters are in effect the
explanation of the concrete terms of that covenant.

The notion of a covenant pervades the Confession because it
pervades the Bible. Would you care to guess how many times the

word covenant, or its other translation, testament, occurs in the Bible? Less than fifty? About a hundred? Or would you venture that 250 is more nearly accurate?

Of course the frequency of a word is no sure sign of its importance. The verbal auxiliary *might* occurs hundreds of time; and the pronouns *ye* and *you* probably reach near to 5000. What then makes a word or idea important?

Read Genesis 12:1-3 and 17:1-14. Are we dealing here with a mere word, an unimportant element of speech; or is the idea of covenant a major concept? Does the covenant of God made with Abraham have any bearing on us who live since the time of Christ? What is the significance of Galatians 3:6-9? And verse 14 of the same chapter? Compare these statements with John 8:56 and Acts 3:25.

In Genesis what land did God promise Abraham? Canaan? But did Abraham ever receive Canaan as his land? Did he expect to get it? What does Hebrews 11:8-10, 13-16 mean? And what people did God promise Abraham as a posterity? The Jewish people? Or the Gentiles? Compare also Luke 1:54,55; 72-75.

With this material now somewhat chaotically in mind, let us see how the Confession reduces it to order. First of all the sovereignty of God is stressed. Man owes obedience to God, his creator. God owes nothing to man. A potter can make any sort of vessel he chooses to, and the clay has no right to complain. This is all the more true in the case of God, for whereas the potter did not create the clay, God created the material out of which he fashioned man.

Today many people think that God as well as the government owes them a living. They regard him as a sort of valet. What is God good for, if he doesn't do what we want him to? A sovereign God who does as *he* pleases and acts for *his own* glory is repulsive to many modern minds. A God to be worth anything, they think, must be subject to men's desires.

The Confession states the Biblical position: if God favors man in any way, it is by some voluntary condescension on God's part. Condescension, grace, mercy; not obligation, necessity, or duty.

Now, this condescension takes the form of a covenant. There is a children's catechism containing the question, What is a covenant? The answer is, a covenant is an agreement between two or more persons. This idea of an agreement has been used to reinforce the notion that God is somewhat less than sovereign. The line argument depends on the assumption that when an agreement is made the two parties must be equal. There are, however, many cases in human affairs where this is not so. Most obviously a treaty of peace or an armistice, though an agreement, is often dictated by the victor. Or, a father may lay down conditions which his son accepts. Even in business agreements the parties are not always equal. Hence the fact that God makes an agreement with man does not imply that man can bargain with God. It is God who sets the terms.

The mistaken interpretation of putting God nearly on a level with man is found in some history books that attempt to describe Puritanism in New England. For example, Miller and Johnson in *The Puritans* (p. 58) write, "The doctrine held that after the fall of man, God voluntarily condescended [correct] to treat with man as with an equal [incorrect] . . . The covenant . . . made it very clear and reasonable how [correct, in a sense] and why [incorrect] certain men are selected. . . . Above all, in the covenant God pledged himself not to run athwart human conceptions of right and justice; God was represented while entering the compact as agreeing to abide by certain human ideas [substantially incorrect]. Not in all respects, not always, but in the main" [a necessary but utterly vague qualification].

Now, Perry Miller does not engage in vilification of the Puritans, as many college textbooks do. Animosity against Calvinism often runs high among college professors. But Perry Miller always tries to be fair. He is not for that reason always accurate. On the page immediately preceding the quotation just made Miller and Johnson also say, "The Puritan theorists worked out a substantial addition to the theology of Calvinism which in New England was quite as important as the original doctrine. This addition or elaboration of the Calvinist doctrine is generally called the 'Covenant Theology' or the 'Federal Theology.' "

Nothing could be farther from the truth. In the first place the Westminster Confession, as we here have it before our eyes, contains this chapter on the covenant. Now the Westminster Confession was composed in the years 1645-1647. The New England

Puritans indubitably were teaching covenant theology at this time, but we can hardly suppose that the Westminster Assembly imported the doctrine from New England. In the second place, a Dutch theologian Cocceius, at the same time, was preaching the doctrine of the covenant with such enthusiasm that he has sometimes been mistakenly identified as the inventor of the doctrine. He surely did not learn it in New England. Nor from the Westminster Confession either. In the third place, the Irish Articles of Religion, adopted in 1615, before there were any Puritans in New England, contains the doctrine of the Covenant. Hence it cannot even be said that the doctrine of the covenant was a reaction by the Synod of Dort in 1620 to the heresies of Arminius. And finally, it was from the Scottish Presbyterians, suffering under Anglican persecutions, that the term Covenanter arose. To locate the origin of federal theology in New England is a blunder only a secularist professor could fall into.

Perry Miller also said, at the end of the quoted material, that God pledged himself not to run athwart human conceptions of right and justice and to abide by certain human ideas. These lines also are substantially incorrect. In the first place human conceptions of justice vary greatly. It has already been pointed out that some people consider the imputation either of guilt or of righteousness to be immoral. But this imputation is essential to the covenant, as we shall more clearly see in later chapters.

In the second place one of the emotional upheavals that saints undergo is the enigma of the suffering of believers. The sturdy Christian may not flinch at outright persecution; but he is sometimes greatly puzzled at other tragedies. Two instances come to mind. First, there was Job. His so-called comforters thought he must have been an exceptionally wicked man to receive such plagues from the hand of God. Neither they nor he knew that God was discomfiting Satan by highlighting Job's faith in and by severe adversity. At the end of the book Job learns that God can do all things and that no divine purpose can be restrained. But the whole incident certainly violated the conception of justice entertained by the comforters. The second instance is that of the man born blind. His neighbors and the disciples themselves thought that this blindness was a punishment of some parental sin. But Jesus

85

tells them that the man was born blind, not because of any particular sin, but in order that the works of God should be made manifest in him.

It is clear therefore that God is under no obligation to conform to human conceptions of justice. So much for the aberrations of learned professors who know so little about Christianity. Let us now return to the main theme of the covenant.

As a matter of fact, the Scriptures speak of two covenants. The terms of the second are more easily seen to be entirely of God's sole decision. But the first covenant is no less so. The first covenant was the Covenant of works, in which God demanded perfect obedience to all his commands and promised eternal life as a reward.

If it is hard to imagine God as demanding less than perfect obedience, it is at least clear that he was under no obligation to promise eternal life as a reward. A man has no more claim on God to be continued in existence than a rock or an atom. This covenant therefore was an instance of condescension or grace on God's part.

It is also to be noted that the reward of Adam's perfect obedience was to have been eternal life for his posterity as well as for himself. This is a still clearer instance of grace, since obviously God could have tested each descendant personally in exactly the same way he decided to test Adam. God did not have to grant eternal life to succeeding generations merely because Adam obeyed.

This idea brings to our attention the interesting relation that God established between Adam and his posterity. It was not merely that Adam was their father. He was, in addition, their representative. His act was to be counted as their act. He acted for and instead of them. This relation was mentioned in the reference to imputed guilt in Chapter VI, and further explanations will be given when we arrive at the relation between Christ and those who believe on him. Chapter VI also made it quite clear that Adam did not fulfill the covenant of works. He disobeyed, and thereby made necessary a second covenant, if anyone was to be saved.

Section III.—Man, by his fall, having made himself incapable of life by that covenant, the Lord was pleased to make a second,[5] commonly called the covenant of grace, whereby he freely offereth unto sinners life and salvation by Jesus Christ, requiring of them faith in him, that they might be saved;[6] and promising to give unto all those that are ordained unto life his Holy Spirit, to make them willing and able to believe.[7]

Section IV.—This covenant of grace is frequently set forth in the Scripture, by the name of a testament, in reference to the death of Jesus Christ the testator, and to the everlasting inheritance, with all things belonging to it, therein bequeathed.[8]

5. Gal. iii. 21; Rom. viii. 3; iii. 20,21; Gen. iii. xv.; Isa. xlii. 6.—
6. Mark xvi. 15,16; John iii. 16; Rom. x. 6.9; Gal. iii. 11.—7. Ezek. xxxvi. 26,27; John vi. 44,45.—8. Heb. ix. 15-17; vii. 22; Luke xxii. 20; 1 Cor. xi. 25.

Section iii needs very little exposition at this place. The fall of Adam has already been mentioned, and with it the need of a new plan of salvation. That this new plan substitutes faith for works will be very fully explained in later chapters.

One small item should no doubt be mentioned here, although it too will be taken up in Chapter IX. The point is the last phrase of section iii, "to make them willing and able to believe." What has previously been said about the total depravity resulting from Adam's fall implies that man in his present sinful condition is unwilling to trust God. The Scripture is exceedingly clear on this point: "There is none righteous, no not one . . . there is none that seeketh after God" (Rom. 3:10-11). Men are in rebellion against God, and therefore God must subdue them. God must make them willing to seek him. Of this more will be said in the chapter on Effectual Calling. But at the moment these ideas should be brought to our attention in preparation for the chapter on Free Will. A careless reading of Chapter IX might give an unattentive person the notion that man is, despite everything already said, in some degree independent of God. Of course he is not. And in fact nowhere is his dependence so striking as in the plan of salvation. Man must depend on God to make him willing.

Section V —This covenant was differently administered in the time of the law, and in the time of the gospel:[9] under the law it was administered by promises, prophecies, sacrifices, circumcision, the paschal lamb,

87

*and other types and ordinances delivered to the people
of the Jews, all fore-signifying Christ to come,[10] which
were for that time sufficient and efficacious, through
the operation of the Spirit, to instruct and build up the
elect in faith in the promised Messiah,[11] by whom they
had full remission of sins, and eternal salvation; and is
called the Old Testament.[12]*

*Section VI.—Under the gospel, when Christ, the
substance,[13] was exhibited, the ordinances in which this
covenant is dispensed are, the preaching of the word,
and the administration of the sacraments of Baptism and
the Lord's Supper;[14] which, though fewer in number,
and administered with more simplicity and less outward
glory, yet in them it is held forth in more fulness, evidence and spiritual efficacy,[15] to all nations, both Jews
and Gentiles;[16] and is called the New Testament.[17] There
are not, therefore, two covenants of grace differing in
substance, but one and the same under various dispensations.[18]*

9. 2 Cor. iii. 6-9.—10.Heb. viii., xi., x ; Rom. iv. 11 ; Col. ii. 11,12 ;
1 Cor. v. 7.—11. 1 Cor. x. 1-4 ; Heb. xi. 13 ; John viii. 56.—12. Gal.
iii. 7-9,14.—13. Col. ii 17.—14. Matt xxviii. 19,20 ; 1 Cor. xi. 23-25.—
15. Heb. xii. 22-27 ; Jer. xxx. 33-34.—16. Matt. xxviii. 19 ; Eph. ii. 15-19.
17. Luke xxii. 20.—18. Gal. iii. 14,16 ; Acts xv. 11 ; Rom. iii. 21-23,30 ;
Ps. xxxii. 1 ; Rom. iv. 3,6,16,17,23,24 ; Heb. xiii. 8.

Section v states the relationship between the Old Testament
and the New Testament. These two are both forms of one Covenant of Grace; but they are different forms. The two parts of the
Bible are not two covenants differing in substance or effect, but
they are different administrations of the one Covenant of Grace.
For this reason one must not suppose that Christ and the Holy
Spirit are absent from the Old Testament. Remember that Christ
said, "Abraham rejoiced to see my day." Paul in Galatians 3:8
says that the gospel was preached to Abraham; and in I Corinthians 10:4 we find that the rock in the wilderness was Christ.
Regeneration, the work of the Holy Spirit, is pictured as clearly
in Ezekiel 36:26 as it is in the third chapter of John.

A certain theologian, now deceased, once wrote, "There are
two widely different, standardized, divine provisions, whereby man,
who is utterly fallen, may come into the favor of God." Is this
statement correct? Does the Bible describe two ways of salvation?
Is the Christian Church the same as, or different from, the Jewish
Church? Can we properly speak of a Jewish Church? Did the
Church begin at Pentecost? Does Acts 7:38 mean that the Church

existed in Moses' day? The Church in the wilderness—can it be said that Christ was in that Church? Did Christ follow the Jews in their wanderings from Egypt to the promised land? See I Corinthians 10:4. And what about Romans 11:16-25? How many olive trees are in the picture? Are both Gentiles and Jews branches of the same olive tree?

Was any devout Jew in Old Testament times saved by keeping the law of Moses? Read Romans 3:9, 10, 20, 23; and James 2:10. Is justification by faith peculiar to the New Testament? In writing Romans was not Paul influenced by Habakkuk 2:4?

In contrast with this modern error, the Westminster doctrine should be insisted upon that since the fall there has been only one method of salvation. Adam, Noah, Abraham, Moses, Peter, Paul, and you and I are saved only through the merits of Christ. Neither conscience nor the Law nor anything else has the power to redeem a sinner.

But surely there were some differences between the Church in the Old Testament and the Church in the New Testament. Yes, there was a difference, and the Confession indicates briefly what the difference was. First, the people of God in old times were not so fully informed as we are. Ephesians 3:4, 5 says that the mystery of Christ was not as fully revealed in other generations as it is now made known to us. Justification by faith and the resurrection, for example, are both in the Old Testament; but we today have a more detailed and explicit knowledge of them.

However, the most obvious difference between the religion of the Old Testament and that of the New relates to the external display in the past and the simplicity of the present. The Old Testament provided for feasts and fasts, for several types of sacrifices, for symbolic offerings, for ritual distinctions among animals, for ceremonies of purification, for sabbatical years and jubilees; and in addition there were the expensive furnishings of the tabernacle or temple and the costly robes and jewels of the priests and High Priest. In the New Testament we may have an upper room or even a commodious auditorium; but the sacraments are reduced to baptism and the Lord's Supper, and beyond these, the activity is chiefly preaching the Word. The Old Testament ceremonies and ritual, and certain of its persons and events, were types, symbols, or anticipatory signs of the reality in Christ. After the Lamb of God came and sacrificed himself on the cross, the Passover Lamb was an anachronism. When the gorgeous veil of the temple was rent in twain, there was no more need for the candlesticks and shewbread. Nor for the temple itself. Nor for the priests. For we all became priests and Christ himself is the High Priest. "There are not therefore two covenants of grace differing in substance, but one and the same under various dispensations."

From this we may conclude that so-called Christian churches which stage colorful processions and spectacular ceremonies, with a priesthood, costly jewels, and many sacraments, either have reverted to Jewish ceremonies whereby they deny that Christ has come, or have invented their own ceremonies whereby they have set themselves up in opposition to God as the arbiter of what is required in worship.

CHAPTER VIII.

OF CHRIST THE MEDIATOR.

Section I.—It pleased God, in his eternal purpose, to choose and ordain the Lord Jesus, his only begotten Son, to be the Mediator between God and man;[1] the Prophet,[2] Priest[3] and King;[4] the Head and Saviour of his Church;[5] the Heir of all things;[6] and Judge of the world:[7] unto whom he did from all eternity give a people to be his seed,[8] and to be by him in time redeemed, called, justified, sanctified and glorified.[9]

1. Isa. xlii.; 1 Pet. i. 19,20; John iii. 16; 1 Tim. ii. 5.—2. Acts iii. 22. —3. Heb. v. 5,6.—4. Ps. ii. 6; Luke i. 33.—5. Eph. v. 23.—6. Heb. i. 2.—7. Acts xvii. 31.—8. John xvii. 6; Ps. xxii. 30; Isa. liii. 10.— 9. 1 Tim. ii. 6; Isa. lv. 4,5; 1 Cor. i. 30.

When we consider how people ignore the laws of God and transgress his commandments without concern, it seems that the doctrine of sin, summarized in Chapter VI of the Confession, must be the most important doctrine of all. And until people acknowledge that their lives offend God, presumably this doctrine is indeed the most important in a practical approach. But when sin is recognized as such, then it will seem that Chapter VIII, which outlines the remedy for sin, is the most important.

Of course, this feeling that one doctrine or one chapter is the most important is purely psychological, momentary, and relative to a particular purpose. One might as well ask which wheel or tire of an auto is the most important. Presumably it is the tire that is about to run over a tack. Otherwise they are all equally important. This is true of the chapters of the Confession because they fit together as a system and are not haphazard and disjointed. It was previously pointed out that the doctrines of predestination and providence underlie effectual calling and the perseverance of the saints; the covenant bears on New Testament baptism; and of course the fall of man necessitates a Redeemer and Mediator. They all fit together.

Chapter VIII is one of the longest chapters in the Confession. It contains a wealth of material.

If a discussion group is studying through this book at the rate of one chapter a week, and if the material in some earlier or later chapters seems too meagre, here is the place to fill in time profitably. To survey the Scriptural teaching on the person of Christ and his work as Mediator takes one pretty well all over the New Testament.

The chapter begins with another reference to God's eternal purpose. What was done, was done because it pleased God to do it. Of course it benefited mankind in the end, but the initiation was simply the good pleasure of the sovereign God. In this instance the particular point is the divine choice of Christ as the Mediator between God and man. Since man by the fall had become wholly inclined to all evil, so that the carnal mind is at enmity against God and cannot possibly be subject to the law of God, not only would salvation require the initiative to come from God, but also there would have to be some form of mediation between the two enemies.

Ordinarily a mediator is a third party, and not one of the enemies. Therefore it might seem at first that an angel would be an appropriate go-between. Now, that there was a deliberate divine choice by which a definite person was selected to fulfill this function should be ascertained by the student through an examination of the first three Scripture references. But it will be seen at the same time that this person was not an angel. The reason is that the mediatorial work in this case required qualifications that angels do not possess. The details are very carefully explained in the Epistle to the Hebrews.

Christ therefore is the chosen Mediator, and his functions entail the duties of prophet, priest, and king. It is a little surprising that the Confession does not say more about these three offices. Sections iv and v cover some of the most important material, but the Shorter Catechism, questions 23-26, and the Larger Catechism, questions 42-45, both of which should be used in conjunction with the Confession, give some details about Christ's offices of prophet, priest, and king, which are not mentioned in the Confession. The Larger Catechism, Q. 32, 36, 38-42, also goes more fully into the idea of a mediator. In Q. 36 the important point is made that Christ is the only mediator (cf. I Tim. 2:5), thus ruling out the claims of the papacy.

Another item mentioned in section i of Chapter VIII of the Confession is that Christ is the Judge of the world. Because of some contemporary distinctions among different judgments, we can well ponder not only Acts 17:31, but especially John 5:22.

But the climax of section i comes in the concluding phrases. The idea is that Christ redeems those people whom the Father gave to him from all eternity. This is a most important idea. In addition to the Scripture references mentioned, we remember what the angel said to Joseph before Christ was born: "Thou shalt call his name Jesus, for he shall save his people from their sins." This divine truth, so frequently mentioned in the Gospel of John, seems to have been slighted in contemporary preaching. Whether this is so or not, the ministers and the people can determine by trying to recollect the last sermon on the subject. A minister should be judged, not only by what he says, but also by what he does not say. If a man openly denies parts of the Confession, we can see clearly that he is unfaithful. But is he not also unfaithful if he refuses to preach some parts? Of course no minister can mention everything in the Confession every week. Yet if a man persistently, year in and year out, avoids one of these main doctrines, is he not unfaithful? The Scripture is God's Word, and it is *all* profitable for doctrine. Let us see that none of it is avoided, omitted, or forgotten.

> *Section II.—The Son of God, the second person in the Trinity, being very and eternal God, of one substance, and equal with the Father, did, when the fulness of time was come, take upon him man's nature,[10] with all the essential properties and common infirmities thereof, yet without sin;[11] being conceived by the power of the Holy Ghost, in the womb of the Virgin Mary, of her substance.[12] So that two whole, perfect and distinct natures, the Godhead and the manhood, were inseparably joined together in one person, without conversion, composition or confusion.[13] Which person is very God and very man, yet one Christ, the only Mediator between God and man.[14]*

10. John i. 1,14 ; 1 John v. 20 ; Phil. ii. 6 ; Gal. iv. 4.—11. Heb. ii.14,16, 17 ; iv. 15.—12. Luke i. 27,31,35 ; Gal. iv. 4.—13. Luke i. 35 ; Col. ii. 9 ; Rom. ix. 5 ; 1 Pet. iii. 18 ; 1 Tim. iii. 16.—14. Rom. i. 3,4 ; 1 Tim. ii. 5.

The first three lines of section ii refer back to the doctrine of the Trinity in Chapter II. Jesus Christ is "very and eternal

God." Unlike angels, the physical universe, and mankind, he never came into existence. He is not a creation. He is the Creator. He is God and equal with the Father.

Since the chapter as a whole deals with the mediatorial work of Christ, the remainder of section ii naturally goes beyond the doctrine of the Trinity and centers on Christ's incarnation. This second Person of the Trinity became man.

If we put ourselves imaginatively in the situation of the early Christians, we can understand how puzzled they were when they tried to think of what sort of a person Jesus Christ was. The initial Jewish complexion of the Church was soon lost, and anyway, the Old Testament did not clearly indicate the nature of the Messiah. The Gentiles, who soon became the overwhelming majority in the Church, could not, with their pagan background, easily understand the nature of Christ. Nothing in paganism gave them any hint. Accordingly it took the Church some centuries to digest the teaching of the Bible. First came the doctrine of the Trinity, formulated by the Council of Nicaea in A.D. 325. The next important advance was to define the doctrine of Christ as one Person with two natures. This was done at Chalcedon in A.D. 451. Those who are interested both in history and in the significance of these definitory statements will enjoy reading Schaff's *Creeds of Christendom* and Shedd's *History of Christian Doctrine*. The latter is particularly full and clear. A modern study of the subject is the useful though somewhat difficult *The Humiliation of Christ* by A. B. Bruce. People miss so much by restricting themselves to Thurber and Wodehouse and neglecting these valuable productions.

The main idea is not too difficult to understand. In order to serve as a mediator, the Son of God had to become man. This is most evident with respect to the crucifixion. Obviously if the mediator was to die on the cross, or die in any way, it was necessary that he have a body. A pure Spirit could not be executed. As it says in Hebrews 2:14, "Since then the children are sharers in flesh and blood, he also partook of the same, that through death he might bring to nought him that had the power of death, that is, the devil."

But the distinguished evangelist, previously mentioned as having no creed, was quite wrong when he described Jesus as

94

"God in a body." What we call the incarnation involves more than God's taking a body. What the second Person of the Trinity took to himself was "man's nature, with all the essential properties and common infirmities thereof." That is, Jesus had a human mind as well as a human body. It was only because he had a human mind that he could advance in wisdom, as well as stature, and in favor with God and men (Luke 2:52).

In addition to the view that Jesus was "God in a body," a theologian by the name of Nestor conceived Jesus Christ to be two different persons: one person purely human, the other purely divine. Another attempt was to conceive of the Savior as neither God nor man, but a sort of "chemical" mixture in which the characteristics of the components were both lost. The student is urged to look up Nestorianism, Eutychianism, and Docetism in a theological encyclopedia. The subject matter is very interesting.

Eventually the Council of Chalcedon, after nearly four hundred years of church history, arrived at the orthodox doctrine that "two whole, perfect, and distinct natures were inseparably joined together in one person, without conversion, composition, or confusion."

This Chalcedonian doctrine is necessary to support the function of Christ's mediatorial office. The reason is that if Christ were a mere man, he could not function as a mediator; nor could he if he were simply God. In both cases he would be confined to one extreme and fail to link the two. If Christ were neither God nor man, but an angel or something else, he would be a barrier between God and man rather than a mediator. But as both God and man, as truly God as man and as truly man as God, Christ can be the Mediator and unite God and men.

In the middle of section ii the Confession states the method God chose to accomplish the incarnation. Christ became man by the Virgin Birth.

On this subject one cannot afford to overlook *The Virgin Birth of Christ* by J. Gresham Machen. This amazing scholar has dealt with just about everything pertaining to the subject, from the genealogies in Matthew and Luke to the claim that Buddha and the Greek gods were virgin born also. In this twentieth century the ordination of unbelieving ministers and the declination from

95

the faith in the larger denominations was initiated chiefly through an attack on the Virgin Birth.

Why this miracle should be harder to accept than any other, such as the floating axe head or Christ's walking on the water, is a puzzle hard to solve. But for some strange reason the Virgin Birth was singled out for special attack. Candidates for the ministry told their presbyteries that they could not affirm the biological miracle of a virgin birth. The modernists defended these candidates on the ground that a belief in the Virgin Birth is not essential. Such a statement is ambiguous and obscures the issue. Doubtless it is possible for some heathen to accept Christ's sacrifice for his sin and be saved without knowing of the Virgin Birth. In this sense belief in the Virgin Birth is not essential. But it is a different question to ask whether or not belief in the Virgin Birth is essential for a Presbyterian ordination. In this latter case it is not a matter of unfortunate ignorance but of deliberate rejection of the Word of God. There is still another question: is the Virgin Birth, the Virgin Birth itself, not a belief in it, essential to God's plan of salvation? Contrary to the modernist attempt to confuse three questions in one, an intellectually honest Christian will avoid ambiguity and will take his ordination vows seriously.

> *Section III.—The Lord Jesus, in his human nature thus united to the divine, was sanctified and anointed with the Holy Spirit above measure;[15] having in him all the treasures of wisdom and knowledge,[16] in whom it pleased the Father that all fullness should dwell,[17] to the end that, being holy, harmless, undefiled and full of grace and truth,[18] he might be thoroughly furnished to execute the office of a Mediator and Surety;[19] which office he took not unto himself, but was thereunto called by his Father,[20] who put all power and judgment into his hand and gave him commandment to execute the same.[21]*

> *Section IV.—This office the Lord Jesus did most willingly undertake;[22] which that he might discharge, he was made under the law,[23] and did perfectly fulfil it;[24] endured most grievous torments immediately in his soul[25] and most painful sufferings in his body;[26] was crucified and died;[27] was buried, and remained under the power of death, yet saw no corruption.[28] On the third day he arose from the dead,[29] with the same body in which he*

96

*suffered;[30] with which also he ascended into heaven, and
there sitteth at the right hand of his Father,[31] making
intercession;[32] and shall return to judge men and angels
at the end of the world.[33]*

15. Ps. xlv. 7; John iii. 34.—16. Col. iii. 3.—17. Col. i. 19.—18. Heb.
vii. 26; John i. 14.—19. Acts x. 38; Heb. xii. 24; vii. 22.—20. Heb. v.
4,5.—21. John v. 22,27; Matt. xxviii. 18; Acts ii. 36.—22. Ps. xl. 7,8;
Heb. x. 5-10; John x. 18; Phil. ii. 8.—23. Gal. iv. 4.—24. Matt.
iii. 15; v. 17.—25. Matt. xxvi. 37,38; Luke xxii. 44; Matt. xxvii. 46.
26. Matt. xxvi., xxvii.—27. Phil. ii. 8.—28. Acts ii. 23,24,27; Acts xiii.
37; Rom. vi. 9.—29. 1 Cor. xv. 3-5.—30. John xx. 25-27.—31. Mark
xvi. 19.—32. Rom. viii. 34; Heb. ix. 24; vii. 25.—33. Rom. xiv. 9,10;
Acts i. 11; x. 42; Matt. xiii. 40-42; Jude 6; 2 Pet. ii. 4.

Section iii further explains Christ's preparation for the work
of mediator. Aside from checking the Scripture references, the
student hardly needs any explanation, for everything here is perfectly clear.

Section iv is also extremely simple. It speaks first of Christ's
obedience. Had Christ been a sinner, he could not have atoned for
our sins, but would have been in the same predicament as all
depraved men. By living a righteous life, that is, by keeping the
whole law, he earned a righteousness that could be imputed to us
who have none.

Next, the section mentions the punishment Jesus took upon
himself for us. These pains were indeed the bodily pains of crucifixion, but also most grievous torments immediately in his soul.

Then follow the statements of his burial, resurrection, ascension, and return to judge the world.

Again the question comes to the fore, why is it harder to
believe in the Virgin Birth than in the Resurrection? The Confession states, repeating the Biblical material, that Jesus rose from the
tomb "with the same body in which he suffered."

Perhaps modernists were forced to attack the Virgin Birth
more openly because they could disguise their unbelief of the
Resurrection by describing it as a vision, or by reducing it to a
spiritual experience of the disciples. But both are equally miraculous, and in a philosophy of so-called scientific law there is no
place for either one. Indeed there is no place for any divine inter-
vention in history. To be quite plain, there is no place for a living,
loving, acting, sovereign God at all.

For all that Karl Barth emphasizes a living, speaking, acting
God, many contemporaries nullify this essential of Christian theology by reducing the historical events of the past to existential

experiences of the present. The fall of Adam is construed, not as an event that happened just once at a certain date, but as a myth or fable picturing the recurring experiences of all men. The Resurrection is divorced from "the third day," and interpreted as an experience of spiritual elevation that you or I might have in the twentieth century. What present experience the fairy tale of the Virgin Birth symbolizes requires more ingenuity to imagine. This existential method of interpretation is a brutal manhandling of the Scripture because the Scripture obviously, evidently, indubitably asserts these things to be actual occurrences as historical as the Peloponnesian War or the British repudiation of Winston Churchill in July 1945.

> *Section V.—The Lord Jesus, by his perfect obedience and sacrifice of himself, which he through the eternal Spirit once offered up unto God, hath fully satisfied the justice of his Father,[34] and purchased not only reconciliation, but an everlasting inheritance in the kingdom of heaven, for all those whom the Father hath given unto him.[35]*

> *Section VI.—Although the work of redemption was not actually wrought by Christ till after his incarnation, yet the virtue, efficacy and benefits thereof were communicated unto the elect in all ages successively from the beginning of the world, in and by those promises, types and sacrifices wherein he was revealed and signified to be the Seed of the woman which should bruise the serpent's head, and the Lamb slain from the beginning of the world, being yesterday and to-day the same, and for ever.[36]*

34. Rom. v. 19; Heb. ix. 14,16; x. 14; Eph. v. 2; Rom. iii. 25,26.—
35. Dan. ix. 24,26; Col. i. 19,20; Eph. i. 11,14; John xvii. 2; Heb. ix. 12,15.—36. Gal. iv. 4,5; Gen. iii. 15; Rev. xiii. 8; Heb. xiii. 8.

Mention was just made of Christ's perfect obedience. Ordinarily we speak of Christ's death as the cause of our salvation. The idea that we are saved by his life has been looked upon with disfavor in orthodox circles because modernists have preached that we earn our salvation by doing good as he did. Now, it is quite certain that we cannot earn our salvation. Men are born sinful, depraved, wholly inclined to all evil, and enemies of God. Nevertheless we are saved, not only by Christ's death, but also by his life. This is a perfectly Scriptural idea, if only we do not deform and contort it as the modernists did. The apostle in Romans 5:10 says, "Much more, being reconciled, shall we be saved by his life." It is the righteousness Jesus earned by his life—theologians call it his active obedience—that he imputes to us, making us righteous in God's sight.

At the same time there is good reason to emphasize his passive obedience, i.e., his sufferings and death. It is essential to understand just what Christ did by dying. The most uninformed Christian knows that Christ's death saves us; but unless one wishes to remain uninformed, one must consider how his death saves us. What is the connection between death and salvation? This question deserves a clear straightforward answer. The contemporary theologians who regard the Bible as myth do not care to give an intelligible answer. When the cross is regarded as a symbol, there remains no way to discover what it symbolizes. If it must be demythologized, how can anyone make sure of its meaning? We can imagine Rudolf Bultmann, as basso profundissimo, singing:

> Ich weiss nicht was soll es bedeuten -
> Das mythologische Kreuz:
> Ein'Tat urgeschichtlicher Zeiten
> Täuscht uns mit trughaften Reiz.

But orthodox Christians, Christians who listen to the Word of God, can answer this question with perfect clarity. The answer is that Christ by his death "hath fully satisfied the justice of his Father, and purchased not only reconciliation, but an everlasting inheritance . . . for all those whom the Father hath given him." The central point of the Christian message, the point which every faithful evangelist must emphasize, the first point that a Christian should understand about salvation, is that Christ's death satisfied divine justice. Today it is customary to call this the doctrine of the atonement; but it used to be called the Satisfaction, and Satisfaction is rather the better name.

When Christians are asked what is their favorite passage, they cite John 3:16, or the twenty-third Psalm, or a portion of Isaiah. And no one can fail to appreciate the beauty of these passages. But if a malevolent demon were to deprive the world of the Bible, and to me was given the heavy responsibility of preserving just a few lines for posterity, I would unhesitatingly pass by the twenty-third Psalm, the beautiful portions of Isaiah, and even John 3:16. I would select Romans 3:25, 26. These Pauline verses do not have the beauty of the Psalms, nor the majestic style of Isaiah, nor the emotional appeal of John 3:16; but they have the heart of the gospel. They explain precisely what Christ did in his death; they show the method of salvation.

At this point, perhaps more so than at others, it is necessary to have a correct conception of God. Chapter II may have seemed either dull, useless, or needlessly lengthy. At this point we need some of that information. People who stress the goodness and love of God and fail to attend to God's righteousness and holiness cannot understand the death of Christ. These people so misunderstand love and goodness that they think God will not punish anybody, or at least not punish them much. God is too good to let anyone perish, they say. Why then did Christ, God's Son, have to suffer so?

The explanation lies in God's perfect justice and righteousness. God defined sin by promulgating laws. He attached a terrible penalty to every infraction of the law.

Today sociologists and penalogists tend to minimize lawlessness. When a man is drunk, commits rape and murder, robs a bank, modern theories call him sick. He is not regarded as a criminal. He is to be rehabilitated, not punished. Modern man has thus lost his sense of justice. Sentimental compassion is expressed for the murderer; no one seems to care about the victim.

This immoral theory is a result of disbelief in God, in the holy and righteous God. It is a result of disbelief in sin and in the punishment of sin. And naturally those who adopt these lax principles cannot accept the idea of atonement or satisfaction.

The gospel, on the contrary, the good news we preach, is that Jesus Christ by his death expiates sin, propitiates his Father, and satisfies divine justice.

We now come to section vi, which is not of the same major importance as the preceding; but it disposes of an interesting speculation that has sometimes plagued the Church. Because Christ died about A.D. 30, some people jumped to the conclusion that no one could be saved before that date. On this theory the Old Testament saints were confined to some place less than heaven and had to await their release until Christ was laid in the tomb.

This theory is supported by a fanciful interpretation of I Peter 3:18-22. These verses are supposed to say that Jesus, during the three days, descended to Noah and other spirits in prison and brought them to heaven.

There are all sorts of things wrong with this interpretation. First, verse 10 speaks of preaching the gospel, not of releasing spirits. Second, the spirits mentioned seem to be unsaved, not Noah and the Old Testament saints, because it was the gospel that was preached to them. Third, if it were all the Old Testament saints, the specific mention of Noah to the exclusion of later times is inexplicable. And fourth, the passage does not say that Jesus preached to anyone during the three days of his entombment. It is rather the Spirit of Christ dwelling in Noah who preached to those who were disobedient in Noah's day. If it seems strained to say that the Spirit of Christ preached as he dwelt in Noah, return to I Peter 1:11 where other Old Testament prophets are said to have tried to understand what the Spirit of Christ which was in them meant to teach in their prophecies.

The subject could be further pursued with profit. It has to do with the nature of Old Testament religion. We shall, however, dismiss it for the time being with the reminder that the gospel was preached to Abraham (Gal. 3:8), and that Abraham rejoiced to see Christ's day: he saw it and was glad.

Section VII.—Christ in the work of mediation, acteth according to both natures; by each nature doing that which is proper to itself;[37] yet by reason of the unity of the person, that which is proper to one nature is sometimes in Scripture attributed to the person denominated by the other nature.[38]

Section VIII.—To all those for whom Christ hath purchased redemption, he doth certainly and effectually apply and communicate the same;[39] making intercession for them;[40] and revealing unto them, in and by the Word, the mysteries of salvation;[41] effectually persuading them by his Spirit to believe and obey; and governing their hearts by his Word and Spirit;[42] overcoming all their enemies by his almighty power and wisdom, in such manner and ways as are most consonant to his wonderful and unsearchable dispensation.[43]

37. Heb. ix. 14 ; 1 Pet. iii. 18.—38. Acts xx. 28 ; John iii. 13 ; 1 John iii. 16.—39. John vi. 37,39 ; x. 15-16.—40. 1 John ii. 1,2 ; Rom. viii. 34.—41.

John xv. 13,15; Eph. i. 7-9; John xvii. 6.—42. John xiv. 16; Heb. xii. 2; 2 Cor. iv. 13; Rom. viii. 9,14; xv. 18,19; John xvii. 17.—43. Ps. cx. 1; 1 Cor. xv. 25,26; Mal. iv. 2,3; Col. ii. 15.

As this is an extra long chapter, let us pass by section vii merely with the admonition to check the Scripture references indicated and others that can easily be found. This abbreviation is all the more excusable, since section viii cannot be passed over in silence.

The first idea in this last section is that God's plans do not fail. How could omnipotence start to do something and be stymied? So it is with Christ too, for he is God. Christ came to save his people. Therefore there is no possibility that any of his people will be lost.

This salvation is not the immediate result of his death. The immediate purpose and result of his death was to propitiate the Father's wrath by satisfying the demands of justice. That is to say, Jesus' death was pointed first toward God, rather than toward men. Jesus offered himself as a sacrifice and sacrifices for sin are offered to God. They are designed to win God's favor—not to produce some change in the person who offers the sacrifice. This is why Jesus was called the Lamb of God. He did in reality what the lambs of the Old Testament did symbolically.

Of course, expiating sin by propitiating the Father would have been no use to us, unless the benefits of this Satisfaction were applied to us. Now, as was said, Jesus never fails. Hence it is absolutely certain that those people whom God had given to him, those persons for whom he died, will be saved. Not one of them will be lost.

Someone is sure to ask, Did not Christ die for all men, and are not some lost?

Let us ask this question a little more pointedly. When Christ was dying on the cross, did he intend to save the wicked people of Sodom and Gomorrah? Did he intend to save Esau? Did he intend to save Judas?

If he did, he failed.

But Christ did not fail. Everyone for whom Christ died is saved. Jesus himself said, All those whom the Father gives to me shall come unto me, and of them I shall lose none (John 6:37-39).

Also, the prophet Isaiah said, "When thou shalt make his soul an offering for sin, he shall see his seed . . . He shall see of

102

the travail of his soul and shall be satisfied" (53:10,11). Would Christ be satisfied with failure?

Christ therefore did not die for all men indiscriminately. He died for all the elect, all his people, all whom the Father gave him. Some verses in the Bible, when read carelessly, seem to say Christ intended to save everybody. One well-known verse is "not willing that any should perish." No, this is not a well-known verse: it is a well-known phrase detached from a poorly known verse. What II Peter 3:9 actually says is, "The Lord . . . is long suffering to us-ward, not willing that any [of us] should perish, but that all [of us] should come to repentance." The *us* of course refers to the author Peter and to those to whom he is writing, viz., "them that have obtained like precious faith with us" (II Peter 1:1). So in other cases also.

The application of the benefits of redemption is not, however, exactly automatic. Christ used certain means of application. First, he intercedes for them; second, he reveals the terms of salvation to them by means of his Word, the Bible; and third, Christ sends the Holy Spirit to them to persuade them to believe the message of salvation.

Remember that all men are dead in sin, enemies of God, haters of righteousness, and lovers of iniquity. They are not willing to believe. Before they can believe, they must be changed. This change of mind, called repentance, is the work, not of a minister, but of the Holy Spirit.

Many times I have preached in rescue missions. Looking at these half-drunken derelicts, these miserable victims of gross sin, one could wonder whether it was any use to preach to them. How can their perverted minds be expected to respond to a Christian sermon? Certainly no natural ground of expectation is possible. But if any of these gutter bums has been given to Christ by the Father, Christ doth effectually communicate redemption to him "effectually persuading them by his Spirit to believe and obey," or, as was stated in Chapter VII, iii on the Covenant, giving them "his Holy Spirit to make them willing and able to believe."

Therefore the preacher need not be discouraged, for God has promised that "my word shall not return unto me void, but it shall accomplish that which I please, and it shall prosper in the thing whereto I sent it."

This is not all. Christ also overcomes the believers' enemies by his almighty power and wisdom in many wonderful ways. Many of these further blessings are explained in later chapters, but the immediately following chapter has more to say about the relation between God and the mind and will of man.

CHAPTER IX.

OF FREE WILL.

Section I.—God hath endued the will of man with that natural liberty that it is neither forced, nor by any absolute necessity of nature determined, to good or evil.[1]

1. Matt. xvii. 12; James i. 14; Deut. xxx. 19.

When a discussion grows excited, there are two possible explanations. Excitement may indicate that the topic is of great importance. Now, in this book on the Westminster Confession every chapter so far has seemed of great importance; and free will is also a matter of importance, though it can hardly be of such importance as the previous chapter on Christ the Mediator. In the second place, excited discussion frequently indicates that the debators are not sure of themselves. When contenders have neglected essential distinctions and have proceeded beyond their resources, the discussion can go on endlessly and without conclusions. As this has often been the case with discussions on free will, it would be wise to see exactly what the Confession says.

"God hath endued the will of man with that natural liberty that it is neither forced nor by any absolute necessity of nature determined to do good or evil." Now, what does the Confession mean by natural liberty? Does a Presbyterian mean the same thing that a Romanist or an Arminian means, when they say that man is free? Are there various concepts of freedom?

Obviously there are various concepts of freedom, and some of them have little to do with the present topic. For example, we say today that American citizens are free men, but that the victims of communistic governments are not free. Freedom therefore has a political and an economic sense; but that is not what concerns us here. Reinhold Niebuhr in *Faith and History* writes pages on freedom; but none of it touches on free will.

Closer to free will is the question whether or not the will of man is free from his intellect. Theologians in the past have discussed this at length. But that the will is free from the intellect is not what the Confession means by natural liberty. Calvin, for example, asserted that "the intellect rules the will"; Charles Hodge said that man's "will was subject to his reason," and Robert J. Breckenridge taught that our primary conception of will includes the notion of its being directed by intelligence. The theology behind all this may be a little intricate, and the matter is mentioned only to show that freedom from intellect is not what Presbyerians mean by the concept of freedom.

What then does the Confession mean by the natural liberty of the will? The remainder of the section quoted answers this question as well as two lines can. Man's will "is neither forced nor by any absolute necessity of nature determined." These words were written to repudiate those philosophies which explain human conduct in terms of physico-chemical law. Although the Westminster divines did not know twentieth century behaviorism, nor even Spinoza, they very probably knew Thomas Hobbes, and they certainly knew earlier materialistic theories. That man's conduc' is determined by inanimate forces is what the Confession denies. Man is not a machine; his motions cannot be described by mathematical equations as can the motions of the planets. His hopes, plans, and activities are not controlled by physical conditions. He is not determined by any absolute necessity of nature.

The freedom of the will has always been a matter of interest and vigorous discussion. In the century following the composition of the Confession the Arminian Dr. Whitby, apparently with great learning, attacked the Calvinistic position, arguing for a different kind of free will. It is reported that Dr. Whitby seemed so convincing that Calvinists were reproached for not being able to answer him. In this situation the Baptist John Gill, previously mentioned, wrote his *The Cause of God and Truth*. Part III chapter V of his work is an extended argument on this subject. Although John Gill in his answer to Whitby examined the materialistic determinism of Thomas Hobbes, and as well the so-called fatalism of the ancient Stoics, the more important question from the standpoint of salvation is the alleged freedom of the will to avoid sin. Arminians no doubt agree with Calvinists in rejecting materialism, mechanism, naturalism, and behaviorism. The difference between the two types of theology has to do with freedom not to sin, freedom to obey God's law, and freedom to act contrary to God's decrees. Can a man will to obey the Ten Commandments? These and related questions are taken up in the following sections.

Section II.—Man, in his state of innocency, had freedom and power to will and to do that which is good and well-pleasing to God,[2] but yet mutably, so that he might fall from it.[3]

Section III.—Man, by his fall and state of sin, hath wholly lost all ability of will to any spiritual good accompanying salvation;[4] so as a natural man, being altogether averse from that good,[5] and dead in sin,[6] is not able, by his own strength, to convert himself, or to prepare himself thereunto.[7]

Section IV.—When God converts a sinner and translates him into the state of grace, he freeth him from his natural bondage under sin,[8] and by his grace alone enables him freely to will and to do that which is spiritually good;[9] yet so as that, by reason of his remaining corruption, he doth not perfectly nor only will that which is good, but doth also will that which is evil.[10]

Section V.—The will of man is made perfectly and immutably free to do good alone in the state of glory only.[11]

2. Eccles. vii. 29; Gen. i. 26.—3. Gen. ii. 16,17; iii. 6.—4. Rom. v. 6; viii. 7; John xv. 5.—5. Rom. iii. 10,12.—6. Eph. ii. 1,5; Col. ii. 13.—7. John vi. 44,65; Eph. ii. 2-5; 1 Cor. ii. 14; Tit. iii. 3-5.—8. Col. i. 13; John viii. 34,36.—9. Phil. ii. 13; Rom. vi. 18,22.—10. Gal. v. 17; Rom. vii. 15,18,19,21,23.—11. Eph. iv. 13; Heb. xii, 23; 1 John iii. 2; Jude 24.

It might appear that there is a hiatus between sections i and ii of this chapter because nothing is said for or against man's freedom and ability to act contrary to God's decrees. Such a hiatus appears only because the chapter on the Divine Decree has already answered the question so definitely. It was not necessary to repeat it again in the Confession. Here, however, permit a reminder that the fact of man's being free from physico-chemical law does not imply that man is free from God's decree. The two types of freedom are logically distinct.

Furthermore, no one can accuse the Confession of going beyond the Bible or of reading into it what is not there. The Bible is as definite as, and by examples far more particular than, the Confession; and in these examples is clearly seen God's control over the wills of men.

A first example, interesting though obscure, is found in Exodus 34:24. The men of Israel were commanded to appear before the Lord three times a year. Such an occasion would give Israel's enemies an excellent opportunity to attack. Therefore, to answer this unspoken objection the Lord immediately assures the Israelites that the enemies during those periods of time will have no such desire. How could this be unless it is the Lord who controlled the desires of the heathen?

In chapter III the passage II Samuel 17:14, which relates how God brought evil upon Absalom through the poor counsel of Hushai, was used to show that God foreordains all events. Here again we emphasize that God foreordains not only external, visible events, but also the decisions and choices of men. Absalom made his choice because God made Absalom choose that way.

Similarly in II Chronicles 10:15 God, in order to fulfill his promise to Jeroboam, caused Rehoboam to adopt evil advice.

Better known than these cases are the words of Paul in Philippians 2:12-13: "Work out your own salvation with fear and trembling, for it is God which worketh in you both to will and to do of his good pleasure." Of course, it is we who work out our own salvation and it is we who will to do so. It was Absalom and Rehoboam who themselves made their choices. But all these choices were determined by God, who works in us according to his good pleasure.

How could it be otherwise? Unless God "governs all creatures, actions, and things" as the Confession V, i says, or "all his creatures and all their actions" as the Catechism 11 says, he would not be omnipotent and could not guarantee the fulfillment of his own prophecies. Man indeed has a natural liberty, a liberty as against nature, a liberty not acknowledged by materialistic philosophy; but Christians should never construe this liberty to the detriment of God's omnipotence and grace.

With this clearly in mind we may turn to the relation of freedom to sin. Section ii states that before the fall Adam had both freedom and ability to please God. Taken by itself this statement causes no difficulty. Where Romanists and Arminians differ from Calvinists is the depth of sin and the extent of its results. The two former theologies do not take sin as seriously as the Calvinists do. In section iii the difference is developed particularly with reference to Romanism; and in this century its contrast with modernism is even sharper.

The point of section iii is that Adam's ability to will what is good was lost by the fall. From that time on man could not choose to will "any spiritual good accompanying salvation." True, a man might will to be honest, to support his family, to discharge most of his obligations as a citizen. In colloquial language these things are called good. But they are not spiritual goods and they have nothing to do with salvation. Furthermore, a man cannot will to be saved. He cannot convert himself, nor even make preparations for conversion. The simple reason is that he is dead in sin.

Section iv now describes a new ability that man receives upon conversion. But first a word should be said about conversion itself, or more precisely, regeneration. That regeneration is not an act of free will must be constantly emphasized. Any attempt to explain the new birth as an act of will makes a man his own savior. Why does the New Testament use the metaphor of birth, if not to exclude all action by the person born? Nor need we rely merely on an inference drawn from a metaphor. In clear literal language John 1:13 states that those who are children of God have been born not of blood (i.e.,not by physical inheritance), nor of the will of the flesh nor of the will of man. Whatever distinction may be made between the will of the flesh (physical impulse?) and the will of man (desire to become a child of God?), the total expression is so broad as to exclude all action of human will in regeneration. Regeneration is an act of God.

Now, when God regenerates, resurrects, and converts a sinner, he frees the sinner from his natural bondage under sin. Although this freedom at the start is not complete, instantaneous sanctification, nevertheless God enables the new born Christian to will and do some spiritual good. The dominion of sin has been broken, the cleansing process has begun, and the convert will inevitably grow in grace.

Complete sanctification, the total eradication of sin, awaits our glorification. And in heaven we shall rejoice, for one thing, because we have no free will—in the Arminian sense of power of contrary choice. For in heaven there is one type of thing that we cannot possibly will to do—viz., to sin.

Since throughout church history the debate on free will has been so lively and excited, it seems wise now to conclude this chapter with a few paragraphs that reveal some of the confusions that have plagued the debate.

The sources of confusion in discussions on free will are chiefly three. First, the discussion is allowed to proceed without anyone's defining the key terms; second, implications are assumed to be valid when actually they are fallacious; and third, more than in any other theological discussion there is a temptation to neglect the express statements of Scripture and to depend on uninspired philosophy, common opinion, and hasty guesswork.

First, as to definition of terms. The Arminian[1] definition of free will is usually the one that is embedded in common opinion. The idea is that in any given situation, all factors and conditions being taken into account, a man can as easily choose this as that. The act of will is supposed not to be an effect of any cause; that is to say, the will is not determined. This idea is given the name of the power of contrary choice, or sometimes, the liberty of indifference. This Arminian definition has the merit at least of being clearcut. The only question is whether or not men can will, desire, or choose this as easily as that.

Upon thinking it over, nearly everyone comes to the conclusion that the above description overestimates man's freedom. The civilization in which we are born, Chinese, African, or American, makes it, if not impossible, at least extremely difficult to desire some things rather than their opposites. Within American society the Christian training one person receives in his youth makes it less easy for him to choose thievery rather than honesty. Fortunately, and sometimes unfortunately, education and upbringing exercise a causative power on the will. Strange would it be if our habitual character and all the factors of life had no effect on our choices. But stranger still would it be if the grace of God and the power of sin had no effect on us. If God cannot control man's will and make us willing to obey him, we are indeed in a

---

1. The Protestant movement, arising out of the Reformation, is divided chiefly into three sections: the Lutheran, the Reformed (which includes the Presbyterian churches), and the Arminian (which is mainly equated with the Methodist churches).

sorry plight, and God is no longer omnipotent. It has previously been shown that the power of sin binds the will so that the unregenerate man can neither seek God (Rom. 3:11) nor be subject to God's laws (Rom. 8:7). It seems clear therefore that man does not have free will in the sense of the power of contrary choice.

The second cause of confusion in this discussion is the acceptance of fallacious implications as valid. Some people jump to the conclusion that if the will is not free, man has no will at all. To them "no free will" means "no will and no choice." But this implication rests on impossible logic. The question is not whether man has a will or not; the question is whether the will a man has and the choices he makes are the results of prior conditions, such as early training, the power of sin, and God's grace. Undoubtedly we will and choose, but it is God who works in us to will according to his good pleasure.

Another commonly held fallacy is that unless the will is free, man is not responsible for what he does. This fallacy, like the preceding, is bad logic; but it also depends on an ignorance of Scripture. The Scripture indicates in several places what the basis of responsibility is; and it is not free will. Consider these three passages. John 15:22 reads, "If I had not come and spoken unto them, they had not had sin; but now they have no cloke for their sin." Luke 12:47,48 reads, "And that servant, which knew his lord's will, and prepared not himself, neither did according to his will, shall be beaten with many stripes. But he that knew not, and did commit things worthy of stripes, shall be beaten with few stripes." In both of these passages knowledge is made the basis of responsibility. And for a third passage, turn to Daniel 5:22, which reads, "And thou, his son, O Belshazzar, hast not humbled thine heart, though thou knewest all this." There are other passages, including the first chapter of Romans, but these must suffice now.

The previous paragraph overlaps and anticipates the third source of confusion in discussions on the will. This source was reliance on common opinions instead of a searching of the Scripture. The Bible never actually mentions free will, as it certainly would have done, if free will had been as important as the Arminians think. The only reference to free will in the Bible is

111

the "free-will" offerings. These have nothing to do with the problem under consideration. Free-will offerings are merely offerings above those required by law. After a person had made all the offerings prescribed by law, he might out of gratitude for God's grace give something additional. This was called a free-will offering. But it has no bearing on the liberty of indifference, the power of contrary choice, the causative power of the intellect on the will, the influence of civilization, or anything else pertaining to this discussion.

That the Confession correctly reports the views of the Protestant Reformers is beyond doubt. In the chapter on Providence a quotation was made from Jerome Zanchius. The passage continues as follows: "That this was the doctrine of Luther, none can deny who are in any measure acquainted with his works, particularly with his treatise *De Servo Arbitrio*, or Freewill a Slave. . . . Among other matters he proves that 'whatever man does, he does necessarily, though not with any sensible compulsion, and that we can do only what God from eternity willed and foreknew we should, which will of God must be effectual and his foresight certain'; . . . adding 'Hereby as with a thunderbolt is man's free will thrown down and destroyed.' "

Finally, to repeat the obvious, the Bible teaches and nothing written here contradicts the fact that man has a will, makes choices, and is responsible for them.

CHAPTER X.

OF EFFECTUAL CALLING

*Section I.—All those whom God has predestinated
unto life, and those only, he is pleased, in his appointed
and accepted time, effectually to call,[1] by his word and
Spirit,[2] out of that state of sin and death in which they
are by nature, to grace and salvation by Jesus Christ;[3]
enlightening their minds spiritually and savingly to understand the things of God;[4] taking away their heart of
stone, and giving unto them an heart of flesh;[5] renewing
their wills, and by his almighty power determining them
to that which is good,[6] and effectually drawing them to
Jesus Christ;[7] yet so as they come most freely, being
made willing by his grace.[8]*

*Section II.—This effectual call is of God's free and
special grace alone, not from anything at all foreseen
in man;[9] who is altogether passive therein, until, being
quickened and renewed by the Holy Spirit,[10] he is thereby enabled to answer this call, and to embrace the grace
offered and conveyed in it.[11]*

1. Rom. viii. 30; xi. 7,8; Eph. i. 10,11.—2. 2 Thess. ii. 13,14; 2 Cor. iii
3,6.—3. Rom. viii. 2-9; Eph. ii. 1-9; 2 Tim. i. 9,10.—4. Acts xxvi. 18; 1
Cor. ii. 10,12; Eph. i. 17,18.—5. Ezek. xxxvi. 26.—6. Ezek. xi. 19; Phil.
ii. 13; Deut. xxx. 6; Ezek xxxvi. 27.—7. Eph. i. 19; John vi. 44,45.—
8. Cant. i. 4; Ps. cx. 3; John vi. 37; Rom. vi. 16-18.—9. 2 Tim. i. 9; Tit.
4,5; Eph. ii. 4,5,8,9; Rom. ix. 11.—10. 1 Cor. ii. 14; Rom. viii. 7; Eph.
ii. 5.—11. John vi. 37; Ezek xxxvi. 27; John v. 25.

The discussion on Chapter VIII section vii alluded to the
unwillingness of derelicts in a rescue mission to accept the Gospel
of Christ. They are happy to accept the meal, the bath, and the
bed, but it takes all this to bribe them to sit through an evangelistic service. They hardly even listen.

But the respectable sinner uptown is just as dead in sin as
the drunken bum. He may be drunk too—of course on better
liquor. If he goes to church, it is for social and business reasons.
And if perchance the Gospel is preached in the kind of church
he attends, he hears no more of it than the derelict.

If an evangelist had to depend solely on his own powers of
persuasion, the job downtown and the job uptown would be not
merely discouraging, but impossible.

Now, the reason that these two jobs, though often discouraging, are not impossible is that God himself does the work. In eternity he began the work by predestinating these two men, and on a certain day in time he effectually calls them. No one can be saved without God's effectual call. Everyone who is born again is "born not of the will of the flesh, nor of the will of man, but of God." Those theologians who, in the interest of an erroneous doctrine of free will, attribute some ability to man's will, contradict John 1:13 and detract from God's grace.

God effectually calls all those whom he predestinated, but no others. From beginning to end the same people are in view. As Romans 8:29-30 says, "Whom he did foreknow, he also did predestinate . . . moreover whom he did predestinate, them he also called; and whom he called, them he also justified; and whom he justified, them he also glorified." No one who enters at the beginning is dropped along the way, and no one is added who did not start.

Someone may be tempted to say that although God undoubtedly calls the elect, he does not call them only, as the Confession says. Does not God call everybody? The answer to this question is to be found by searching the Scripture. John 12:39, 40 says, "They could not believe, because Esaias said again, He hath blinded their eyes and hardened their heart, that they should not see with their eyes nor understand with their heart, and be converted, and I should heal them." In Romans 11:7 we read, "Israel hath not obtained that which he seeketh for; but the election hath obtained it, and the rest were blinded." Since God does all that he pleases (Ps. 135:6), and since his causative power is omnipotent, it follows that he has not called the lost, but the elect only.

Of course, ministers and evangelists call people too. That is, they preach the Gospel publicly. But the effective call, the call that actually produces the proper response, comes from God alone.

Consider these passages. "I will put a new spirit within you; and I will take the stony heart out of their flesh, and will give them a heart of flesh, that they may walk in my statutes . . . and they shall be my people, and I will be their God" (Ezek. 11:19,20). Can the stony heart prevent God from performing this operation? See the similar words in Ezekiel 36:25-27, which also adds, "Then

114

will I sprinkle clean water upon you and ye shall be clean . . . and I will put my spirit within you and cause you to walk in my statutes." Is God's causative power effective? Can God cause this result? If an effect does not occur, there could not have been any *cause* whatever, could there? God's call is surely effectual, for Isaiah 55:11 says, "My word . . . shall not return unto me void, but it shall accomplish that which I please." No human will can prevent the effect which God intended to produce.

Turning from the Gospel in the Old Testament to the Gospel in the New Testament we find that in Acts 13:48 "as many as were ordained to eternal life, believed." It does not say, as some try to twist it, "as many as believed were ordained to eternal life." The divine ordination comes first and causes the belief. The fact and power of God's call are also seen in II Thessalonians 2:13,14, "God hath from the beginning chosen you to salvation . . . whereunto he called you by our gospel." In order not to multiply quotations, the student is invited to look up these additional references: John 5:21, 15:16, and 6:37; II Cor. 4:6; Eph. 2:5; Phil. 2:13; I Thess. 5:9; Jas. 1:18.

There are some Christians, even some who have been raised in Presbyterian homes and churches, who dislike the idea of determinism. These people, to varying degrees, have been infected with the Arminian notion of a free will, a will independent of God. But the Confession is not afraid of determinism. Note carefully that the effectual or effective call occurs by God's "renewing their wills, and by his almighty power determining them to that which is good, and effectually drawing them to Jesus Christ." This is determinism as powerful as, yea, rather, more powerful than any alleged physical determinism. The sinner comes "freely," i.e., voluntarily, not in spite of but because of the fact that God controlled his will and made him willing.

The reason it is so necessary to insist on divine determinism and to rebut any doctrine of a will free and independent of God's causative power is that man since the fall is dead in sin, cannot will to accept Christ, and is wholly dependent on grace. Thus section ii not only ties in with section i, but also depends on chapter VI.

Probably the majority of Christians, if they hear Biblical preaching year after year, absorb some vague notion of three or four or half a dozen doctrines. What is usually overlooked is the fact that these doctrines form a system. They are logically connected. The doctrine of sin necessitates the doctrine of effectual calling; and the absolute need of grace rules out all human merit and what is ordinarily called free will. Calvinism means free grace, not free will. The two are logically incompatible. Therefore section ii notices that here "man . . . is altogether passive therein, until quickened and renewed by the Holy Spirit."

To be quickened, to be resurrected from a valley of dry bones, to be born again, is not an act of will at all. The person who is being born is altogether passive. By the process of birth or resurrection he is given certain powers. Before he is alive, he has none. Thus it is that God's effectual call enables a man "to embrace the grace offered and conveyed in it."

> *Section III.—Elect infants, dying in infancy, are regenerated and saved by Christ through the Spirit,[12] who worketh when and where and how he pleaseth.[13] So also are all other elect persons, who are incapable of being outwardly called by the ministry of the Word.[14]*

12. Luke xviii. 16; Acts ii. 38,39; John iii. 3,5; 1 John v. 12; Rom. viii. 9.—13. John iii. 8.—14. 1 John v. 12; Acts iv. 12.

Section i had indicated that God calls men by his Word and Spirit. The derelict and the leader of society are to hear the Gospel preached. This is part of the ordinary process. And since most of the activity recounted in the Bible has to do with ordinary adults, there is not much said about children who die in infancy and imbeciles who cannot understand language. Section iii takes up this point.

When I was a boy, in those calm happy days before World War I, a neighbor of ours was an old-fashioned free-thinker. The type is now extinct. The boys of our street used to sit with him and his lovely wife on their front steps in the summer evenings. We discussed perpetual motion and tried to emulate Benjamin Franklin in the invention of small gadgets. One evening the free thinker with judicious approval noted that the Presbyterians were improving because they had just repudiated their traditional doctrine of infant damnation. This doctrine was supposed to teach that all who die in infancy are lost, and naturally Presbyterians must be a heartless people to hold such a pitiless position.

116

Of course the old gentleman was mistaken, as free thinkers usually were on all matters Christian.

Presbyterians had never held that all who die in infancy are lost. What the Confession is interested in, is whether any dying in infancy can be saved. If salvation unexceptionally depended on hearing, understanding, and accepting the Gospel, no child who died in infancy could be saved. Nor could any imbecile. Section iii declares that infant salvation is possible.

Now, of course, Presbyterians, repeating the words of Jesus himself, believe in hell, outer darkness and gnashing of teeth, in a fire that is not quenched, and in everlasting punishment. If anybody wishes to accuse us of believing in the sort of God Jesus believed in, we can only plead guilty. And I rather suspect that it is Jesus' concept of God that dismays nineteenth century free thinkers and contemporary neo-orthodox theologians.

But the Confession neither asks nor answers how many who die in infancy are saved. For all the Confession says, all may be lost or all may be saved. The Bible gives no number or proportion; neither does the Confession, for the Confession claims, and claims justly, to summarize the Bible. The proof texts given in the footnote are taken as sufficient to show that all elect persons, whether infants or adults, who are incapable of being outwardly called by the preaching of the Word, are regenerated and saved notwithstanding.

> Section IV.—Others not elected, although they may be called by the ministry of the word,[15] and may have some common operations of the Spirit;[16] yet they never truly come unto Christ, and therefore cannot be saved;[17] much less can men not professing the Christian religion be saved in any other way whatsoever, be they ever so diligent to frame their lives according to the light of nature and the law of that religion they do profess;[18] and to assert and maintain that they may, is very pernicious, and to be detested.[19]

15. Matt. xxii. 14.—16. Matt. vii. 22 ; xiii. 20,21 ; Heb. vi. 4,5.—17. John vi. 64-66 ; viii. 24.—18. Acts iv. 12 ; John xiv. 6 ; Eph. ii. 12 ; John iv. 22 ; xvii. 3.—19. 2 John 9-11 ; 1 Cor. xvi. 22 ; Gal. 1. 6-8.

But though some persons may be regenerated apart from the preaching of the Word, no one can be saved by a different message.

117

Today it is very popular and democratic to say that all religions are equally good—because equally useless. In voting for governmental officials it is unpatriotic to consider their religion because religion has no bearing on important questions. Religion is a matter of personal superstitions or odd practices in which everybody should be indulged so long as they do not affect business or politics. As the head of a college history department told me: religion has its proper place in life, but one should not allow it to dominate.

Presbyterians therefore are fanatics. I mean real Presbyterians—not those who merely have their names enrolled in churches with the word Presbyterian in the title. Presbyterians are fanatics because they believe that men not professing Christian religion cannot be saved in any other way whatsoever, be they ever so diligent to frame their lives according to the light of nature and the law of that religion they do profess. To maintain that all religions are of equal value, or to suppose that any other one affords salvation, is very pernicious and to be detested.

Presbyterians hold that there is only one name in which men may be saved. So they are fanatics! Away with them! Let them be crucified!

Unfortunately many ministers in the large denominations have substituted a social and political theory for this glorious gospel of grace. A recent president of Princeton Seminary advocated the admission of Red China into the United Nations. *The Christian Century* is full of socialist political propaganda. The World Council emasculates doctrine, repudiates Protestantism by admitting the Greek Catholic organization that persecutes evangelicals, and raises no voice against state control of churches. Certainly it raises no voice to proclaim effectual calling.

How sad it is when ministers and professedly Christian organizations forsake the gospel of grace to preach something else! The outright denial of Biblical doctrines, in other words, heresy, is bad; but even apart from outright denial, the substitution of another message is almost if not altogether as bad. Whether people are lost because they have heard the Scriptures denied or because they simply have not heard the Scripture, makes little difference. The servants of Christ have been given a message to proclaim, and failure to proclaim it cannot be excused on the ground that the substitute was socialistic politics instead of outright heresy.

Sincere, conservative preachers ought to take stock of themselves too. It is all too easy to forget some parts of the message because we are so interested in some other parts. It is so easy to become lopsided. Then our people will become lopsided too. One excellent method of avoiding this unfortunate result is to preach a series of sermons on the Westminster Confession; at least we should review the thirty-three chapters to determine what we have not preached on for some time.

Chapter XI.

OF JUSTIFICATION.

Section I.—Those whom God effectually calleth he also freely justifieth;[1] not by infusing righteousness into them, but by pardoning their sins and by accounting and accepting their persons as righteous: not for anything wrought in them, or done by them, but for Christ's sake alone; not by imputing faith itself, the act of believing, or any other evangelical obedience, to them as their righteousness; but by imputing the obedience and satisfaction of Christ unto them,[2] they receiving and resting on him and his righteousness by faith: which faith they have not of themselves; it is the gift of God.[3]

Section II.—Faith, thus receiving and resting on Christ and his righteousness, is the alone instrument of justification;[4] yet is it not alone in the person justified, but is ever accompanied with all other saving graces, and is no dead faith, but worketh by love.[5]

1. Rom. viii. 30; iii. 24.—2. Rom. iv. 5-8; 2 Cor. v. 19,21; Rom. iii. 22, 24,25,27,28; Tit. iii. 5,7; Eph. i. 7; Jer. xxiii. 6; 1 Cor. i. 30,31; Rom. v. 17-19.—3. Acts x. 44; Gal. ii. 16; Phil. iii. 9; Acts xiii. 38,39; Eph. ii. 7,8.—4. John i. 12; Rom. iii. 28; v. 1.—5. James ii. 17,22,26; Gal. v. 6.

Do you expect to go to heaven when you die? Virtually everybody does. If you should ask a dozen different people why they expect to go to heaven, what answers do you think they would give? A Lutheran girl told me that she had behaved commendably through life and so she was sure she would go to heaven. (Luther would never have given that answer.) A doctor of no particular denomination said that although he had done a few bad things, he had done a great deal of good, and so he expected to go to heaven. And a utility repairman guessed that the Church would get him through. But these answers bring to mind the Negro spiritual: "Everybody talking 'bout heaven ain't going there."

If you were an elder of a Presbyterian session, and an applicant for communicant membership gave some such answer, would you vote to receive him?

In general there are only two plans of salvation. The first plan has several varieties, but basically it is a purely human plan of salvation by works. Its sole drawback is that the works do not work. Heaven's requirements are too stringent, and we cannot make the grade. The second plan is the divine plan of justification by faith.

During the Middle Ages, a one-thousand-year period of ignorance and superstition, this doctrine of justification by faith was hardly known at all. Some small groups, the Waldensians, the followers of Wycliffe, the followers of Huss, and perhaps a few isolated unknown individuals, knew its meaning. But the vast majority thought that they could earn entrance into heaven by fasting, by giving money to the church, by whipping themselves, by walking up the stone steps of churches on their knees, or by doing other uncomfortable works of penance. If in this way they did not earn sufficient merits to enter heaven, their lack could be made up either by having transferred to them some merits from people who had done more than God required and so had some merits to spare, or ultimately by suffering for a longer time after death in purgatory.

In the early fifteen hundreds Martin Luther chiefly, but also Ulrich Zwingli, followed a little later by John Calvin and many others, rediscovered the teaching of the New Testament and by God's grace preached it so effectively that it revolutionized the world. Even in Spain and Italy, as well as in France, large numbers heard, accepted, and rejoiced in these good tidings; though within a century in these three countries the evangelicals were exterminated by persecution, by being burnt at the stake, and by brutal, wholesale massacre.

These people were evangelicals. The word *evangelical* is derived from the Greek word meaning good news or gospel; and while the word in the twentieth century has been claimed by some groups not properly entitled to it, its original use indicated those people who believed in justification by faith.

In the United States evangelicals are no longer burnt at the stake. Even in France, the land of St. Bartholomew's massacre, the Protestants are not persecuted. But of course the followers of Christ must with much tribulation enter the Kingdom of heaven. Sin still abounds on every side, and contemporary secularism has its own methods of hindering the spread of the gospel.

121

In Spain, in South America, and in Italy oppression has been and still is heavier than in other western lands. In Greece the official church harasses the evangelicals; and under communist rule there is no telling what Christians must suffer. Mohammedan lands too have recently enacted laws against the preaching of the Gospel. From all of which it is clear that much of the world wants a different way of salvation; and though one nation may differ from another in various details, they all agree on some sort of salvation by some sort of works, but, above all, not salvation by faith in Jesus Christ.

Since the Protestant Reformation revolted against a Roman Catholic background, it was natural that the authors of our Confession should first contrast justification by faith with certain Romish ideas. Hence the first sentence of section i states that God's method of justification is not that of infusing righteousness into sinners.

This Romish view, the infusion of righteousness, is essentially the notion that God graciously gives us ability to do good works. If we use this ability and earn enough merits, God will forgive our sins because of our efforts and works. These works include, as indicated above, the giving of alms, flagellation and other ascetic practices, and, as with the monk Tetzel, contributions for the erection of St. Peter's in Rome:

> Wenn ein Thaler in dem Kasten klingt,
> Ein' Seele aus Hölle in den Himmel springt.

Or, as best I can make it out,

> When your dollar in Rome's coffer lies
> A soul from hell to heaven flies.

Now the Romanists admit and insist (we have no desire to misrepresent them) that meritorious works are possible only through God's grace; but at the same time forgiveness of sin is conditioned on our doing these works.

This view is diametrically opposed to the whole New Testament; and the doctrine of justification by faith, not works, is so important that a Lutheran theologian wrote, "Let this be held in purity, and all doctrine remains pure, the Church is master of all foes and heresies. Let it be obscured and adulterated, and all is lost."[1]

However, beyond exposing an error that dominated Europe for a thousand years, it is most necessary to state positively what justification is. If it is not an infusion of grace, then what is it?

To discover what justification is, it is best first to see how the word is used in the New Testament. Luke 7:29 says that the publicans justified God. Now certainly, the publicans did not infuse grace into God, nor did they give him any ability to do good works. Far from making God righteous, they declared that he was already righteous. It should be completely obvious that the publicans produced no change whatsoever in God's character.

That justification does not refer to a subjective change is seen also in other verses. There is the figure of speech in Matthew 11:19, "Wisdom is justified of her children." Luke 10:29 says, "But he, willing to justify himself . . ." where the lawyer did not intend to alter his character but intended to defend it. He meant to declare that he was already just.

That justification is a declaration is more clearly seen when we notice how the New Testament contrasts it with condemnation. Matthew 12:37, even though the exegesis be somewhat complicated, clearly contrasts justification and condemnation. So too Romans 8:33-34 says, "It is God that justifieth. Who is he that condemneth?" The same contrast is also found in Romans 5:16 and 18. Other verses, though they do not explicitly use the two words, imply the same contrast, such as John 3:18.

From this contrast we may conclude that since the verb *condemn* does not mean to make a person guilty or to make his character evil, but means to declare that he already is guilty, the verb *justify* does not mean to make a man just, or to improve his character, but means to declare that he is now just, not guilty, innocent. Indeed a good verb to contrast with *condemn* is *acquit*. A judge acquits a man when he declares that the man is not guilty. Justification then is a judicial act. It is God's declaration that this sinner is not guilty, but righteous.

But how can this be so? How can a sinner be righteous? It should be clearly understood that even faith itself is not the basis

---

1. I. A. Dorner, *A System of Christian Doctrine*, tr. by Cave and Banks, Vol. IV, p. 199.

of justification. The ground or basis of justification is the object in which the faith rests; that is, Christ and his righteousness. God acquits a sinner, declares him not guilty, on the basis of Christ's righteousness having been imputed to him. Sometimes the expressions are shortened in Scripture, as in Romans 4:5, so that faith is mentioned while the object of the faith is left understood; but this is because the true basis of justification had been clearly expressed a few verses before, in Romans 3:21-26. Then again, the great passage in Romans 5:12-19 shows that as it was one act of one man that brought condemnation, so it was by the righteousness of one man alone that justification is possible.

The Arminians, even though they were born Protestants, broke away from the Lutheran and Calvinistic teaching and took one or more steps backward toward Rome. They held that the demands of the law were lowered to the level of "evangelical obedience" and on the basis of this quite human obedience, we are justified. But in addition to running counter to the previous references which exclude works, this impinges on the holiness of God by picturing him as satisfied with less than perfection. The Scripture does not teach that God lowers his requirements. On the contrary, God requires and supplies complete sinlessness. Christ not only bore our penalty on the cross, but in his life he perfectly obeyed his Father. It is the personal righteousness of Christ's sinless obedience that is put to our account, on the basis of which we are declared not guilty. Read the same references again. Cf. also Tit. 3:57; Eph. 1:7; I Cor. 1:30; Phil. 3:9; and even Jer. 23:6, for, remember, the Gospel is in the Old Testament and with it justification by faith.

It has been necessary to insist that justification is a judicial act of acquittal, for only so can salvation be by grace. However, the ordinary idea of acquittal does not exhaust the Biblical concept of justification. Section i also says that God pardons the sins of those who are justified and accepts their persons as righteous. Perhaps the idea of pardon needs no explanation, for its meaning is easily understood; but the idea of acceptance needs to be distinguished from both pardon and acquittal. The governor of a state may pardon a convicted official without restoring him to favor and to his previous office. Appointments to office, if honest, would depend on the future conduct of the pardoned man.

But it is otherwise with Biblical justification; for if favor with God depended on our future conduct, eventual salvation would be based on our works—clearly contrary to Scripture—and we could never have an assurance of success. When our position depends on Christ's merits instead of our own, we need have no fear.

Of course there are objections raised against the doctrine of justification by faith. Section ii takes care of the most important one. If justification, acquittal, pardon, and acceptance were the last words of the Confession and of Calvinism, there might indeed be a serious objection. Someone has parodied a gospel song so as to make it say,

> Free from the law, O blessed condition,
> I can sin as I please and still have remission.

And in the time of the Apostle Paul, objectors argued that justification by faith alone encouraged men to sin. That they raised this objection in Paul's day shows clearly that Paul did not teach justification by works. But in Romans 6 Paul shows with equal clarity that the objection is unfounded.

Justification is God's judicial act of acquittal, but acquittal never comes to a man without regeneration and effectual calling. God never pardons a man without removing his heart of stone and supplying him with a heart of flesh. Christ's perfect righteousness is never imputed without the sinner's being raised from the dead and given a new life. Faith in Christ, then, is always accompanied by other saving graces; and the second chapter after Justification in the Confession is Sanctification. We shall come to it shortly.

But we would be in a bad way, as Luther and Calvin well knew, if we had to depend on our own merits for acquittal, pardon, and acceptance with God. For this, only Christ's righteousness is sufficient, and with Christ's righteousness we can be sure of heaven.

Section III.—Christ, by his obedience and death, did fully discharge the debt of all those that are thus justified, and did make a proper, real and full satisfaction, to his Father's justice in their behalf.[6] Yet, inasmuch as he was given by the Father for them,[7] and his

*obedience and satisfaction accepted in their stead,[8] and
both freely, not for anything in them, their justification
is only of free grace;[9] that both the exact justice and
rich grace of God might be glorified in the justification
of sinners.[10]*

6. Rom. v. 8-10,19 ; 1 Tim. ii. 5,6 ; Heb. x. 10,14 ; Dan. ix. 24,26 ; Isa.
liii. 4-6,10-12.—7. Rom. viii. 32.—8. 2 Cor. v. 21 ; Matt. iii. 17 ; Eph. v.
2.—9. Rom. iii. 24 ; Eph. i. 7.—10. Rom. iii. 26 ; Eph. ii. 7.

We come now to section iii. Earlier it was suggested that
Chapter VI on Sin was the most important chapter in the Confession; and still earlier a similar suggestion was made. But here
we come to what is *really* the most important material! Of course,
different things are most important for different purposes. What
is logically basic is most important in one sense, and in another
sense the complete and perfect development of the basis. Section
iii here is most important in the sense that this is the part of the
message that most directly and immediately applies to sinners.
It is and must be the central point in all evangelism. It is the
doctrine that must be constantly repeated and emphasized in the
pulpit. For it is the statement of how a sinner can be saved.

Sin leaves man without merit. He has no righteousness; he
is guilty of rebellion against God; he is subject to the penalty that
God has imposed. That penalty is eternal death in hell.

Now, God is righteous. He will not lower the law nor remit
the punishment for infraction. If God were less than perfect, he
might just forget sin, pay no attention to it, accept men without
any Atonement whatever. This seems eminently sensible to many
modern minds, either because they think that sin is trivial, or
because they conceive of God as "love without righteousness."
Such people are hard put to it to explain why Christ was crucified. Possibly they take it just as an unfortunate tragedy. But they
cannot see in Christ's death a sacrifice for sin, an atonement, a
deliberate act of God.

The Bible has a totally different story to tell. The story is
that Jesus bore our sins in his own body on the tree. The story
is that God made Jesus to be sin for us, though he knew no sin,
that we might be made the righteousness of God in him. This
is the story, the greatest story ever told, the story of God's grace,
a grace combining, not separating, love and righteousness.

126

God did not lower his holy law, did not remit the penalty, did not just forget the whole thing. On the contrary, Jesus paid the penalty by suffering the death we should have suffered.

The person who accepts Christ as his substitute is saved. The person who refuses has not the slightest possibility of ever arriving in heaven. This then is the most important doctrine.

But being the heart of the Christian gospel, it produces great antagonism. Some men try to undermine it surreptitiously. Others attack it directly.

Once more we shall mention the present professor of Systematic Theology in Princeton Seminary in order to see what views are well received in the United Presbyterian Church.

Professor Hendry (pp. 111, 112, 135-137) comments:

> "hath fully satisfied the justice of his Father." The interpretation of the atoning work of Christ which is presented here . . . is unbiblical. It combines a genuinely Biblical conception (sacrifice) with another (satisfaction) which is not Biblical. . . . In no passage in the New Testament where the death of Christ is represented as sacrifice is it suggested that it produced an effect on God, either in the "satisfaction" of his "justice" or in the alteration of his disposition toward men. . . . forgiveness is the free gift of God . . . it does not first have to be procured from him by the fulfillment of some condition on the part of Christ. . . .
>
> If God's grace is contingent on "a proper, real, and full satisfaction" of his justice, grace is not sovereign, and justification cannot be *only* of free grace."

Concerning Dr. Hendry's views the following points must be made. First, if the Westminster Confession is so unbiblical as he thinks it is, and if, as is obvious, he does not accept the doctrine of the Confession, why did he take ordination vows in a church whose official creed is this Confession?

Second, the Confession, contrary to what Dr. Hendry says, is fully Biblical, and his accusations are untrue. Dr. Hendry said that the phrase "hath fully satisfied the justice of his Father" (Confession VIII, v) is unbiblical. But the Apostle Paul in Romans 3:26 says that Christ died in order to declare God's righteousness, and in particular in order that God might be both just himself as well as the justifier of him who believes in Jesus. Here the apostle explicitly gives Christ's death the purpose of preserving the justice of God.

The preceding verse (Rom. 3:25) not only prepares for the emphasis on maintaining God's righteousness and justice, but also contradicts Dr. Hendry's statement that the New Testament never indicates that Christ's death produced an effect on God, either in the satisfaction of his justice or in the alteration of his disposition toward men. Romans 3:25 explicitly calls Christ a propitiation. To propitiate means to appease, to render favorable, to turn aside wrath. This is precisely what Christ did.

Note that the word is *propitiation*, not *expiation* as the Revised Standard Version mistranslates it. The RSV would give the impression that neither the King James translators nor the American revisers knew Greek. But on the Greek word Souter's lexicon has "(original idea, *propitiation* of an angry god), (a) *a sin offering*, by which the wrath of the deity shall be appeased, *a means of propitiation*. Rom. iii 25; (b) *the covering* of the ark . . ."

Now, if anyone prefers Liddell and Scott to Souter, he will find the same two meanings, and Romans 3:25 is cited for the meaning *propitiation*.

This is sufficient to show that Dr. Hendry's statement is false.

The third point is slightly, but only slightly, more complicated. Dr. Hendry argues that forgiveness does not have to be procured from God by the fulfillment of some condition on the part of Christ. Dr. Hendry gives a reason for this, but first let us compare the statement with Scripture.

Acts 20:28 reads, "feed the church of God, which he hath purchased with his own blood." This verse is often used to show that Jesus, who shed his blood, was himself God, the second Person of the Trinity. But for the present purpose let us note that his blood *purchased* the church. Liberals will complain at the base notion of a commercial transaction, but Paul, whose words they are, was never troubled on this score. The church had to be purchased and Jesus bought it: "Ye are bought with a price" (I Cor. 6:20 and 7:23); and II Peter warns against false prophets and false teachers who deny "the Lord that *bought* them." If, as Dr. Hendry claims, Christ did not have to fulfill any condition in order to save us, why did he have to be crucified? Why indeed did he have to come to earth at all?

Dr. Hendry proposes a reason or argument for his unscriptural thesis. He says that if Christ had to do something to

128

procure our forgiveness, grace is not sovereign and justification cannot be said to be "only of free grace."

This is just nonsense, for two reasons. In the first place, even if Christ did nothing to satisfy divine justice or to propitiate the Father, still if he did anything at all to influence, affect, or benefit the sinner, he was fulfilling a condition; and on Dr. Hendry's argument this would be inconsistent with free sovereign grace. Now, for the third time, we ask, Why did Christ have to die? If there were no conditions to fulfill, there was no need of his doing anything.

But there was a condition, and this leads to the second reason for labeling Dr. Hendry's thesis nonsense. Christ had to pay the penalty for sin and satisfy divine justice. But it is ridiculous to say that this is inconsistent with free grace. It was sovereign grace that brought our Lord to earth; it was sovereign grace that induced him voluntarily to pay the penalty for our sins; and it is sovereign grace that effectually calls the elect. How in the world can anyone be so confused as to think that the active and passive obedience of Christ is inconsistent with sovereign grace? It *is* sovereign grace. And those to whom sovereign grace is extended will preach it as such.

> *Section IV.—God did, from all eternity, decree to justify all the elect;[11] and Christ did, in the fulness of time, die for their sins and rise again for their justification.[12] Nevertheless, they are not justified until the Holy Spirit doth in due time actually apply Christ unto them.[13]*

11. Gal. iii. 8; 1 Pet. i. 2,19,20; Rom. viii. 30.—12. Gal. iv. 4; 1 Tim. ii. 6; Rom. iv. 25.—13. Col. i. 21,22; Gal. ii. 16; Tit. iii. 4-7.

Sometimes a student wants to go beyond the most obvious, essential, and elementary parts of a doctrine and examine some of its more advanced implications. This would result if one should try to answer the question, When is a man justified? Conversion, faith in Christ, and a developing sanctification are conscious events in a temporal sequence. But justification is a judicial act on the part of God. And if God's decree to justify the elect is an eternal decree, does it follow that we were justified before we were born, before the foundation of the world? Section iv does not quite say this. It places the actual justification at a point of time within our life span. Abraham Kuyper in his excellent volume *The Work of the*

Holy Spirit, chapter XXXII, may not have a very different view, but he at least expresses himself in a different way. It would be worthwhile to read him. Also, in Chapter XXXIX he has a very interesting passage on faith as the gift of God. One should be willing to take the time to get such books as this one and to spend some time in careful study.

> *Section V.—God doth continue to forgive the sins of those that are justified;*[14] *and although they can never fall from the state of justification,*[15] *yet they may by their sins fall under God's fatherly displeasure, and not have the light of his countenance restored unto them until they humble themselves, confess their sins, beg pardon, and renew their faith and repentance.*[16]
>
> *Section VI.—The justification of believers under the Old Testament was, in all these respects, one and the same with the justification of believers under the New Testament.*[17]

14. Matt. vi. 12; 1 John i. 7,9; ii. 1,2.—15. Luke xxii. 32; John x. 28; Heb. x. 14.—16. Ps. lxxxix. 31-33; li. 7-12; xxxii. 5; Matt. xxvi. 75; 1 Cor. xi. 30,32; Luke i. 20.—17. Gal. iii. 9,13,14; Rom. iv. 22-24; Heb. xiii. 8.

Sections v and vi can be dismissed with a very brief comment. The remark in section v that those who are justified, acquitted, declared righteous, will never later be "un-acquitted" is discussed fully in the later chapter on the perseverance of the saints. Section vi was treated sufficiently in the chapter on the Covenant. All that the student needs to do is to review that previous material and further meditate on the Scripture references.

CHAPTER XII.

OF ADOPTION.

*All those that are justified, God vouchsafeth, in,
and for his only Son, Jesus Christ, to make partakers of
the grace of adoption:[1] by which they are taken into the
number, and enjoy the liberties and privileges of the children of God;[2] have his name put upon them,[3] receive the
spirit of adoption;[4] have access to the throne of grace
with boldness;[5] are enabled to cry, Abba, Father;[6] are
pitied,[7] protected,[8] provided for,[9] and chastened by him
as by a father;[10] yet never cast off,[11] but sealed to the day
of redemption,[12] and inherit the promises,[13] as heirs of
everlasting salvation.[14]*

1. Eph. i. 5; Gal. iv. 4,5.—2. Rom. viii. 17; John i. 12.—3. Jer. xiv.
9.; 2 Cor. vi. 18; Rev. iii. 12.—4. Rom. viii. 15.—5. Eph. iii. 12; Rom.
v. 2.—6. Gal. iv. 6.—7. Ps. ciii. 13.—8. Prov. xiv. 26.—9 Matt.
vi. 30,32; 1 Pet. v. 7.—10. Heb. xii. 6.—11. Lam. iii. 31.—12. Eph. iv.
30.—13. Heb. vi. 12.—14. 1 Pet. i. 3,4; Heb. i. 14.

Chapter XII of the Westminster Confession, on adoption, is
rather short, consisting of only one section; yet it undoubtedly
merits at least a short discussion. The section states that all
those who are justified are also made children of God by adoption
and thereby enjoy certain liberties and privileges.

Justification, being a judicial act, is entirely external to us;
it gives a new standing before God, but it does not effect any subjective change within us. There are, however, certain inevitable
concomitants. Justification is always and without exception accompanied by regeneration, adoption, and sanctification. Now,
regeneration and sanctification, unlike justification, produce subjective changes in us. They have nothing to do with our objective
position before God. Adoption, on the other hand, has reference
both to the external relationship of position and to the subjective
changes of character. It is a complex concept that includes both
factors which occur separately in justification and regeneration.
Adoption expresses the truth that "now are we the sons of God."
The chapter in the Confession lists the factors in sonship.

During the past hundred years as modernism developed,
the doctrine of adoption has been slighted by those disloyal

ministers who have rejected the infallibility of the Bible. In its place they have preached a natural and universal Fatherhood of God and a natural and universal brotherhood of man. Now, the Scriptures have considerable to say about the Fatherhood of God, but they have little or nothing to say about a natural and universal Fatherhood.

One verse that might be so understood is Paul's use of a quotation from a Stoic poet, "for we are also his offspring." Possibly the poet had some notion of a universal Fatherhood, but Paul used the quotation only to stress that God is a Spirit and that men were created in God's image. Another verse is Ephesians 3:15, "Of whom the whole family in heaven and earth is named." But this family is more reasonably understood as the family of the redeemed than as the human race as a whole.

In contrast with these few and doubtful verses, the Scriptures speak many times and clearly of God's Fatherhood in relation to a portion of mankind. Of the Pharisees, Jesus said, "ye are of your father the devil"; but he taught his disciples to pray, "Our Father." The most familiar figure of speech by which entrance into the Christian life is described is that of a new birth. Not all men, but some only are born again, not by their own will, but of God; and thus God gives them authority to become sons of God. Quite evidently they were not natural-born sons, otherwise they would not have needed to be born again. If men must be born again, those who are not born again are not children of God.

The figure of a new birth is appropriate to the new life that then commences. So also is the figure of the resurrection. Men who were dead in sin are raised in Christ to a life they did not previously have. But the Scriptures also describe this change as adoption. Children of another father are adopted by God and become a part of the Christian family. Here too the previous conclusion follows: if a man becomes a child of God by adoption, he could not have been a child of God by nature. And for the same reason it is clear that the Bible does not teach the universal Fatherhood of God nor the universal brotherhood of man. It speaks about sheep and goats, and about a final and irremediable division between them.

Adoption brings certain privileges that are denied to those not adopted. First, they receive God's name, and as members of the family can now call God, Abba, Father. They are pitied, protected, and provided for. They are sometimes even chastened by God as a Father, "yet never cast off, but sealed to the day of redemption, and inherit the promises as heirs of salvation."

It is comforting to know that the act of adoption cannot be annulled; the new birth can never be undone; the resurrection to newness of life can never be reversed. Later in the Confession this is more fully stated in the chapters on the assurance of salvation and the perseverance of the saints.

By rejecting the Scriptural position liberals sometimes put themselves into uncomfortable positions. Their notion of the universal Fatherhood of God depends on the unity of the human race. Now, orthodox Christians believe in the unity of the human race on the basis that all human beings living today are descended from Adam and Eve. But if the modernists wish to say that the opening chapters of Genesis are false, and if the neo-orthodox existentialize the account and make it a fable of present day affairs, then how can they be sure that all men are brothers? If they replace the creation of Adam and Eve with an evolutionary mutation from lower animals, how can they know that there was only one mutation? Why could not such an evolutionary event have happened several times? There is just as much evidence that it happened a dozen times as that it happened once. Hence the unity of mankind is left without support and so also the Fatherhood of God.

Of course, there is a deeper perplexity. The modernist notion of a universal Fatherhood of God and a universal brotherhood of man is strictly a physical or biological concept. There is nothing spiritual about it. If there were, it would be necessary to conclude that Stalin and Hitler were spiritually related to God in the same way in which Augustine, Luther, and Calvin were. Now Christians admit that all men are born sinners. Naturally Stalin and Calvin were brothers. But God adopted and regenerated Calvin; he gave him a new nature; he raised him from spiritual death. The result is, as St. Augustine showed at such length in his *City of God*, that God's grace broke the natural unity of the human race and founded in opposition to the world a City of God. If the modernists still wish to claim spiritual unity with Hitler and Stalin, we don't. We have been adopted into a different family.

133

Chapter XIII.

OF SANCTIFICATION.

Section I.—*They who were effectually called and regenerated, having a new heart and a new spirit created in them, are further sanctified really and personally, through the virtue of Christ's death and resurrection,[1] by his Word and Spirit dwelling in them;[2] the dominion of the whole body of sin is destroyed,[3] and the several lusts thereof are more and more weakened and mortified,[4] and they more and more quickened and strengthened in all saving graces,[5] to the practice of true holiness, without which no man shall see the Lord.[6]*

Section II.—*This sanctification is throughout in the whole man,[7] yet imperfect in this life: there abide still some remnants of corruption in every part:[8] whence ariseth a continual and irreconcilable war; the flesh lusteth against the Spirit, and the Spirit against the flesh.[9]*

Section III.—*In which war, although the remaining corruption for a time may much prevail,[10] yet, through the continual supply of strength from the sanctifying Spirit of Christ, the regenerate part doth overcome:[11] and so the saints grow in grace,[12] perfecting holiness in the fear of God.[13]*

1. 1 Cor. vi. 11; Acts xx. 32; Phil. iii. 10; Rom. vi. 5,6.—2. John xvii. 17; Eph. v. 26; 2 Thess. ii. 13.—3. Rom. vi. 6,14.—4. Gal. v. 24; Rom. viii. 13.—5. Col. i. 11; Eph. iii. 16-19.—6. 2 Cor. vii. 1; Heb. xii. 14.—7. 1 Thess. v. 23.—8. 1 John i. 10; Rom. vii. 18,23; Phil. iii. 12.—9. Gal. v. 17; 1 Pet. ii. 11.—10. Rom. vii. 23.—11. Rom. vi. 14; 1 John v. 4; Eph. iv. 15,16.—12. 2 Pet. iii. 18; 2 Cor. iii. 18.—13. 2 Cor. vii. 1.

One reason why Presbyterians should study the Westminster Confession is that the Presbyterian denominations have adopted it as their doctrinal platform. This is what Presbyterians believe. If then someone asks what the difference is between Presbyterians and some other group, and this question arises every so often, the person who knows the Confession can answer authoritatively.

A reason why others than Presbyterians should study the Westminster Confession is that it forms an excellent summary of the main teachings of the Bible. To be sure, it is a summary only. It is not a complete theological treatise; it does not furnish an exhaustive account of the doctrines; it is not the equivalent of a seminary course. Further, it is a summary of only the main doctrines of the Bible. There is much else in the Bible, all of which is useful; but the doctrines enumerated in the Confession are the most important.

In our present study we have now come to the chapter on Sanctification. Sanctification is a favorite theme among some people. There are for example the pietistic groups. The pietists are a very quiet people, devout, with an air of holiness. They are not very strong on the other Biblical doctrines, but they are calmly determined to lead a pious life.

Then too there are the holiness groups, sometimes called Holy Rollers. These people are very noisy, or as one evangelist I heard boasted (using the name of his denomination), "I'm an old fashioned, shouting, stomping, singing, crying . . . ." Such people want sanctification and holiness in a lightning flash and clap of thunder. Because of their emotionalism, these groups are somewhat disdained by the larger denominations. People who stomp and cry are queer. Indeed they are. We do not approve of them. But let us remember, as too many people are willing to forget, that Hebrews 12:14 exhorts us to "follow peace with all men and holiness, without which no man shall see the Lord."

In the Greek text *peace* is feminine; *holiness*, or the process of becoming holy, is masculine; the relative pronoun *which* is masculine singular: therefore the verse says that no man can see the Lord without going through a process of becoming holy.

The comments that follow are grouped around two points which call for emphasis. First, the relation of sanctification to justification must be explained; and second, something must be said about detailed directions for living a holy life.

The chapter on Justification quoted a caricature of a gospel song:

> Free from the Law, O blessed condition,
> I can sin as I please and still have remission.

This of course is a caricature. It is not what the gospel song says and it is not what the doctrine of Justification teaches. Those who make this objection against the doctrine should remember that there is another hymn:

He died that we might be forgiven,
He died to make us good.

These lines state that Christ's purpose was at least two-fold. He died that we might be forgiven, that we might receive remission from sin; but he also died to make us good. He died in order to diminish and finally to eradicate our sinning.

In this third stanza of "There Is a Green Hill Far Away," the doctrines of justification and sanctification are conjoined. Naturally, the limitations of hymnology do not permit an explanation of the conjunction: it would seem that forgiveness and being made good are two results, otherwise unrelated, of Christ's death. But the Confession of Faith, Chapter XIII, and still more explicitly Paul, in Romans 6 and elsewhere, make sanctification the purpose or aim of the preceding stages of salvation.

A study of Romans 6 is an important prerequisite for understanding the Confession on sanctification. In the first five chapters of Romans, Paul has explained the doctrine of justification by faith. On the basis of Christ's righteousness imputed to us God justifies us—he acquits us and declares that we are not guilty of sin. He asserts that the law cannot impose its penalty on us, and further, he receives us as righteous. Toward the end of this explanation Paul says (Rom. 5:20) that where sin abounded, grace did much more abound.

Such is the frailty of the human mind, infected as it is by the disease of sin, that it is frequently subject to false inferences. Nothing could better illustrate the truth of this than years of experience in the classroom. Every successive group of students in physics confuses the weight of water in a bucket with the pressure on the bottom. Year after year in logic the students make the same mistakes of conversion and contraposition. In the world at large the same types of mistakes are made, though the regularity of occurrence usually remains unnoticed.

When, therefore, Paul says that where sin abounds, grace much more abounds, the very human, though completely mistaken, inference is drawn that we should continue in sin that grace may continue to abound. Because of this human tendency to invalid inference, Paul must defend his doctrine of justification against the charge that it ministers to immorality. Hence the apostle proceeds with the doctrine of sanctification.

The connection between justification and sanctification is often misunderstood. These two phases of Christian experience are sometimes thought to be connected with the conjunction *but*. We are justified by faith, *but* we must now be holy so as not again to fall into condemnation. Other people would connect justification and sanctification with the conjunction *and*, as if they were two completely unrelated facts that for some mysterious reason were forced into a connection. In truth, these two conjunctions, the *but* and the *and*, are far from accurate The connection is better expressed by a *therefore*. We are justified by faith, *therefore* we should not sin. Or, in view of Romans 6:14 (For sin shall not have dominion over you), we may put it even more strongly and say, we are justified, therefore we do not sin. Of course these phrases are too short to summarize accurately all the material in Romans 6; but we could hit the truth with a fair degree of faithfulness by paraphrasing a Scriptural expression and saying, justification is the straight gate and sanctification is the narrow way that leads to glory. Or, to be less picturesque, it is the purpose of justification to produce holy lives.

Paul, then, faces the question, shall we continue in sin that grace may abound? The main point of the answer as it is given in the first fourteen verses is very plain. It is briefly this: No one who comes to Christ for salvation from both the guilt and the power of sin, can possibly want to continue sinning. Christ's suffering and death on the cross was an expiation of sin. When a man comes to Christ he so identifies himself with Christ in this purpose that he can truly say, I am crucified with Christ, or, simply, as in Romans 6:8, we are dead with Christ. If a man does not thus identify himself with Christ's purpose to destroy sin, if instead of grief and hatred of sin he cherishes the notion that he may continue in sin that grace may abound, that perhaps he can wait a few years after regeneration for a subsequent act of sanctification, the conclusion is inevitable that he knows nothing of Christ and has never truly applied to the Lord for salvation. To put the matter very bluntly, it is a psychological impossibility to trust in Christ's shed blood and to want to continue in sin.

From this it follows that as Christ was raised from the dead by the glory of the Father, even we also, who died with him, shall be in the likeness of his resurrection and walk in newness of life.

The significance of verses four and five is not grasped if we consider Christ's resurrection and our walking in newness of life as a mere analogy. Paul is not saying, as Christ dies and rises, so the believer dies and rises. The believer and Christ are more intimately united than such an interpretation would allow. Rather, we must take verses four and five to mean, *because* Christ dies and rises, the believer dies and rises also. If we are united with Christ in his death, then, as the branches derive their life from the vine, we receive our Christian life from the resurrection life of Christ.

Sanctification, therefore, is not some instantaneous crisis in our life which happens one year or ten years after our regeneration. Sanctification is just that process of becoming more and more like Christ which begins when we pass from death to life. Sanctification is nothing other than the Christian life itself, with its tribulation, patience, experience, and hope. Accordingly, Paul exhorts us not to yield our members as instruments of unrighteousness unto sin, but to yield ourselves unto God. Our members, then, become members of righteousness.

When we consider the omnipotence of God, we may wonder why he does not accomplish the work of purification and sanctification in us instantaneously. God could, no doubt, make us perfect all at once, but, nonetheless, he takes time. Some people chafe under the burden of becoming righteous slowly; they look for some short-cut. If God justifies by faith, they ask, why does he not also sanctify by faith? And because of impatience, a few Christians try to satisfy themselves with a perfection which, though not perfect, is at least apparently attainable all at once.

The Scriptures, however, teach something different. We have seen that our members must be instruments of righteousness; in the verses following (Rom. 6:16 ff.), we have the illustration of slavery or servitude, which obviously is not an instantaneous act, but a continuous condition of life. The point is stressed in other passages of Scripture. Philippians 2:12,13 says, work out your own salvation with fear and trembling. Of course, God works in us; the point to be noted is that it is a work and not a single act.

Or we may turn to Galatians 6:5, which says, every man shall bear his own burden. The Christian life, then, has burdens that take time to bear. Or again, in I Corinthians 3:9, we are laborers together with God. Therefore we should not indulge ourselves in the hope of an easy, instantaneous sanctification, but rather run with patience the race that is set before us.

In the words of Isaac Watts:

> "Must I be carried to the skies
> On flowery beds of ease?"

The Christian life, then, is not a life of sin, but of struggle against sin. We must reckon ourselves dead unto sin, but alive unto God. Such a conception not only answers the question in the first verse about continuing in sin, it also excludes the notion that we may live in a state, not of constant sinning, but merely of lazy indifference.

In fact, this is the distinction between the question in verse one and the question in verse fifteen. Verse one asks, Should we remain in habitual sin? Verse fifteen narrows the question to a single sin asking simply, Shall we sin? Not only do the two verses refer to a different amount of sinning, so to speak, but there is also a difference in the mental attitude. Verse one asks, Should we sin *in order that* grace may abound? In other words, it examines a case of wicked calculation. Verse fifteen considers only lazy indifference: Shall we sin *because* we are not under the law? We have escaped the penalty for sin, and of course we do not want to live in sin, but an occasional sin now and again does not matter much because we are not under law but under grace.

Lazy indifference may not be so heinous as wicked calculation, but it is equally excluded from the consistent Christian life. Paul answers the question by the illustration of slavery. The major premise, found in verse sixteen, repeats in substance the teaching of Christ that no man can serve two masters. The minor premise, found in verses seventeen and eighteen, points out with thanksgiving that Christians are no longer servants of sin, but have become the slaves of God. The conclusion is obvious. God is our master, and him alone ought we to serve.

And in this service we bring forth fruit unto holiness and the end everlasting life.

Thus there is no gap between justification and sanctification; they are not separated by a *but*; they are not violently conjoined by an *and*; on the contrary, they are related with a *therefore*. To repeat, justification is the straight gate and sanctification is the narrow way that leads to glory.

What a difference it makes whether one enters that gate and walks that way, or whether one continues to be the slave of sin. To be sure, slavery to sin provides some security, for sin is a just master and will pay its wages; it will not cheat a person of what he deserves. But who can be content with the wages of sin? For the wages of sin is death, but the gift of God is eternal life through Jesus Christ our Lord.

To this point the discussion has been in general rather than in particular terms. General principles are useful and in fact necessary; but they sometimes meet the cynical reaction of a politician who characterizes his opponent as being against sin and for motherhood. There was also the old time colored preacher who preached constantly on heaven and hell, since once he preached on chicken stealing and it dampened the enthusiasm.

There is a pertinent white version of this colored story, for the race involved is not the black, the yellow, or even the white race: it is the story of the human race. However, the white version, especially the American version, has to do with falsification of our income tax returns. When we preach against sin, the first thing that comes to mind is murder, adultery, theft, drunkenness, and profanity. Of course, the avoidance of these gross sins is elementary in the Christian life. If some convert has been saved out of such a life and still finds that these things tempt him, he must pray for grace and strength to conquer the inclinations of the flesh; and we older Christians must in kindness and love encourage and help him along.

But as we progress in the Christian life, we discover subtler temptations. We would not think of shop-lifting—that is theft; but we might falsify our income tax return. And what an argument we can compose to justify ourselves! The income tax is so arranged as to benefit the dishonest and to penalize the honest man. The big shots hide their income or bribe the collector. Why should I pay my complete share when these scoundrels evade thousands of dollars of tax, or a hundred thousand? So, I shall pad my deductions and forget some of my income. A plausible argument, isn't it?

However, the income tax is not the first unjust tax to be inflicted on a people. The Roman taxes of Christ's day were outrageous. Yet, Christ commands his followers to pay their taxes. Strange though it may seem, we are sanctified by paying taxes.

Perhaps paying taxes is not a sufficiently vigorous activity to satisfy American practicality. There is further the communication (contributing) to the necessities of the saints; the practice of hospitality; rejoicing with them that do rejoice, and weeping with them that weep. Or, do we look on other people as a nuisance?

There are also other sins to avoid and other means of sanctification. The sins are not so spectacular as murder; nor are these virtues so observable as great deeds of public service. For example, if one wishes to attain that state of sanctification by which he can qualify as an officer in the church, there are the instructions to rule well one's own house, having one's children in subjection; besides this, and probably because of this, the candidate for office must be apt to teach, able to exhort, slow to wrath.

Even if the office is no more than that of usher, the Scripture tells him not to shunt a man in blue jeans into a corner while showing special attention to a visitor in striped pants and cutaway coat.

Such lowly activity does not appeal to popular imagination. The American Christian, influenced by American culture, is on the whole more extrovert, activist, and practical than the European Christian. Our gospel songs verge on jazz; the hymns of the French church are worshipful and majestic. We go in for organizations and vigorous evangelism; the European is more devotional and contemplative. We are apt to disparage theory and exalt practice.

However, when one reads the exhortations to holy living in the Bible, and sees the emphasis on a pure conscience, peace, joy, self-control, one may conclude that after all the quiet devotion of the European Christian may be closer to the ideal than American activism. Our zeal for organization has often turned the church into a country club and has altered the role of the minister from that of pastor, preacher, and teacher to that of business administrator. This is not conducive to sanctification. Nor do the hillbilly gospel songs accord with worship as well as Bach chorales.

For further pointers on personal sanctification and for a vivid portrayal of the wiles of the devil in frustrating our attempts to grow in grace, by all means read, if you have not already done so, C. S. Lewis' *Screwtape Letters*, written to the imp Wormwood.

CHAPTER XIV.

OF SAVING FAITH.

Section I.—*The grace of faith, whereby the elect are enabled to believe to the saving of their souls,[1] is the work of the Spirit of Christ in their hearts[2] and is ordinarily wrought by the ministry of the word;[3] by which also, and by the administration of the sacraments and prayer, it is increased and strengthened.[4]*

1. Heb. x. 39.—2. 2 Cor. iv. 13; Eph. i. 17-19; ii. 8.—3. Rom. x. 14,17.—4. 1 Pet. ii. 2; Acts xx. 32; Rom. iv. 11; Luke xvii. 5; Rom; i. 16,17.

The first section of this chapter contains two main ideas: (1) faith is the work of Christ's Spirit within us, and (2) faith is ordinarily produced through the Word of God.

Point one involves the relationship and cooperation between the Spirit and our minds. Many people are puzzled by the idea that the Spirit of God and the mind of man can cooperate in one and the same mental act. A theory of free will has led these people to suppose that the human mind is impervious to the control of the Spirit. But this is not what the Bible says. That the Spirit can in fact operate on our minds and cause us to turn to God has already been discussed in the previous chapters, from which we may now repeat Psalm 65:4, "Blessed is the man whom thou choosest and causest to approach unto thee." Here in this chapter it is more explicitly said that faith is produced in the souls of the elect by the Holy Spirit. Faith is indeed something that we do; it is our own mental activity; but it is an activity that could not have been initiated by any decision of a free will, nor produced by ordinary human striving. Faith is the gift of God. We do indeed work out our own salvation; we are the actors; but we work it out in fear and trembling because it is God who works in us so as to cause us not only to do something, but to will to do it in the first place. And all of this is according to God's good pleasure. If therefore the Spirit works faith in us, we have faith; if he does not, we don't.

In this connection it is desirable to study carefully Ephesians 1:15-20. Verse 15 records that Paul had heard of the great faith

143

of the Ephesians. This is a matter of thanksgiving. Then Paul prays that God may give them further wisdom and revelation, that he may increase their knowledge and enlarge their understanding. These additional blessings, which Paul asks God to bestow on the Ephesians, and indeed the measure of faith they already have (for verse 19 speaks of us who believe), are the result of God's mighty power, the same mighty power he displayed when he raised Christ from the dead. Thus it is that wisdom, knowledge, understanding, and faith are produced in our souls by the power of God.

The second point is that this work of God in our minds, causing us to believe, is ordinarily, one might say always, accomplished by means of the Word. We do not deny that God can regenerate an imbecile, an insane person, or a dying infant. In these cases the person is mentally incapable of the activity of faith so that he must be saved apart from an understanding of the Word. But this is not so where the usual mental operations are not impeded. A sane man must believe the Gospel; the Gospel contains events of history and the explanations of those events; all of this is good news; and one must be told the news before he can believe it. As the apostle says, "How shall they believe in him of whom they have not heard?" Since saving faith comes only through the Word of God, one can easily understand why we place such a great emphasis on the Word and on its being preached; for the apostle adds, "How shall they hear without a preacher?"

Emphasis on preaching the Word is important for the contrast between Christianity and other forms of religion. For example, the sacramentarianism of Rome has little need of preaching. Romish priests celebrate mass in a belief that mass works their salvation automatically. Probably some priests never preach a sermon in their whole life. But Protestantism was first and foremost a rediscovery of God's message, and the message or good news had to be told and believed.

Today, however, Protestantism has fallen low; or, more accurately, many religious leaders who are not Romanists have fallen. There is a desire for symbolism; even the words of Scripture are divested of their plain meaning and turned into symbols or pointers of—who knows what? The meaning of Scripture is so

144

far undervalued that Emil Brunner says that God can reveal himself in false statements as easily as in true statements. But if it makes no difference whether God's Word is true or false, it obviously makes no difference what the preacher says. It might be better if he said nothing. Preaching is thus relegated to an inferior position. Otto Dibelius, a prominent German theologian, once wrote, "Preaching, pedestalled on the person of the preacher, now stands too much in the foreground." If he had meant that much modern preaching is simply the word of man, in which the preacher preaches himself, the statement would have been true and would have been an indictment of modernism. But we suspect a distaste for all preaching. Paul Tillich also wishes to supplant preaching with other forms of worship, particularly art and music. The Word is relegated to the background. It reminds us of the sentiments of Goethe as he has Faust translate the first verse of John's Gospel:

Tis writ, "In the beginning was the Word."
I pause, perplexed! Who now will help afford?
I cannot the mere Word so highly prize;
I must translate it otherwise.

Goethe's and Tillich's objection to preaching presupposes a type of religion that is anti-intellectual. Goethe's religion was romantic and emotional; Tillich's religion is artistic or aesthetic. So also apparently is Reinhold Neibuhr's. He writes, "I prefer a liturgical church with as little sermon as possible." It is true that Niebuhr thinks that the church needs sermons, at least once in a while, but not too often. He tells of going to an Episcopal cathedral with his wife, but going late so that they can miss the sermon, yet hear the litany. His wife declares "We Anglicans do not need a sermon if we have the service. There is more genuine religion in a well-sung litany than in any sermon." Niebuhr records that he agrees with his wife in this and adds that "a good boys' choir covers a multitude of sermons" (*Applied Christianity*, pp. 29,42). Note that the litany must be "well-sung," and that the boys' choir must be "good." This purely aesthetic experience (which they say is better than any sermon on the Atonement or Resurrection) is what Dr. Niebuhr and his wife call "genuine religion." But it is not genuine Christianity.

In addition to aesthetic religion there is also activistic religion, a form especially popular in the United States. Americans like to be doing something, doing something active. They do not care to sit and study. In Europe the student who earns the highest grade in his class receives the applause of the school. Here it is the football star. In religion this urge to action was expressed in the so-called social gospel of the early twentieth century. Perhaps most of you have forgotten the Inter-church World Movement that tried to manage a steel strike just after World War I. Today we have left-wing demonstrations of various sorts until law and order is in danger of collapsing altogether. But again, while this may be a religion, it is not Christianity.

Christianity is not a romantic religion where feeling and emotion suffice. Nor is it an aesthetic religion where faith and sermons are unnecessary. Christianity is a definite faith. It includes the doctrines of the Atonement and the Resurrection, and it requires a knowledge of these doctrines, an intellectual assent to them, a faith that can and must be preached.

Historic Protestantism has always made preaching the central part of the worship service because it is by preaching that faith is produced and propagated. The magic of sacramentarianism will not do, nor the aesthetic enjoyment of good singing. There is a message to be told, and faith cometh by hearing and hearing by the Word of God.

Note well now that it is not enough for us to insist on the necessity of faith merely. Not any kind of faith will do. The social gospel is a faith too, but it is an alien faith. It is a faith in man, in governmental control, or, more recently, in the United Nations. But faith in man is not Christianity, for Psalm 39:5 says, "Verily, every man at his best state is altogether vanity"; and Psalm 62:9 says, "Surely men of low degree are vanity, and men of high degree are a lie: to be laid in the balance they are altogether lighter than vanity." This covers the United Nations too, for Psalm 146:3 warns us, "Put not your trust in [government officials] nor in the son of man, in whom there is no help."

Nor is it enough to insist even on faith in God, for the phrase faith in God is often used without any Christian content. In our present theological circumstances there is need to insist that saving faith is not just any type of vague or foreign religious faith. Articles in popular magazines often recommend religion and faith. Apparently any faith will do. Attend the church of your choice. All that is necessary is to avoid being an atheistic communist. But this is not the Christian message. Saving faith is definitely and emphatically faith in Jesus Christ, who died and rose again. Jesus said, "if ye believe not that I am he, ye shall die in your sins." Peter said, "there is none other name under heaven . . . whereby we must be saved." And Paul said, "A man is not justified by the works of the law, but by the faith of Jesus Christ." Pleasant opinions may keep us happy for a time; strong subjective belief may cure imaginary diseases; but it is Christ only that raises us from the death of sin. Saving faith is faith in Christ.

> *Section II.*—*By this faith, a Christian believeth to be true whatsoever is revealed in the Word, for the authority of God himself speaking therein,[5] and acteth differently upon that which each particular passage thereof containeth; yielding obedience to the commands,[6] trembling at the threatenings,[7] and embracing the promises of God for this life and for that which is to come.[8] But the principal acts of saving faith are, accepting, receiving and resting upon Christ alone for justification, sanctification and eternal life, by virtue of the covenant of grace.[9]*

5. John iv. 42 ; 1 Thess. ii. 13 ; 1 John v. 10 ; Acts xxiv. 14.—6. Rom. xiv. 26.—7. Isa. lxvi. 2.—8. Heb. xi. 13 ; 1 Tim. iv. 8.—9. John i. 12 ; Acts xiv. 31 ; Gal. ii. 20 ; Acts xv. 11.

Section ii expands our view of saving faith. Not only does the Spirit of God use the Word in producing faith: what is equally important is that the Word is the object of faith. Saving faith is faith in Christ, we have said. So it is. But we must be careful not to empty the name of Christ of its New Testament meaning. Some ecclesiastical leaders want to restrict faith in Christ to such an extent that Christ becomes a mere name about which nothing is to be said. The general tenor of modern religion is so antagonistic to doctrine that the Virgin Birth, the two natures in one Person, and even the Atonement are said to be unessential. One must believe in Christ, they say, but not in a Christ who pre-existed as the second Person of the Trinity, not in a Christ who was virgin-born, not in a Christ who rose from the grave. What Christ then do they believe in? The answer is, no real Christ at all. They have put their faith in an empty name; or, better, they have disguised their lack of faith by pious terminology.

Other religious leaders are more conservative. They may believe in the Deity of Christ and even in the Virgin Birth. They claim the title of evangelical. But they reject Moses as the author of the Pentateuch; they place the book of Daniel two or three centuries after the time of Daniel; and perhaps they doubt the reality of hell. Such a picking and choosing from among all the Biblical details shows that these so-called conservatives are using a criterion of truth other than the Bible itself. For Old Testament affairs they accept Wellhausen and his destructive criticism; for their doubts on hell they submit to the guidance of the modern civilized conscience. What they happen to accept from the Bible is accepted also on such a basis. In other words they do not accept any verse in the Bible "for the authority of God himself speaking therein." If they accepted even one verse on God's authority, they would believe "to be true *whatsoever* is revealed in the Word," that is, all of it. For the Bible is the Word of God, as Chapter I said, and God speaks the truth.

The importance of such an extensive and detailed revelation as the Bible is should be clearly understood. Without a detailed revelation, our religious life would be impossible to organize. How could we determine on what day to hold public worship; or even whether we should assemble once a week or once a month? How could we determine whether to have two sacraments, seven, or none at all? How even could we determine what is right and wrong in daily conduct? And, to repeat, how could we know even one bit of information about Jesus?

Yet this empty religion is the religion of many ministers in the large denominations. They assemble in their ministerial meetings to discuss the affairs of their church. How do they resolve their arguments?

Having attended such meetings, I can report that they remind me of a bunch of boys arguing about a ball game. One boy says that the ball should be a sphere three inches in diameter; the next boy says, No, it should be an oval about a foot long; the third boy offers a compromise—the ball should be both spherical and a foot in diameter, but he insists that there should be five, not nine or eleven boys on each side. And then a truly ecumenical

148

spirit declares that such creedal discussions are trivial: the important thing is that they should all play one big ball game.

But vacuous ecumenism is not Christianity. The Confession continues by saying that the principal acts of saving faith are accepting Christ alone for justification, sanctification, and eternal life. The empty name Christ, emptied of justification and sanctification as defined in Chapters XI and XIII, and emptied also of eternal life, is of no value whatever and cannot be an object of faith.

Since the Confession says that saving faith accepts everything that is revealed in the Word, this is a good time to review some of the preceding chapters and to stress again their concatenation. Note that the gift of faith belongs to the elect. Is it not obvious that if God wishes to give faith to anybody, he must choose the recipients? But to choose is to elect. Further, the choice or election of one individual rather than another cannot be made on the basis of a foreseen faith, because this is a choice of those to whom the faith is to be given. Any other than this Biblical construction dilutes and in effect denies the grace of God.

Since it is this pure and free grace that enables a man to believe, it is clear that he could not have believed without this work of the Holy Spirit. Cf. I Cor. 2:14; 12:3; II Cor. 3:14; 4:4,6. Thus the Biblical idea of saving faith is consistent with the Biblical idea of total depravity. And if Christ is the Logos, the Reason or Logic of God, and if we are created in God's image, why should not the evident logic and consistency of the Scriptures satisfy our rational minds? Some people talk as if they favor an irrational religion; but Presbyterians have escaped such insanity.

To say that God has foreordained whatsoever comes to pass and that he gave us his grace before the world began (II Tim. 1:9) does not, of course, preclude the use of ordinary means. God chose to give us faith by means of the ministry of the Word: cf. Matt. 28:19,20; Rom. 10:12,17; I Cor. 1:21; and while he has determined to what extent the faith of each one will develop and bear fruit, still growth in grace occurs through the administration of the sacraments and through prayer.

Section III.—This faith is different in degrees, weak or strong;[10] may be often and many ways assailed and

149

weakened, but gets the victory:[11] growing up in many to the attainment of full assurance through Christ,[12] who is both the author and finisher of our faith.[13]

10. Heb. v. 13,14; Rom. iv. 19,20; Matt. vi. 30; viii. 10.—11. Luke xxii. 31,32; Eph. vi. 16; 1 John v. 4,5.—12. Heb. vi. 11,12; x. 22; Col. ii. 2.—13. Heb. xii. 2.

Faith exists in different degrees. Jesus remarked that the faith of the centurion was greater than that of anyone in Israel. He also spoke of faith as small as a grain of mustard seed. Then there was the father of the boy with the dumb spirit: he said, "Lord, I believe. Help thou mine unbelief." Such a faith, however weak, is still saving faith.

The Apostle tells us, "If thou shalt confess with thy mouth that Jesus is Lord and shalt believe in thy heart that God hath raised him from the dead, thou shalt be saved." The degree of belief is immaterial to the fulfillment of this divine promise.

In the history of theology attempts have been made to give a psychological account of this faith. Such accounts must be so framed as to allow for these degrees of conviction. Since the discussions were originally in Latin, the components of faith were said to be *notitia, assensus,* and *fiducia,* i.e., knowledge, assent, and trust or confidence.

That there are degrees of knowledge is easy to understand. Some people know more, some people know less. But all Christians must know something. The thief on the cross may not have known of the Virgin Birth; he certainly did not know of the resurrection; but he was not so ignorant as some people imagine him. Although we cannot be sure of it, he probably knew something of Jesus' preaching. Jesus had been a popular preacher and it is likely that an enterprising criminal would have mingled among the crowds. Discount as speculation if you wish his knowledge of Jesus' sermons, yet he could hardly have failed to hear of Jesus' many miracles. Maybe he didn't believe them; but he must have heard about them. There is no speculation at all involved in asserting that he knew the charge on which Christ was condemned. If he could not read the superscription, he certainly heard what the Pharasaic mob was shouting. Further, he knew that he was guilty and that Jesus was innocent. Also, somehow he caught the idea that the disciples regarded Jesus as Lord; and this might explain the superscription. Then when he saw Jesus'

150

bearing and heard his prayer on the cross he learned something more. We should therefore not underestimate the thief's knowledge.

The necessity of knowledge has already been emphasized. A person cannot believe good news until he knows what the good news is. When told, he may of course refuse to believe; or he may give his assent. It was when the thief saw Jesus' bearing and heard the prayer that he gave his assent. Jesus claimed to be King and Lord; he claimed a kingdom, obviously a kingdom not of this world. The thief then believed these claims and cried, "Lord, remember me when thou comest into thy kingdom." Knowledge and assent therefore are obviously necessary to faith. Knowledge has different degrees or quantities; but it is not evident that an act of assent has degrees.

The further question as to the components of faith regards the status of *fiducia*. The Apostle said, if thou shalt believe, thou shalt be saved. But to assent to the good news is to believe. What else can be required?

A Latin dictionary may throw some light on the terminology. The Latin word *fides*, translated *faith*, means: *trust* (in a person or thing), *confidence, reliance, credence, belief*. The Latin word *fiducia* means: *trust, confidence, reliance, assurance*. This reduces the old analysis of faith to a tautology: faith is composed of knowledge, belief, and faith. Or we might retranslate it: Confidence is composed of knowledge, assent, and confidence. Clearly therefore the listing of *fiducia* as a component of *fides* is not very enlightening.

Charles Hodge, the great Presbyterian theologian of the nineteenth century, wrote, "Faith in the widest sense of the word is assent to the truth, or the persuasion of the mind that a thing is true. In ordinary language we are said to believe whatever we regard as true. The primary element of faith is trust" (*Systematic Theology*, III, p. 42). Appealing to etymology Hodge continues, "To believe, then, is to live by or according to, to abide by, . . . or adopt as a *rule of life*; and, consequently, to think, deem, or judge right . . ." A few lines further on: "To regard a thing as

151

true is to regard it as worthy of trust, as being what it purports to be."

Hodge continues with about twenty-five pages on the psychological nature of faith, plus an equal number with other subtitles, which nonetheless have to do with this psychology. Some of this discussion is vitiated by too great a reliance on the popular "faculty psychology" of the nineteenth century. Just how an author can eliminate from his thought the influence of the philosophy of his own day is by no means clear. When Hodge comments on Romans, there is a minimum of cultural distortion; but in the philosophic asides scattered through his *Systematic Theology*, he is as vulnerable as anyone else. Accordingly, whether it is Hodge or another theologian whom we are reading, the definitions of the terms should be examined, and, all the more, the usage of the terms that are not defined.

The attempt to define faith or belief, and to state its components, has embarrassed secular psychologists as well as Christian theologians. The secular scholars have met with as little success. Terms such as acceptance, conviction, affirmation, or assertion are merely synonyms. The Würzburg school in Germany reached an indescribable *Bewusstseinslagen*, consisting of neither ideas nor volitions. The phrases of other schools are equally unenlightening. Bertrand Russell analyzed belief into either words, images or both. In one place he describes belief as an image or set of words accompanied by a "belief-feeling." These attempts to define belief, it is true, envisage only perceptual beliefs, that is, the belief that I see a dog or an auto in front of me. Since strictly religious belief would be still more difficult to analyze because of its presumably greater complexity, such a study will probably incline us to stay a little longer with easier matters before addressing ourselves to almost insuperable difficulties.

Now, the remainder of section iii is largely an anticipation of what is to follow. That there are degrees of faith is clear from the Scriptural references; that faith eventually gains the victory in the life of the Christian will be discussed in Chapter XVII; assurance is the subject of Chapter XVIII; and that Christ is the author and finisher of our faith has been emphasized in what precedes. Let us repeat it: Faith is the gift of God; it is not the production of a free will; nor does it grow strong by mere effort alone, for although we must be diligent to make our calling and election sure, it is Christ, not ourselves, who develops and completes the work he began.

CHAPTER XV.

OF REPENTANCE UNTO LIFE.

Section I.—Repentance unto life is an evangelical grace,[1] the doctrine whereof is to be preached by every minister of the gospel, as well as that of faith in Christ.[2]

Section II.—By it a sinner, out of the sight and sense, not only of the danger, but also of the filthiness and odiousness of his sins, as contrary to the holy nature and righteous law of God, and upon the apprehension of his mercy in Christ to such as are penitent, so grieves for and hates his sins, as to turn from them all unto God,[3] purposing and endeavoring to walk with him in all the ways of his commandments.[4]

1. Zech. xii. 10 ; Acts xi. 18.—2. Luke xxiv. 47 ; Mark i. 15 ; Acts xx. 21. —3. Ezek. xviii. 30,31 ; xxxvi. 31 ; Isa. xxx. 22 ; Ps. li. 4 ; Jer. xxxi. 18, 19 ; Joel ii. 12,13 ; Amos v. 15 ; Ps. cxix. 128 ; 2 Cor. vii. 11.—4.Ps. cxix. 6,59,106 ; Luke i. 6 ; 2 Kings xxiii. 25.

This chapter begins with the assertion that repentance is an evangelical grace, i.e., an unmerited favor accompanying the Gospel, and that every minister ought so to preach it. Well, of course, this is precisely what the Scripture teaches. But to do so, the minister needs to know what repentance is. A person who does not know what repentance is, cannot preach it. A person who has only some fuzzy notion of what repentance is can preach it only fuzzily. A man who has a clear and accurate idea of repentance can preach it clearly and accurately. And a cleric who has a false view of repentance turns people away from God. Definitions and precise concepts are extremely important, and in this age woefully lacking. Every student who wishes to be a faithful minister, and every Christian who wants to live up to the name he bears should take pains to learn what sin, regeneration, justification, and repentance signify.

First, then, let us have a paragraph on the meaning of repentance and then later a little history and explanation.

The first point is to describe what repentance is. Such a description is necessary because irreligious people and people of non-Christian religions do not know the Christian meaning of the word. These people often think that repentance means being sorry for your sins. Now it is true that repentance includes sorrow for sin, but it includes more. It is possible to be sorry for sin without repentance. A person may be sorry that he committed a crime because it got him into trouble. Such sorrow is not repentance. Repentance includes a godly sorrow for sin that recognizes sin for what it really is. And because the penitent recognizes sin for what it really is, namely an offence against God, repentance also includes a turning to God. More specifically it includes a turning to God because of the apprehension of God's mercy in Jesus Christ. This turning is called conversion, so that conversion is a part of repentance. Then further, hatred of sin and turning to God carries with it a desire to obey God's commandments. These three aspects of repentance (sorrow, conversion, obedience) can be summed up in the etymological meaning of the word, which is, "a change of mind." Repentance therefore is a change of mind with respect to sin and God. From this description it will be seen that repentance is not an act that occurs just once or several times sporadically: it is a lifelong habit, a continuing state of mind, a fixed disposition or temperament.

A little history and explanation are now in order. This history is a bit unfortunate. As the Christian church spread through the Latin-speaking west, the need for a Latin translation of the Bible became more and more evident. Several attempts were made. Jerome's was the best and it came to be called the Vulgate or commonly received version.

Jerome's translation, however, had some serious defects, one of which was that he translated the Greek noun *metanoia* as *poenitentiam* and the verb as *poenitentiam agite*. This means, *do penance*. It is from this translation that the Romish doctrine of penance arose, and also the misleading term *repentance*. It is misleading because this etymology connects repentance with penance and penalty. Penance centers attention on an external act and obscures the internal mental attitude which the original Greek word so specifically designated.

It is true that repentance should produce certain external acts. Undoubtedly we should bring forth fruits meet or suitable to repentance. Sometimes restitution is required; sometimes it is impossible; for although we can restore stolen goods, we cannot restore a reputation damaged by malicious gossip. But even when possible the more important thing is not the external act: the important thing is the state of mind from which the act springs.

The Roman church, with the word *poenitentiam* in its official Vulgate, developed the doctrine of penance, which is a penalty imposed by a priest. Perhaps originally the priests made the penalty fit the crime; but after a little time irrelevant penalties were imposed, such as walking up stairs on your knees, beating yourself with a whip, abstaining from meat, or finally, paying a money fine to the church. Reference has already been made to Tetzel's financial success in raising funds to build St. Peter's.

There is a story, perhaps not literally accurate, but at least symbolically appropriate, that the true meaning of justification dawned upon Luther's mind when he was doing penance by walking up the stone steps of a church on his knees. For some time afterward he was still puzzled by the Latin words, *poenitentiam agite*: do penance. Were the Romanists right after all? Was the sale of indulgences legitimate?

Then Melanchthon showed him the Greek original. The word is not *do penance*, but *change your mind*. What we call repentance therefore is not an external act but a sincere inward state of mind.

The Pharisees and their forerunners in Israel, like the Romanists, preached a legalistic external religion. This was one of the curses of later Judaism, a curse and depravity that the prophets rebuked: "Rend your hearts and not your garments!"

Unfortunately the English word *repentance* still carries the notion of pain and penalty and so obscures the New Testament doctrine. If it does not connote penance, at least it emphasizes sorrow for sin and points us to the past instead of the present and future. It is true, of course, that repentance includes sorrow for past sin. But there may be sorrow for sin when there is no repentance whatever. The fact is that the King James Version uses the word repentance to translate two quite different Greek words. In Matthew 27:3 Judas "repented." But he did not "change his mind." It would be better to say, Judas regretted that he betrayed Christ. He was sorry, and for many people this is repentance. But Judas was far from the meaning of the other word.

156

Another and more complicated example is II Cor. 7:8-10. It reads, "Though I made you sorry with a letter, I do not repent (regret) though I did repent (regret) . . . For godly sorrow worketh repentance to salvation not to be repented of (regretted); but the sorrow of the world worketh death."

Sorrow for sin therefore is not enough. It must be godly sorrow; for a worldly sorrow, like that of Judas, worketh death.

At the same time sorrow, even godly sorrow, is not all there is to repentance. Repentance is a complete change of mind, the adoption of a wholly new outlook on life.

Imagine a young man, well-educated, with great ability, favored by the officials of government. He has been educated to hate Christianity; and being a resident of a somewhat totalitarian country, he obtains permission to harass the Christians.

Then suppose something happens to change his mind. He becomes convinced that his old views were wrong. He now believes that Christianity is true. He is so convinced that he preaches the faith he once persecuted and himself suffers persecution at the hands of his former superiors. This is repentance, and the young man was Paul. Repentance then is no superficial emotion of regret or remorse, felt one day and forgotten the next. It is a permanent intellectual revolution. It is a life established on new principles, a life lived until death, in obedience to the Lord Jesus Christ.

Now that we know what repentance is, and have seen its outstanding example in the person of the Apostle Paul, we can better understand the opening statement of section i that repentance is an evangelical grace, i.e., an unmerited favor from God. In view of what it is, it can be nothing other than a divine gift. When the early Jewish Christians first heard Peter's account of the conversion of Gentiles, they were amazed: they apparently did not expect Gentiles to repent. But they were not amazed or uncertain that repentance was a gift of God. After they heard what Peter had to say, "They glorified God, saying, Then hath God also to the Gentiles granted repentance unto life." In fact the unexpected conversion of Gentiles could only make clearer the fact that repentance is a gift from God, for human nature as totally depraved cannot voluntarily manufacture a holy hatred for sin, nor turn to God in a new life whose activities include repentance.

Section III.—Although repentance be not to be rested in, as any satisfaction for sin or any cause of the pardon thereof,[5] which is the act of God's free grace in Christ,[6] yet is it of such necessity to all sinners that none may expect pardon without it.[7]

Section IV.—As there is no sin so small but it deserves damnation,[8] so there is no sin so great that it can bring damnation upon those who truly repent.[9]

Section V.—Men ought not to content themselves with a general repentance, but it is every man's duty to endeavor to repent of his particular sins particularly.[10]

5. Ezek. xxxvi. 31,32 ; xvi. 61-63.—6. Hos. xiv. 2,4 ; Rom. iii. 24 ; Eph. i. 7.—7. Luke xiii. 3,5 ; Acts xvii. 30,31.—8. Rom. vi. 23 ; v. 12 ; Matt. xii. 36.—9. Isa. lv. 7 ; Rom. viii. 1 ; Isa. i. 16,18.—10. Ps. xix. 13 ; Luke xix. 8 ; 1 Tim. i. 13,15.

The next step in the doctrine of repentance is its necessity to salvation. Section iii says that repentance is "of such necessity to all sinners that none may expect pardon without it." This is what the Scriptures definitely assert. It could not be plainer. Acts 17.30 declares, "God . . . commandeth all men everywhere to repent." It is not enough, however, to say that repentance is necessary: we must know just what its necessary place or function is. Repentance is not necessary in order to be regenerated, as if regeneration were a reward for a prior repentance. It is the other way around: repentance is a necessary consequence of regeneration. This order is important because if it were reversed, it would detract from the full sufficiency of Christ's atonement on the cross. Let us see why.

Because of the necessary connection between repentance and pardon, the Unitarians, modernists, and liberals have fallen into an error somewhat similar to a Roman Catholic error. Both groups mistakenly hold that repentance constitutes a ground for pardon and a satisfaction for sin. The liberals adopt a moral influence theory of the atonement and teach that God accepts man on the ground of repentance, understanding repentance more as mere sorrow for sin without much apprehension of God's mercy in Christ. The Romanists take repentance to mean penance—a penalty prescribed by the priest, by which the sinner atones for his sin. This is an impertinent attempt to supplant the perfect satisfaction of Christ. Never forget that Jesus paid it all. Repentance, according to the Scriptures and our Confession, is not a satisfaction for sin; though there is no pardon without repentance.

158

Even some good evangelicals get things backwards. For example, when the original articles from which this study developed were published in *The Southern Presbyterian Journal,* a gentleman in a letter to the author asserted that repentance precedes rather than follows regeneration. His reason for so asserting was a list of verses that he had collected. These verses in one way or another taught that repentance is essential to salvation, e.g., Except ye repent, ye shall all likewise perish; repent ye therefore and be converted; God commandeth all men everywhere to repent. But it is one thing to say, as the Bible assuredly does, that repentance is essential to salvation, and quite another to say that repentance precedes regeneration. Note that justification, sanctification, and indeed glorification are essential to salvation; but they are not prior to regeneration. In addition to the fallacious inference that "essential to the whole" means "prior to a given part," the gentleman, so it seems, made two false identifications. The first of course is that salvation is to be identified with regeneration. The second is that repentance is an act that can take place in a short space of time. Perhaps there could be some carry over from the Romish notion of penance. Penance may take seven minutes, seven hours, or seven days; but then it is over with. Similarly this act of repentance is supposed to take a short time and then the sinner is ready to be born again.

The original article had already made it clear that repentance is a lifelong process. Here the emphasis is placed on the fact that it cannot occur before regeneration. The reason is plain. Repentance is a command of God, and therefore obedience to this command is pleasing to God. Therefore repentance either follows after or accompanies faith. Repentance cannot precede faith. Both faith and repentance, since they are pleasing to God and are therefore spiritually good, cannot occur before the new birth because a man dead in sin can neither please God, do any spiritual good, or exhibit any process, factor, or result of spiritual life. Are we not therefore permitted to conclude with Q.E.D?

> *Section VI.—As every man is bound to make private confession of his sins to God, praying for the pardon thereof;*[11] *upon which, and the forsaking of them, he shall find mercy;*[12] *so he that scandalizeth his brother, or the Church of Christ, ought to be willing, by a private or*

public confession and sorrow for his sin, to declare his repentance to those that are offended;[13] who are thereupon to be reconciled to him, and in love to receive him.[14]

11. Ps. li. 4,5,7,9,14 ; xxxii. 5,6.—12. Prov. xxviii. 13 ; 1 John i. 9.—13. James v. 16 ; Luke xvii. 3,4 ; Josh. vii. 19 ; Ps. li.—14. 2 Cor. ii. 8.

What section vi says is clear to all. A godly sorrow for sin leads to confession. We must confess our sins to God and beg pardon through Christ. Then, too, when one of our sins particularly injures our neighbor, we are bound to confess that sin to him and seek his pardon. Or, if our sin is one that scandalizes the church, we should be willing to confess publicly.

What section vi does not say should also be made clear to all. Neither the Confession nor the Scripture says anything about confessing our sins to a priest. This is a non-Christian invention of Rome.

The Romish sacrament of Penance gives rise to their practice of confession. The priest, in order to impose a penalty and to forgive, or retain, sins, must know not only the sin itself, but also its causes and circumstances, which might aggravate or perhaps alleviate the sin. Unless the priest is fully told such details, "the sins themselves are neither entirely set forth by the penitents, nor are they clearly known to the judges; and it cannot be that they can estimate rightly the grievousness of the crimes, and impose on the penitents the punishment which ought to be inflicted on account of them" (Council of Trent, Fourteenth Session, Chapter V).

Thus the Romish church imposes a practice not sanctioned by Scripture; claims to weigh the gravity of sins, which a more modest appraisal of human wisdom would not countenance; and by imposing a penalty, which Christ only could suffer, gives the sinner a sense of meriting his salvation.

CHAPTER XVI.

OF GOOD WORKS.

Section I.—Good works are only such as God hath commanded in his holy word,[1] and not such as, without the warrant thereof, are devised by men, out of blind zeal, or upon any pretence of good intention.[2]

Section II.—These good works, done in obedience to God's commandments, are the fruits and evidences of a true and lively faith;[3] and by them believers manifest their thankfulness,[4] strengthen their assurance,[5] edify their brethren,[6] adorn the profession of the gospel,[7] stop the mouths of the adversaries,[8] and glorify God,[9] whose workmanship they are, created in Christ Jesus thereunto;[10] that, having their fruit unto holiness, they may have the end, eternal life.[11]

1. Mic. vi. 8; Rom. xii. 2; Heb. xiii. 21.—2. Matt. xv. 9; Isa. xxix. 13; 1 Pet. i. 18; Rom. x. 2; John xvi. 2; 1 Sam. xv. 21,23.—3. James ii. 18, 22.—4.Ps. cxvi. 12,13; 1 Pet. ii. 9.—5. 1 John ii. 3,5; 2 Pet. i. 5-10.—6. 2 Cor. ix. 2; Matt. v. 16.—7. Tit. ii. 5,9-12; 1 Tim. vi. 1.—8. 1 Pet. ii. 15.—9. 1 Pet. ii. 12; Phil. i. 11; John xv. 8.—10. Eph. ii. 10.—11. Rom. vi. 22.

Many people in the pews, and not merely liberal ministers in the pulpits, express a distaste for doctrine and theology. They want something practical. Well, who can deny that good works are practical?

Unfortunately for those who dislike theology and a detailed confessional statement, there cannot be much progress in good works unless it is known what works are good and what works are evil. And who can deny that a definition of good works is theological, doctrinal, and creedal? The popular disjunction between doctrine and practice, between theology and life, between knowing and doing, is a false one. To fix an auto engine, one must know some theory. The theory of practice must precede the practice of theory.

What then are good works? Are they those actions a benevolently intentioned gentleman may happen to enjoy? Is a substantial donation to an orphanage, hospital, or church a good work? Strange as it may seem to non-Christians, and even to uninstructed Christians, the answer is that these actions are not necessarily good. They may be good; but again they may not be. What then makes a work or action good?

Section i gives the definition of good works and distinguishes them from works that are not good. In conformity with the definition of sin, given in an earlier chapter, the first part of this section teaches that every distinction between good and evil is found in the Bible. To be sure, the heathen know that there is some distinction between right and wrong, and they regularly violate their consciences; but by and large they do not know in particular what acts are right because their consciences are unenlightened. This explains why the Greeks thought it right to murder unwanted infants and why the Hindus thought it right to burn widows. The Biblical revelation therefore is essential to a knowledge of what works are good.

The second part of this section teaches the same truth in a negative form. Without the warrant of the Bible an act done with good intentions is not a good work. The blind zeal and arrogant authority of Romanism imposes practices, such as genuflection, crossing oneself, using holy water, kissing the big toe of St. Peter's image, which are not good works at all. Where in the Bible is any of this? Or where in the Bible are we taught to offer prayers for the dead? Since all these are beside the commandments of God, they are superstitious practices that God abominates. These are the things Paul had in mind in Colossians 2:18,23, where he speaks of the sins of voluntary humility and will worship.

Next, section ii asserts that good works, i.e., obedience to God's revealed commandments, are the result and evidence of true faith. The relation between faith and works is really very simple and easy to understand, even though from age to age so many people entertain confused notions about it. The relation is that faith is the cause of good works and good works are the effect of faith. This simple causal relation removes the notion that good works are the basis of our justification and, as well, the notion that good works are unnecessary in a salvation accomplished by sovereign grace.

Although the great danger and error in any age is the repudiation of God's grace in favor of a salvation by works, there is also a less widespread danger, found among those who stress

162

God's grace, of minimizing or ignoring good works. This antinomianism, to use a technical term, has been alluded to before. Here a particular example may be mentioned. During the last fifty years various local churches and small mission boards, though they stress Christ's substitutionary atonement, have turned their backs on the full Biblical teaching of the Westminster Confession and have written for themselves abbreviated and diluted statements of faith. Often these statements consist of no more than half a dozen sentences. Now, if these modern creeds simply omitted most of the Bible, that would be bad enough. But occasionally they contradict the Bible. I remember one that asserts "we are saved without works." Well, it is true that we are justified apart from works. The sole ground of justification is Christ's merit. But we are not saved without works—unless, like the thief on the cross, we die immediately upon our regeneration. But for those that live, a true faith produces good works. There is an agricultural expression which puts the matter succinctly enough: faith is the root and works are the fruit. We cannot be saved without them.

This in no way detracts from God's grace. The life that works itself out in this way is itself a life from above. It was initiated by the supernatural act of regeneration. The faith, the roots for the fruits, is the gift of God. And the works themselves are done in the power of the Spirit, who works in us both to will and to do, as he pleases.

> *Section III.—Their ability to do good works is not at all of themselves, but wholly from the Spirit of Christ.[12] And that they may be enabled thereunto, besides the graces they have already received, there is required an actual influence of the same Holy Spirit to work in them to will and to do of his good pleasure:[13] yet are they not hereupon to grow negligent, as if they were not bound to perform any duty unless upon a special motion of the Spirit; but they ought to be diligent in stirring up the grace of God that is in them.[14]*

12. John xv. 4-6 ; Ezek. xxxvi. 26-27.—13. Phil. ii. 13 ; iv. 13 ; 2 Cor. iii. 5.—14. Phil. ii. 12 ; Heb. vi. 11,12 ; 2 Pet. i. 3,5,10,11 ; Isa. lxiv. 7 ; 2 Tim. i. 6 ; Acts xxvi. 6,7 ; Jude 20,21.

The previous paragraph anticipated the teaching of section iii. Indeed section iii was anticipated by the chapter on sanctification, for the material on good works is not logically distinct from it, but is rather an explication of its details. This section therefore indicates that good works, far from being inconsistent with salvation by grace, are themselves the effect of grace. Unless we were given an ability to do good works, an ability which the unregenerate man does not have, we could not do them. The section incorporates the wording of Philippians 2:13, that God works in us, of his own good pleasure, to the end that we may be able to do these good works.

For this reason, if a man does no good works, and particularly if he is known for evil works, we may well doubt the sincerity of his Christian profession, and if he is not a member of the church we would do well to reject his application for membership until he can make a *credible* profession. Regeneration and the consequent faith inevitably produce sanctification; and if no progress is visible, there is no evidence that the individual believes in Christ at all.

The strong stress on the need of power from the Holy Spirit in order to do good works does not mean that the Spirit gives us knowledge of what is good in addition to and beyond what the Bible teaches. Near the end of section iii we are warned not to grow negligent as if we are not bound to perform any duty unless upon a special motion of the Spirit. The Spirit gives us power, not knowledge.

Mystics and people who talk a great deal about guidance miss this point. Among my circle of acquaintances there is a man who went out into his farmyard one evening before supper to feed the chickens. He stayed so long that his wife came out to see if anything was wrong. Nothing physical was wrong, but something spiritual was. There he stood in the middle of the chicken yard, waiting for guidance from the Spirit as to whether he should feed the chickens. No guidance is necessary and no guidance will be granted. The Old Testament already has instructed us to take care of our animals.

What is perhaps worse than this is a prayer for guidance as to whether or not one should do something sinful. There was a man about to enter the ministry who said he had no guidance about getting out of the liquor business, but he would pray about it. There are ministers who pray whether or not to cooperate with apostasy. Should they continue to contribute their money and their

164

names to support anti-biblical publications for Sunday School use? Or should they separate themselves from this sort of evil? Such prayers are sinful. The Bible has already said that we should not do evil that good may come. Our guidance is already before us. To ask for more is a repudiation of what God has spoken. A prayer for strength from the Spirit to do what is already known to be right would be a much more commendable prayer.

Section IV.—They who in their obedience attain to the greatest height which is possible in this life, are so far from being able to supererogate, and to do more than God requires, as that they fall short of much which in duty they are bound to do.[15]

Section V.—We cannot, by our best works, merit pardon of sin, or eternal life, at the hand of God, by reason of the great disproportion that is between them and the glory to come, and the infinite distance that is between us and God, whom by them we can neither profit, nor satisfy for the debt of our former sins;[16] but when we have done all we can, we have done but our duty, and are unprofitable servants;[17] and because, as they are good, they proceed from his Spirit;[18] and, as they are wrought by us, they are defiled and mixed with so much weakness and imperfection, that they cannot endure the severity of God's judgment.[19]

Section VI.—Yet, notwithstanding, the persons of believers being accepted through Christ, their good works also are accepted in him;[20] not as though they were in this life wholly unblamable and unreprovable in God's sight;[21] but that he, looking upon them in his Son, is pleased to accept and reward that which is sincere, although accompanied with many weaknesses and imperfections.[22]

15. Luke xvii. 10; Neh. xiii. 22; Job ix. 2,3; Gal. v. 17.—16. Rom. iii. 20; iv. 2,4,6; Eph. ii. 8,9; Tit. iii. 5-7; Rom. viii. 18; Ps. xvi. 2; Job xxii. 2,3; xxxv. 7,8.—17. Luke xvii. 10.—18. Gal. v. 22,23.—19. Isa. lxiv. 6; Gal. v. 17; Rom. vii. 15,18; Ps. cxliii. 2, cxxx. 3.—20. Eph. i. 6; 1 cxliii. 2.—22. Heb. xiii. 20,21; 2 Cor. viii. 12; Heb. vi. 10; Matt. xxv. 21,23.

Regeneration and justification inevitably produce sanctification; but perfect obedience to God's commands is impossible in this life because of the effects of sin remaining in us. Still more impossible is the ability to do more than God requires. Of all the idiotic notions what can be sillier than the Romish claim

that some men have been more holy, more perfect, more righteous than God requires? This is worse, even, than the Arminian
claim to instant and complete sanctification.

Of course if we cannot actually obey all of God's commandments, it immediately follows that we cannot do more than he
commands.

If it were possible for us to do more than God commands,
these works would be meritorious and could be used to cancel
past sins. The Roman church not only allows these extra works
to cancel the past sins of this super-good individual, but even
applies them to the sins of other people. Now, obviously, this
conflicts with the sufficiency of Christ. In fact, carried to its
logical conclusion, it makes Christ's sacrifice unnecessary. For
if we can be so excessively good that we can spare merits for
other people, we must have been good enough to have earned a
sufficient amount for ourselves. And with such unlimited ability,
we need not depend on Christ's merits at all.

Of course the Romanists try to maintain the necessity of
Christ's sacrifice, but they make no pretense of maintaining
Christ's sufficiency. We can think of them as singing:

> Christ has paid in part.
> Thanks to him I say.
> Sin had left a bluish stain.
> He washed it somewhat gray.

The modernist version of course puts it a little differently:

> Jesus lived and died
> Quite respectably.
> We can always do the same
> Much more successfully.

> Jesus on the cross
> Bore no sins away.
> He could never pay my debt.
> There was no debt to pay.

*Section VII.—Works done by unregenerate men,
although, for the matter of them, they may be things
which God commands, and of good use both to themselves and others,*[23] *yet, because they proceed not from*

166

a heart purified by faith,[24] *nor are done in a right man-*
ner, according to the Word,[25] *nor to a right end, the*
glory of God,[26] *they are therefore sinful, and cannot*
please God or make a man meet to receive grace from
God.[27] *And yet their neglect of them is more sinful and*
displeasing unto God.[28]

23. 2 Kings x. 30,31 ; 1 Kings xxi. 27,29 ; Phil. i. 15,16,18.—24. Gen. iv.
5 ; Heb. xi. 4,6.—25. 1 Cor. xiii. 3 ; Isa. i. 12.—26. Matt. vi. 2,5,16.—27.
Hag. ii. 14 ; Tit. i. 15 ; Amos v. 21,22 ; Hos. i. 4 ; Rom. ix. 16 ; Tit. iii. 5.—
28. Ps. xiv. 4 ; xxxvi. 3 ; Job xxi. 14,15 ; Matt. xxv. 41-43,45 ; xxiii. 23.

Section vii shows why unregenerate men can never do any
good works at all. Since a good work is an act of obedience to
God, its motive must be pure. This explains why, at the beginning of this chapter, a donation to a church or hospital was not
called good. Of course, God commands us to care for widows
and orphans. But God does not approve of donations to these
worthy causes, when the motive is publicity, social standing, or
some such thing. Such a donation is actually a sin.

Take a further example. In ordinary conversation we would
not be likely to say that the plowing of a field in the spring
was a sin. Maybe we would not call it a "good work"; though
perhaps we might insofar as it was the farmer's means of supporting his family. But at any rate, few people would call it a
sin. Yet the Scripture says, "The ploughing of the wicked is
sin" (Prov. 21:4).

Another example is prayer. Isaiah condemns the sacrifices,
the prayers, the attendance of the people at the temple. They
were going through the external motions of worshiping God, but
their praying was sin.

The Confession acknowledges that it would be a worse sin
for the unregenerate farmer not to plow his field and let his
family starve. Perhaps it would be a worse sin not to give a donation to the orphanage. But I cannot help thinking that it would
be better not to pray at all than to fall under Isaiah's condemnation. God requires pure motives.

Motivation is stressed in Mark 9:41. It is not just the giving
of a cup of cold water that is good; it is giving the water in
Christ's name. This is why the Christian life is so difficult. To do
the correct external actions is relatively easy, though some young
Christians find it hard at times. But it is much harder, and it requires a lifelong struggle, to maintain pure motives.

167

CHAPTER XVII.

OF THE PERSEVERANCE OF THE SAINTS.

Section I.—They whom God hath accepted in his Beloved, effectually called and sanctified by his Spirit, can neither totally nor finally fall away from the state of grace; but shall certainly persevere therein to the end, and be eternally saved.[1]

Section II.—This perseverance of the saints depends not upon their own free will, but upon the immutability of the decree of election, flowing from the free and unchangeable love of God the Father;[2] upon the efficacy of the merit and intercession of Jesus Christ;[3] the abiding of the Spirit, and of the seed of God within them;[4] and the nature of the covenant of grace;[5] from all which ariseth also the certainty and infallibility thereof.[6]

Section III.—Nevertheless they may through the temptations of Satan and of the world, the prevalency of corruption remaining in them, and the neglect of the means of their preservation, fall into grievous sins;[7] and for a time continue therein;[8] whereby they incur God's displeasure,[9] and grieve his Holy Spirit;[10] come to be deprived of some measure of their graces and comforts;[11] have their hearts hardened,[12] and their consciences wounded;[13] hurt and scandalize others,[14] and bring temporal judgments upon themselves.[15]

1 Phil. i. 6; 2 Pet. i. 10; John x. 28,29; 1 John iii. 9; 1 Pet. i. 5,9.—2. 2 Tim. ii. 18,19; Jer. xxxi. 3.—3. Heb. x. 10,14; xiii. 20,21; ix. 12-15; Rom. viii. 33-39; John xvii. 11,24; Luke xxii. 32; Heb. vii. 25.—4. John xiv. 16,17; 1 John ii. 27; iii. 9.—5. Jer. xxxii. 40.—6. John x. 28; 2 Thess. iii. 3; 1 John ii. 19.—7. Matt. xxvi. 70,72,74.—8. Ps. li. 14.—9. Isa. lxiv. 5,7,9; 2 Sam. xi. 27.—10. Eph. iv. 30.—11. Ps. li. 8,10,12; Rev. ii. 4; Cant. v. 2-4,6.—12. Isa. lxiii. 17; Mark vi. 52, xvi. 14.—13. Ps. xxxii. 3,4; li. 8.—14. 2 Sam. xii. 14.—15. Ps. lxxxix. 31,32; 1 Cor. xi. 32.

One evening as I was conducting the mid-week prayer meeting, an elderly, white-haired gentleman asked for one of his favorite hymns: "How Firm a Foundation." The hymn has six long stanzas, and as the meeting was very informal I wondered aloud which of the six we could omit. Not the first, of course—it speaks of the Word of God as the foundation of our faith; not the second because we need the aid and strength of God's omnipotent hand; the third or fourth? The old gentleman interrupted my wondering by insisting that this was a good hymn and that we could sing it all. We did, and as we reached the fifth stanza, everyone else in the room saw in it the picture of the grand old man who had requested the hymn:

> E'en down to old age all my people shall prove
> My sovereign, eternal, unchangeable love.
> And when hoary hairs shall their temples adorn,
> Like lambs they shall still in my bosom be borne.

He too sang it with vigor, and he sang the sixth stanza too:

> The soul that on Jesus hath leaned for repose
> I will not, I will not desert to his foes.

Now it was a bit strange that this gentleman should have requested this hymn and should have sung it with such praise and devotion. For he did not like Calvinism; all his life he had been an Arminian; he did not believe in "eternal security," as he called it; and he had been telling his friends so for years. Even now he would have disowned the name of Calvinism. But could it be that without realizing it he had now come to believe, and that his earlier Arminian views had changed with the color of his hair?

If it is strange that this lovely Arminian saint could become at least somewhat of a Calvinist without knowing it, it is far more strange that anyone who bases his faith on the firm foundation of God's Word could ever be an Arminian. The Scripture verses are too numerous to mention.

But some may be puzzled at the doctrine of perseverance and think that it ascribes too much will power to frail humanity. Such an objection rests on a misunderstanding. Section ii of this chapter clearly says that "this perseverance of the saints depends not upon their own free will, but upon the immutability of the decree of election." I remember a conversation with another Arminian. He had been fulminating against the doctrine of election and I replied that election was the basis of our assurance of salvation. The Arminian's contempt rose in his face as he charged me with substituting the doctrine of election for the crucifixion of Christ. Well of course, our salvation is based on the active and passive obedience of Christ; but our assurance requires some reason to believe that the benefits of Christ's work are permanently applied to ourselves. Small comfort it is indeed if we are saved at breakfast and lost at noon. Let us emphasize the fact: the Arminians can have no sure hope of entering heaven. They must always entertain the uncomfortable feeling that they will finally be lost. Obviously no man can depend on his own power to persevere in grace; for, first, human nature is weak, and, second, grace is not something we can earn or keep. And if the Arminian refuses to admit that God causes his elect to persevere, what reasonable expectation can he have of heaven?

The Roman Catholic doctrine, to which the Arminians reverted in their revolt against the Reformation, is expressed in the decrees of the Council of Trent. One section reads, "If anyone maintain that a man once justified cannot lose grace, . . . let him be accursed." Only a massive ignorance of the Scriptures allows for such a position.

Philippians 1:6 says, "he which hath begun a good work in you will perform it until the day of Jesus Christ." Language could hardly make it plainer that if God starts the good work in a sinner, he will complete it. The ARV reads, "will perfect it." The RSV reads, "will bring it to completion." The Greek verb means, to accomplish, to complete, or to finish. Is there any conceivable way by which this verse could be harmonized with Arminianism?

If Philippians 1:6 is as clear as it is possible for language to be, John 10:28,29 is still clearer: "And I give unto them eternal life; and they shall never perish, neither shall any man pluck them out of my hand. My Father, which gave them me, is greater than all; and no man is able to pluck them out of the Father's hand."

How some people have squirmed to avoid these verses. Those who insist on a free will independent of God say that although other men cannot pluck a child of God from the Father's hand, the man himself is free to do so. But the verse says no man can do so: this includes the man himself. Another act of desperation is to argue that although no *man* can pluck the child from the hand of God, the devil can do so. But once more, the phrase *no man* in the KJV is in the original *no one*. So it is translated in the ARV. And in any case the verse says that Christ gives his sheep eternal life. Would it be eternal if it ceased after five days or five years? The verse also says that they shall never perish. How long and how sure is *never*? It would seem that no one could misunderstand this language.

Then for good measure we shall add I Peter 1:5, which speaks of the regenerate as those "who are kept by the power of God through faith unto salvation ready to be revealed in the last time." Why belabor the obvious? And still the Scriptures, addressed as they are to stubborn rebels against God, repeat the same idea time after time. Cf. II Tim. 2:19; Jer. 31:3, and 32:40; I John 2:19; and Isa. 55:11.

Of course, the perseverance of the saints does not mean sinless perfection or a life free from struggle and temptation. Eradication of our corrupt nature is a long and difficult process and will not be completed until we are glorified. As long as the present life continues, we may become careless of the means of grace, our hearts may be temporarily hardened, we may fall into grievous sins. Thus we may harm others and bring temporal punishment upon ourselves. God does not promise to carry us to the skies on flowery beds of ease. But praise his name, he promises to carry, drag, or push us there. So, and only so, we arrive.

What should be particularly noted in this section is how the doctrine of perseverance fits in with all the other doctrines. God is not irrational or insane. What he says hangs together; it forms a logical system. Election, total depravity, effectual calling, sovereign grace, and perseverance are mutually consistent. God does not contradict himself. But Arminian saints do. They may be grand old men, loved by all who know them. But not until the message of the Bible persuades them of God's sovereign, unchangeable love, can they really sing

> That soul, though all hell should endeavor to shake,
> I'll never, no, never, no never forsake.

CHAPTER XVIII.

OF ASSURANCE OF GRACE AND SALVATION

*Section I.—Although hypocrites, and other unre-
generate men, may vainly deceive themselves with false
hopes and carnal presumptions of being in the favour
of God and estate of salvation;[1] which hope of theirs
shall perish;[2] yet such as truly believe in the Lord Jesus,
and love him in sincerity, endeavouring to walk in all
good conscience before him, may in this life be certainly
assured that they are in the state of grace,[3] and may re-
rejoice in the hope of the glory of God; which hope shall
never make them ashamed.[4]*

*Section II.—This certainty is not a bare conjectural
and probable persuasion, grounded upon a fallible hope;[5]
but an infallible assurance of faith, founded upon the
divine truth of the promises of salvation,[6] the inward
evidence of those graces unto which these promises are
made,[7] the testimony of the Spirit of adoption witnessing
with our spirits that we are the children of God;[8] which
Spirit is the earnest of our inheritance, whereby we are
sealed to the day of redemption.[9]*

1. Job viii. 13,14; Mic. iii. 11; Deut. xxix. 19; John viii. 41.—2. Matt.
vii. 22,23.—3. 1 John ii. 3; iii. 14,18,19,21,24; v. 13.—4. Rom. v. 2,5.—
5. Heb. vi. 11,19.—6. Heb. vi. 17,18.—7. 2 Pet. 1,4,5,10,11; 1 John ii. 3;
iii. 14; 2 Cor. i. 12.—8. Rom. viii. 15,16.—9. Eph. i. 13,14; iv. 30; 2 Cor.
i. 21,22.

In the study of our Confession one theme becomes more
and more vivid as we proceed from chapter to chapter. It is that
the Confession and the Bible teach a system of doctrine. God
does not ramble in his message to us. His thoughts are not
desultory and disconnected. On the contrary God speaks with
logical consistency. Therefore the later chapters of the Confession
depend on the earlier.

The new creed now in process of adoption by the United
Presbyterian Church reflects a far different view of logic, the Bible,
and God. In the past, after the candidate for ordination had solemnly affirmed that he believed "the Scriptures of the Old and New
Testaments to be the word of God, the only infallible rule of faith
and practice," he then had to reply in the affirmative to the question, "Do you sincerely receive and adopt the Confession of Faith

of this Church, as containing the system of doctrine taught in the Holy Scriptures?" Therefore, in addition to the infallibility of Scripture, the ordination vows commit every Presbyterian minister to a certain system of doctrine.

The new creed, on the contrary, tries to give the impression that there is no system of doctrine in the Bible. The Scripture is regarded as a hodge-podge of unsystematic, conflicting views. The text is: "The words of Scripture are the words of men, conditioned by the language, thought forms, and literary fashions of the places and times at which they were written. They reflect views of life, history, and the cosmos which were then current . . . The variety of such views found in the Bible . . ." (lines 192-198). The Scriptures are called the words of men; the new creed does not call them the Word of God, nor does it say that the Scriptures are the revelation of God. No suggestion of eternal and unchangeable truth is to be found. Consequently the Bible gives no logical and consistent message. The views of the different authors differ; and the modern minister must pick and choose from among them and adapt their suggestions to the common opinions of the twentieth century. It was thus that the so-called "German Christians" reinterpreted the Bible by Nazi principles. It is thus that the United Presbyterian Church is reinterpreting the Bible as a message of civil rights. But when the issue of civil rights is no longer popular, a different message will be distilled out of Scripture. These different messages, Nazism, civil rights, and whatever comes next, have no logical connection with each other, because the Bible, instead of teaching one definite system, is an illogical confusion of many systems.

On the basis of this new creed, one of two implications necessarily follows. If the Bible is God's word, then God is irrational. If the Bible is not God's word, it can have no ecclesiastical authority. And in fact, the creed effectively removes authority from Scripture and assigns it to the church itself. True, the new creed says "The church has received the Old and New Testaments as the normative witness to this revelation and has recognized them as Holy Scripture"; but the emphasis falls on the church, not on the Scripture, for the Scripture is only a witness to a non-scriptural "revelation." Then further down, to finish a sentence already started, "The variety of such views found in the Bible shows that God has communicated with men in diverse cultural conditions. This gives the church confidence that he will continue to speak to men in a changing world and in every form of human culture" (lines 197-201).

Now, if God's communication with men in the Scripture is put on a level with God's continuing communication in every form of human culture, including abstract art, race riots, and the Beatles, it follows that there is nothing really normative or authoritative in Scripture, and everyone must depend on the infinite wisdom of the General Assembly—properly manipulated, of course.

In contrast with all this, Presbyterians believe in Scripture alone. They believe that Scripture teaches a logical system of doctrine. They sincerely adopt the Westminster Confession as containing the system taught in the Holy Scriptures. And they see clearly that predestination ties in with irresistible grace and that both are consistent with the perseverance of the saints.

This is true in the case of assurance also. If God had not begun a good work in us, totally depraved as human nature is, the work would not have begun. If God did not intend to complete that good work in us, it would not be completed. And if there were the slightest possibility that it would not be completed, we could not have the comfort of assurance. Though someone might suppose (if he assumes a different content in the divine decree) that God could have decided to begin and to finish the work in us without also granting assurance as a part of that work, it cannot be denied that assurance presupposes and depends on perseverance and irresistible grace. The trouble with Arminianism is that it is illogical. It retains parts of the Biblical message, but because of its unscriptural theory of free will rejects other parts.

An Arminian may be a truly regenerate Christian; in fact, if he is truly an Arminian and not a Pelagian who happens to belong to an Arminian church, he must be a saved man. But he is not usually, and cannot consistently be assured of his salvation. The places in which his creed differs from our Confession confuse the mind, dilute the Gospel, and impair its proclamation.

The Arminian system holds (1) that God elects persons to eternal life on the condition of their reception of grace and their perseverance as foreseen; (2) that Christ died, not as the substitute for certain men, definitely to assume their penalty, but to render a chance of salvation indifferently possible to all men; (3) that all men have the same influence of the Holy Ghost operating on them, so that some are saved because they cooperate, and others are lost because they resist, thus in effect making salvation depend on the will of man; and (4) that since salvation is not made certain by God's decree nor by Christ's sacrifice, and since man's will is free or independent of God's control, a regenerate man can unregenerate himself and ultimately be lost.

In contrast the Calvinist, the Confession, and the Bible teach (1) that election is unconditional and that sovereign grace is irresistible; (2) that Christ offers us salvation and not merely a chance of salvation (there is quite a difference, you know— our grocery stores offer a chance of a car with every purchase, and we have received dozens of chances, but they have not offered us a Ford or a Chevrolet yet); (3) that human cooperation is not the cause of regeneration, which depends on God and not on the will of man; and (4) that the new birth begins an eternal life, i.e., a life that does not end in a year or two.

It must of course be said, and this chapter of the Confession says it first, that many people entertain false hopes of God's favor. A converted Chinese, who had been an exponent of Zen for years, told me that during that time he was very much assured of his favored state. There must be many other such cases in the several pagan religions. We all know that there are many such cases among the sects and religions of this country. Yet they cannot all be right because they are so inconsistent one with another.

This false assurance is found among nominal Christians too. Job 8:13-14 says, "The hypocrite's hope shall perish, whose hope shall be cut off, and whose trust shall be a spider's web." A spider's web, as I have seen them in the early morning sunlight sparkling with dew, can be very beautiful. But it cannot be used to tie a Christmas package to send through the mail. So too heathen religions may have a certain attractiveness; and yet the hope of those who trust in them shall perish.

In the time of Micah, much later than Job, there was a great deal of wickedness. The government was corrupt. Justice perished in bribery. The people worshiped images. There was theft and violence; and the religious leaders were preaching a false message. The picture could have been photographed today. This year there have been riots in New York, Philadelphia, Chicago, and Berkeley. Murder and rape are committed on the streets of New York without protest and without help extended to the victims. Violent demonstrations are encouraged by high government officials. The fabric of our society is disintegrating.

In such a situation the prophet Micah spoke: "They build up Zion with blood . . . the heads thereof judge for reward and the priests teach for hire. . . . Yet will they lean upon the Lord and say, 'Is not the Lord among us? None evil can come upon us.' "

The same warning is found in the New Testament also. The liberals are fond of asserting that the Old Testament is a severe book of wrath, while the New is full of sweetness and light. But the New Testament is even more severe than the Old. Matthew 7:22-23 reads, "Many will say to me in that day, Lord, Lord, have we not prophesied in thy name . . . ? And then will I profess unto them, I never knew you."

This is severe, and very strange. These people against whom Jesus shall shut the door of heaven are not the secularists who openly despise religion. These are the people who attend church regularly, the ones who do the work, who boast of their success. These are the religious leaders, who talk of leading the church of Christ. But Jesus says, I never knew you. False assurance is a common thing.

Yet it is possible to have a true assurance and rejoice in a hope that will not disappoint. The Scriptures say it is possible and urge us to attain to that state. John wrote his first epistle especially to teach us this lesson.

When we think of the Reformation, we usually think first of the doctrine of Justification by Faith. But the Reformers also discovered assurance. The proper word is *discovered*, for they came out of a medieval background of superstition and fear. In the Cluny Museum in Paris I saw the face of a devil, made of leather, wood, and whatnot, with glaring eyes and a tongue that wagged, which was used in those dark days to scare the credulous. This of course stimulated the sale of indulgences. To such fearful people the Reformers preached a message of hope.

176

The Romanists soon saw that they must take steps to combat this hope. Accordingly in 1560 they made it official. The Council of Trent (Sixth Session, chap. IX) decreed, "It is not to be said that sins are forgiven or have been forgiven to anyone who boasts of his confidence and certainty of the remission of his sins and rests on that alone; seeing that it may exist, yea, does in our day exist among heretics and schismatics." Thus the assurance the Reformers expressed was taken as a proof that they were not Christians.

Section III.—This infallible assurance doth not so belong to the essence of faith, but that a true believer may wait long, and conflict with many difficulties, before he be partaker of it:[10] yet, being enabled by the Spirit to know the things which are freely given him of God, he may, without extraordinary revelation, in the right use of ordinary means, attain thereunto.[11] And, therefore, it is the duty of every one to give all diligence to make his calling and election sure;[12] that thereby his heart may be enlarged in peace and joy in the Holy Ghost, in love and thankfulness to God, and in strength and cheerfulness in the duties of obedience,[13] the proper fruits of this assurance: so far is it from inclining men to looseness.[14]

Section IV.—True believers may have the assurance of their salvation in divers ways shaken, diminished and intermitted; as, by negligence in preserving of it; by falling into some special sin, which woundeth the conscience and grieveth the Spirit; by some sudden or vehement temptation; by God's withdrawing the light of his countenance, and suffering even such as fear him to walk in darkness, and to have no light;[15] yet are they never utterly destitute of that seed of God, and life of faith, that love of Christ and the brethren, that sincerity of heart and conscience of duty, out of which, by the operation of the Spirit, this assurance may in due time be revived,[16] and by the which, in the meantime they are supported from utter despair.[17]

10. 1 John v. 13; Isa. l. 10; Mark ix. 24; Ps. lxxxviii; lxxvii. 1-12.—11. 1 Cor. ii. 12; 1 John iv. 13; Heb. vi. 11,12; Eph. iii. 17-19.—12. 2 Pet. i. 10.—13. Rom. v. 1,2,5; xiv. 17; xv. 13; Eph. i. 3,4; Ps. iv. 6,7; cxix. 32.—14. 1 John ii. 1,2; Rom. vi. 1,2; Tit. ii. 11,12,14; 2 Cor. vii. 1; Rom. viii. 1,12; 1 John iii. 2,3; Ps. cxxx. 4; 1 John i. 6,7.—15. Cant. v. 2,3,6; Ps. li. 8,12,14; Eph. iv. 30,31; Ps. lxxvi. 1-10; Matt. xxvi. 69-72; Ps. xxxi. 22; lxxxviii.; Isa. l. 10.—16. John iii. 9; Luke xxii. 32; Job xiii. 15; Ps. lxxiii. 15; li. 8,12; Isa. 1,10.—17. Mic. vii. 7-9; Jer. xxxii. 40; Isa. liv. 7-10; Ps. xxii. 1; lxxxviii.

Have you ever tried to adjust a lawnmower? The revolving blades are too far from the fixed cutting blade and the grass slips through. So we tighten the bolts on both sides, only to find that one side is too loose and the other so tight that the blades cannot revolve. Then we try again and get it out of balance the other way around. So too we may upset the perfect balance of the Bible: one man is too loose on one side and another on another.

This happens with views of assurance. Some men, perhaps most, vainly deceive themselves with a false assurance that they are worthy of heaven. Because of this others jump to the conclusion that assurance is impossible. Since, however, it has already been shown that the Scripture teaches the assurance of grace and salvation, the remaining question is how we may attain that assurance.

To begin to distinguish between presumption and true assurance, one may begin by noting the title of the chapter—Assurance and Grace. The unregenerate are not assured of *grace*: they believe that they are good enough to deserve heaven. But the assurance spoken of in the Confession is a result of faith in Jesus Christ. It is an assurance that can be found only in those who love him in sincerity and who endeavor to walk in all good conscience before him. The Pharisees were no doubt very sure of themselves. Their great sin was spiritual pride. The assurance of grace, however, accompanies humility and a sense of unworthiness. The distinction is clear to anyone who wishes to see it.

I John 2:3; 3:14,19,24, and 5:13 tell us how we may obtain assurance of salvation. Do we love the brethren? Are we humble or proud? Cf. I Cor. 15:9,10; Gal. 6:14. Do we teach transgressors the way of the Lord? Cf. Ps. 51:12,13; II Pet. 1:5.

On this subject Jonathan Edwards has some inmportant things to say in his *Treatise Concerning Religious Affections*. This treatise runs over 350 pages and cannot be reproduced here, unfortunately. If Edwards' work seems too long at first, one may begin with Part III, Sections xii, xiii, xiv. The titles, which like the treatises and its sentences are long too, are, Gracious and holy affections have their exercise and fruit in Christian practices (22 pages); Christian practice or holy life is a manifestation and sign of the sincerity of a professing Christian, to the eye of his neighbors and brethren (14 pages); and Christian practice is a

178

distinguishing and sure evidence of grace to persons' own consciences (40 pages, all worthwhile).

On the other hand we must not say that assurance is a necessary and inseparable concomitant of faith. Some overly enthusiastic evangelists insist that unless a man is sure he is saved, he is not saved at all. They sometimes use a jingle: "I was there when it happened, and I ought to know." Just imagine a baby three months old making such a claim!

If assurance were a necessary concomitant of faith, the Scriptures would not exhort the faithful to press on to assurance. But the Scripture references contain such exhortations.

Indeed, while it is impossible to lose one's faith or salvation, assurance may be shaken, diminished, and intermitted. There is such a thing as backsliding, both sudden and gradual. The Christian may fall into sin and lose his assurance. This is graphically portrayed in Bunyan's great work, *Pilgrim's Progress*. Christian and Hopeful disobey their instructions, leave the path to the Celestial City, and climb over the fence, where, after the storm, they are caught by Giant Despair and thrust into the dungeon of Doubting Castle.

In general, one must be extremely cautious, not merely in asserting that faith and assurance are inseparable, but in making any universal statement of the psychology of Christians. The New Testament records a number of conversions, and psychologically they were all different, in fact very different. The New Testament and church history as well give abundant evidence of the infinite variety of Christian experience.

Not only because of particular sins and temptations, but also because of differences of temperament, of upbringing, of education, and of the cultural and historical conditions of one's age, no one pattern of experience fits everybody. Some are too fearful of presumption, others are not fearful enough. Elijah went to heaven in a fiery chariot, but Jeremiah may have died in despondency. Assurance of salvation, like other blessings, does not come to all Christians; but it is a part of the fulness of God's grace which we may legitimately and consistently hope to enjoy.

It is therefore most hazardous to insist that a man is not saved unless he conforms to some familiar pattern. Such patterns

179

are familiar largely because the evangelist has had a limited experience. Just consider the difference between Paul and Timothy, for instance. Their lives were so different; their childhood homes and conversions were so different; their subjective experiences had little if anything in common. There was something the same, however, not only for Paul and Timothy, but for all of us too. It is not something subjective. What is the same is the object of our faith, and this object is the same yesterday, today, and forever.

CHAPTER XIX.

OF THE LAW OF GOD.

*Section I.—God gave to Adam a law, as a cove-
nant of works, by which he bound him, and all his
posterity, to personal, entire, exact and perpetual obedience; promised life upon the fulfilling, and threatened
death upon the breach of it; and endued him with power
and ability to keep it.*[1]

*Section II.—This law, after his fall, continued to
be a perfect rule of righteousness; and, as such, was
delivered by God upon Mount Sinai in ten commandments, and written in two tables;*[2] *the first four commandments containing our duty toward God, and the
other six our duty to man.*[3]

1. Gen. i. 26,27; ii. 17; Rom. ii. 14,15; x. 5; v. 12,19; Gal. iii. 10,12;
Eccles. vii. 29; Job xxviii. 28.—2. James i. 25; ii. 8,10-12; Rom. xiii.
8,9; Deut. v. 32; x. 4; Ex. xxxiv. 1.—3. Matt. xxii. 37-40.

This chapter begins by repeating some material from chapters VI and VII. In the beginning God imposed certain laws on
Adam. These laws are not all spelled out in the early chapters of
Genesis. In fact all that is explicitly commanded is that Adam
and Eve should propagate the race, subdue nature, cultivate
Eden, and should not eat of the tree of the knowledge of good
and evil.

It is implied, however, that Adam was to observe the Sabbath day and worship God. And, after the fall at least, he was to
offer certain sacrifices. Moreover the story of Cain and Abel
requires us to believe that God had forbidden murder. It would
seem likely therefore that God had given Adam all the Ten
Commandments. Later, after the flood, these commands were
repeated.

Now, unfortunately, among the fundamentalists a certain
group talks so as to give the impression that God gave no laws
before the days of Moses. These people divide time into several
dispensations which are distinguished by different plans of salvation. They speak of a dispensation of conscience, a later dispensation of human government; and only with Moses is the

dispensation of law supposed to begin. This dispensational view, in addition to being inconsistent with Genesis, is directly contradicted in Romans 5:13,14. These verses say, "until the law (here Paul refers to the Mosaic law) sin was in the world"; that is to say, people before the time of Moses were sinners. "But," continues Paul, "sin is not imputed where there is no law. Nevertheless (sin very obviously was imputed before the days of Moses because) death reigned from Adam to Moses, even over (infants) that had not sinned (voluntarily) after the similitude of Adam's transgression." Accordingly, there must have been law between Adam and Moses because the penalty for disobedience was exacted.

There is further evidence of a moral law imposed by God on man before and apart from the Mosaic code as such. God not only gave specific commands, such as to keep the Sabbath day and to subdue nature, but he also provided man with an innate moral endowment, referred to in Romans 1:32 and 2:15. This is the law written on the hearts of even the heathen. How extensive it was in the case of Adam is hard to say; and since the fall has defaced the image of God in man, these innate moral principles are woefully ineffective. But in a preceding chapter it was said that responsibility is based on knowledge. The heathen, who have never heard the Gospel of salvation, are nonetheless responsible for their sins because of this original endowment of knowledge which is part of the divine image in which man was created.

The dispensationalists go on and place a dispensation of grace after the dispensation of law. In this dispensation, i.e., the present age, law has no place. But once again the Scripture contradicts such a view. The three chapters of Romans where our freedom from the law of sin and death is most emphasized are far from disparaging the law. In addition to the strong insistence on the necessity of a righteous life (Rom. 6:2,6,12,15; 8:1,4,13), Paul asserts that the law is holy and good (Rom. 7:12), spiritual (7:14), a delight to the godly man (7:22), and the rule of service (7:25).

The Scriptures do not in fact speak of being free from the law, that is, from the moral law whether expressed in the Ten Commandments or elsewhere. Romans 6:18,22 speak of being free from sin. Romans 7:3 refers to a widow who is no longer bound to her deceased husband—she is free to marry again; but she is not free to commit adultery. Romans 8:2 says that one law has freed us from another law. The only sense in which we are free from the moral law is that we are free from its penalty. We are never free to disobey God's commands.

> *Section III.—Besides this law, commonly called moral, God was pleased to give to the people of Israel, as a Church under age, ceremonial laws, containing several typical ordinances: partly of worship, prefiguring Christ, his graces, actions, sufferings and benefits;[4] and partly holding forth divers instructions of moral duties.[5] All which ceremonial laws are now abrogated under the New Testament.[6]*
>
> *Section IV.—To them, also, as a body politic, he gave sundry judicial laws, which expired together with the state of that people, not obliging any other now, further than the general equity thereof may require.[7]*
>
> *Section V.—The moral law doth for ever bind all, as well justified persons as others, to the obedience thereof;[8] and that not only in regard of the matter contained in it, but also in respect of the authority of God, the Creator, who gave it.[9] Neither doth Christ in the gospel any way dissolve, but much strengthen this obligation.[10]*

4. Heb. ix. 1; Gal. iv. 1-3; Col. ii. 17.—5. 1 Cor. v. 7; 2 Cor. vi. 17; Jude 23.—6. Col. ii. 14,16,17; Dan. ix. 27; Eph. ii. 15,16.—7. Ex. xxi.; xxii. 1-29; Gen xlix. 10; 1 Pet. ii. 13,14; Matt. v. 17,38,39 ;1 Cor. ix. 8-10.—8. Rom. xiii. 8-10; Eph. vi. 2; 1 John ii. 3,4,7,8.—9. James ii. 10, 11.—10. Matt. v. 17-19; James ii. 8; Rom. iii. 31.

In addition to these pre-Mosaic laws, God gave to his chosen people a ceremonial law or ritual. These sacrifices, sacraments, and procedures were typical of the full Gospel yet to be revealed. The Church in the Old Testament was the Church as a minor; in its immaturity, though it was the heir, it was placed under a tutorship. But the tutorship was temporary. For Christ fulfilled the old types and his death did away with those preparatory sacrifices. Thus the Church in the New Testament is continuous with the Church in the Old; and since we are Christ's, we are Abraham's seed, and heirs according to the promise (Gal. 3:23; 4:7).

The Old Testament also prescribed certain civil laws for the nation of Israel. The details of these laws are not obligatory on other nations, though the principles of equity that underlie them are.

But to say that Christians are no longer subject to the moral law is to say that Christians are free to worship idols, use profanity, ignore the Lord's Day, commit murder, adultery, and theft, and to live a life that the New Testament plainly condemns (Cf. Rom. 13:8-10; I Cor. 7:19; Eph. 6:2; I John 2:3,4,7,8). Christ does not dissolve our obligation; he strengthens it (Cf. Matt. 5:19; Rom. 3:31).

> *Section VI.—Although true believers be not under the law as a covenant of works, to be thereby justified or condemned,[11] yet is it of great use to them, as well as to others: in that, as a rule of life, informing them of the will of God and their duty, it directs and binds them to walk accordingly;[12] discovering also the sinful pollutions of their nature, heart and lives;[13] so as, examining themselves thereby, they may come to further conviction of, humiliation for, and hatred against sin;[14] together with a clearer sight of the need they have of Christ, and the perfection of his obedience.[15] It is likewise of use to the regenerate, to restrain their corruptions, in that it forbids sin;[16] and the threatenings of it serve to show what even their sins deserve, and what afflictions in this life they may expect for them, although freed from the curse thereof threatened in the law.[17] The promises of it, in like manner, show them God's approbation of obedience, and what blessings they may expect upon the performance thereof,[18] although not as due to them by the law as a covenant of works;[19] so as a man's doing good, and refraining from evil, because the law encourageth to the one and deterreth from the other, is no evidence of his being under the law, and not under grace.[20]*
>
> *Section VII.—Neither are the forementioned uses of the law contrary to the grace of the gospel, but do sweetly comply with it;[21] the Spirit of Christ subduing and enabling the will of man to do that freely and cheerfully which the will of God revealed in the law requireth to be done.[22]*

11. Rom. vi. 14; Gal. ii. 16; iii. 13; iv. 4,5; Acts xiii. 39; Rom. viii. 1.—
12. Rom. vii. 12,22,25; Ps. cxix. 4-6; 1 Cor. vii. 19; Gal. v. 14,16,18-23.
—13. Rom. vii. 7; iii. 20.—14. James i. 23-25; Rom. vii. 9,14,24.—15.
Gal. iii. 24; Rom. vii. 24,25; viii. 3,4.—16. James ii. 11; Ps. cxix. 101,104,
128.—17. Ezra ix. 13,14; Ps. lxxxix. 30-34.—18. Lev. xxvi. 1-14; 2 Cor.
vi. 16; Eph. vi. 2,3; Ps. xxxvii. 11; Matt. v. 5; Ps. xix. 11.—19. Gal.

ii. 16 ; Luke xvii. 10.—20. Rom. vi. 12,14 ; 1 Pet. iii. 8-12 ; Ps. xxxiv. 12-16 ; Heb. xii. 28-29.—21. Gal. iii. 21.—22. Ezek. xxxvi. 27 ; Heb. viii, 10 ; Jer. xxxi. 33.

Section vi gives several indications of how the law is of use to Christians. Not only are there these applications to our private lives, but also anyone who has a position of responsibility in the church must pay attention to the law.

For example, a certain denomination, of which I am not a member, sponsored a Christmas service in which part of the worship (what word shall I use?) was performed by a troupe of ballet dancers. When I remarked, upon being pressed for an opinion, that ballet was a bit incongruous with divine worship, one of their ministers replied that any exercise that stimulates love of humanity is appropriate in church. Then I tried to tell him of the Puritan principle and of the law of God from which we should not turn aside, either to the right hand or to the left. And, since this minister expatiated on love versus law, I quoted "if ye love me, keep my commandments." But he concluded the conversation, politely enough, by saying that my viewpoint appeared legalistic to him.

Some ministers who prefer to be known as evangelicals rather than as liberals also attempt to substitute love for law. But they never explain how love can decide what is right and what is wrong. Does love tell us to keep the Sabbath day holy or does it tell us to watch TV in the evening? Does love tell us to tithe our income, or give more, or to give less? Is it not clear that love cannot give directions in any specific case? What is needed is law, i.e., divine precepts that are applicable to particular situations. This is not legalism. Legalism or justification by works is the unscriptural teaching that man can merit heaven by his own efforts. And it is especially strange when modernists, who have rejected the gracious sacrifice of Christ, should accuse anyone of being legalistic. But the meanings of words often get twisted these days, both in religion and in politics.

The moral law also provides principles for the conduct of our civil affairs. It does not spell out the details, but it sets limits and furnishes norms. For example, II Corinthians 12:14 teaches us that children should not lay up for their parents, but parents for their children. At first this seems to have little to do with national and state law. But does it not follow by good and necessary consequence that a nation should not accumulate an astronomical debt and pass it on to the next generation? No doubt, in time of war, as in times of emergencies in a family, the budget may be unbalanced. It is also true that in exceptional cases, cases of misfortune and tragedy, children may have to provide for their parents. But the general principle is that each generation should take care of itself and if possible hand on to the next, not debts, but assets. Thus the policy of the United States Government stands condemned as immoral and anti-Christian.

Not only in fiscal irresponsibility has the United States violated the law of God. While it was quite proper for the Supreme Court to prohibit the imposition of officially composed prayers in the schools—the prayer in question was utterly devoid of Christian sentiment—the Boards of Education and other lesser officials have seized the opportunity to harass Christian activity. The Gideons are prevented from giving New Testaments to children, though no tax money is used to buy the Testaments. The University of California prohibits Christian girls from having a house or sorority of their own. They call it religious segregation. Christian girls must be forced to live with the type that frequents the beaches of Fort Lauderdale. That is democracy. Surely a review of history teaches the evils of governmentally enforced religion. We do not want an established church. But also we do not want an established atheism. School officials who interfere with Christian activity should be relieved of their jobs.

There is a story going the rounds that a teacher saw several boys on their knees in a corner. When she came near, she saw that they were shooting craps. She breathed a sigh of relief, for she had been in mortal terror that they might have been praying.

The connection between Christian principle, the education of children, and the affairs of state is exemplified in the Air Cadet scandal of 1965. In the Air Academy at Colorado Springs there was widespread cheating on examinations. Its magnitude is clear from the fact that about one hundred cadets had to resign. They had been discovered to be morally unfit for the rank of an officer. The nation loses a hundred officers because of mass cheating. And how did this occur? Well, this wholesale dishonesty came by way

186

of the products of our public schools. The public schools are for-bidden to teach Christian standards. These young men had been raised under the influence of a materialistic, statist, godless system. Success is what counts. But this time they were not suc-cessful. They got caught. How many others in other schools are not caught?

This is the corruption that permeates our national life. From the office of the President on down there are scandals, murder, syndicates, riots and destruction of property, not to mention the much-advertised sexual decay among the fraternities and sorori-ties as they gather for their wild festivities.

Evil education has been warping American youth for years. There is no easy way to reverse the trend. Atheism and immorality are entrenched. One thing that is needed is powerful preaching of the law of God. Right is right because God commands it. Wrong is what God forbids. There is no other basis for moral distinctions. If, however, the world will not hear the preaching of righteousness, if it loves its sins as the people of Sodom did, then at least we can examine our own lives and see if there is any wicked way in us. The law of God is a lamp on our pathway and a light to our feet. By taking heed thereto a young man, and an older man too, may correct his ways.

CHAPTER XX.

OF CHRISTIAN LIBERTY
AND LIBERTY OF CONSCIENCE.

Section I.—The liberty which Christ hath purchased for believers under the gospel, consists in their freedom from the guilt of sin, the condemning wrath of God, the curse of the moral law;[1] and in their being delivered from this present evil world, bondage to Satan, and dominion of sin,[2] from the evil of afflictions, the sting of death, the victory of the grave, and everlasting damnation;[3] as also in their free access to God,[4] and their yielding obedience unto him, not out of slavish fear, but a childlike love and willing mind.[5] All which were common also to believers under the law;[6] but under the New Testament, the liberty of Christians is further enlarged in their freedom from the yoke of the ceremonial law, to which the Jewish Church was subjected,[7] and in greater boldness of access to the throne of grace,[8] and in fuller communications of the free Spirit of God than believers under the law did ordinarily partake of.[9]

1. Tit. ii. 14; 1 Thess. i. 10; Gal. iii. 13.—2. Gal. i. 4; Col. i. 13; Acts xxvi. 18; Rom. vi 14.—3. Rom. viii. 28; Ps. cxix. 71; 1 Cor. xv. 54-57; Rom. viii. 1.—4. Rom. v. 1,2.—5. Rom. viii. 14,15; 1 John iv. 18.—6. Gal. iii. 9,14—7. Gal. iv. 1-3,6,7; v. 1; Acts xv. 10,11.—8. Heb. iv. 14,16; x. 19-22.—9. John vii. 38,39; 2 Cor. iii. 13,17,18.

Freedom and liberty are grand words. Until the recent tidal wave of communism and socialism, they have been the watchwords of the American people. But the Confession is not here speaking of political liberty or the freedom from tyrannical governments. The subject is spiritual freedom. We must therefore know the meanings of our terms. To speak intelligibly, one must think logically and follow unambiguous definitions. In an earlier chapter we saw that the phrase "free from the law" had a scriptural and an unscriptural interpretation. A Christian should know the difference. Clear definitions are more useful than existential experiences.

The liberty spoken of here in section i is "the liberty which Christ has purchased"; it consists in freedom from the guilt of sin, the wrath of God, and the curse or penalty of the moral law.

It includes also free access to God in childlike love. Further than this the New Testament enlarges the liberty of believers by freeing them from the requirements of the ceremonial law. In this age we may without sin eat bacon and oysters, as the Jews could not. And while freedom from guilt and access to God are of first importance, freedom from ceremonial law involves some very practical matters of daily living. The Levitical requirements, designed as they were as pedagogical instruments, were burdensome; and the Pharisaic multiplication of them interrupted the daily schedule with nuisances at every turn. We would appreciate this freedom more, had we experienced these annoyances.

> *Section II.—God alone is Lord of the conscience,*[10] *and hath left it free from the doctrines and commandments of men which are in anything contrary to his word, or beside it, in matters of faith or worship.*[11] *So that to believe such doctrines, or to obey such commandments out of conscience, is to betray true liberty of conscience;*[12] *and the requiring of an implicit faith, and an absolute and blind obedience, is to destroy liberty of conscience and reason also.*[13]
>
> *Section III.—They who, upon pretence of Christian liberty, do practice any sin, or cherish any lust, do thereby destroy the end of Christian liberty; which is, that, being delivered out of the hands of our enemies, we might serve the Lord without fear, in holiness and righteousness before him, all the days of our life.*[14]
>
> *Section IV.—And because the powers which God hath ordained, and the liberty which Christ hath purchased, are not intended by God to destroy, but mutually to uphold and preserve one another; they who, upon pretence of Christian liberty, shall oppose any lawful power, or the exercise of it, whether it be civil or ecclesiasical, resist the ordinance of God.*[15] *And for their publishing of such opinions, or maintaining of such practices, as are contrary to the light of nature, or to the known principles of Christianity, whether concerning faith, worship or conversation; or to the power of godliness; or such erroneous opinions or practices, as either in their own nature, or in the manner of publishing or maintaining them, are destructive to the external peace and order which Christ hath established in the Church; they may lawfully be called to account, and proceeded against by the censures of the Church.*[16]

189

10. James iv. 12; Rom. xiv. 4.—11. Acts iv. 19; v. 29; 1 Cor. vii. 23; Matt. xxiii. 8-10; 2 Cor. i. 24; Matt. xv. 9.—12. Col. ii. 20,22,23; Gal. i. 10; ii. 4,5; v. 1.—13. Rom. x. 17; Rom. xiv. 23; Isa. viii. 20; Acts xvii. 11; John iv. 22; Hos. v. 11; Rev. xiii. 12,16,17; Jer. viii. 9.—14. Gal. v. 13. 1 Pet. ii. 16; 2 Pet. ii. 19; John viii. 34; Luke i. 74,75.—15. Matt. xii. 25; 1 Pet. ii. 13,14,16; Rom. xiii. 1-8; Heb. xiii. 17.—16. Rom. i. 32; 1 Cor. v. 1,5,11,13; 2 John 10,11; 2 Thess. iii. 14; 1 Tim. vi. 3-5; Tit. i. 10,11,13; iii. 10; Matt. xviii. 15-17; 1 Tim. i. 19,20; Rev. 2,14,15, 20; iii. 9.

Section ii very clearly states the principle of liberty of conscience. This is a most important and most practical element of the Protestant Reformation, for the Romanists were and are very similar to the Pharisees.

Matthew 15:9 reads, "In vain do they worship me, teaching for doctrines the commandments of men." The Pharisees had accused the disciples of Jesus of having transgressed the tradition of the elders. Indignantly Jesus asks the Pharisees why they transgress the commandments of God by their tradition. The point Jesus uses for an example is the Pharisaic method evading obedience to the fifth commandment. They allowed a man to dedicate his financial resources to God so that, although he continued to enjoy full use of his money, he did not have to take care of his aged parents.

Matthew 23 continues Jesus' indignation against the Pharisees. They laid heavy ceremonial burdens on men's shoulders. For example, they made rules as to what dishes should be washed in running water and what dishes should be washed in standing water. The Talmud is full of such regulations. It has substituted the tradition of the elders for the commandments of God.

Romanism and Anglicanism do the same thing; that is, they impose their own regulations on their people without any warrant from God's Word. Where does the Bible require us to make the sign of the cross? When did God command us to eat fish instead of meat on Fridays? Who decided that the clergy should not marry. Not only do Romish regulations go beyond Scriptural requirements, they completely reverse Scriptural precedent. For example, the Roman church forbids its members to eat breakfast before going to mass. Even when mass is permitted in the evening, a person must not have eaten within three hours. But Jesus instituted his Supper immediately after a full meal of roast lamb.

The Anglicans quite generally, after the accession of Elizabeth, reintroduced many Romish practices. For example, in the early years of Queen Elizabeth's reign a large number of ministers

190

petitioned that the sign of the cross in baptism be abolished, as well as kneeling at the Lord's Supper and bowing at the name of Jesus. The lower house of the Convocation voted 43 to 35 to grant the petition; but when the proxies were counted the superstitious practices won by a vote of 59 to 58. By a majority of one the Episcopal churches continued to sign infants with the sign of the cross in baptism.

The chief objection to these rites is that they have no warrant whatever in Scripture. They appeared as a human invention of the Patristic period along with the practice of exorcism to drive away evil spirits and of putting a mixture of milk and honey in the baby's mouth.

These and other medieval superstitions continue today in ritualistic churches. But as the Elizabethan and Jacobite church fell from the purity it had under Edward VI, some of the Reformed churches have in this century begun a similar descent.

The twentieth century church in America seems to have fallen into a curious self-contradiction. The lust for power and control over men and organizations has produced an almost papal claim to authority on the part of bureaucratic ecclesiastical officials. When the majority speaks (and the officials manipulate the majority) it is the voice of God. Yet with all this unscriptural claim to authority, the officials and their obedient servants are horrified at the thought of censuring or excommunicating a minister who denies the virgin birth or the resurrection. No doubt such a thought strikes too close to home.

Some years ago a young man presented himself to a presbytery for ordination. As he was known to believe that the boards and agencies of that church were infiltrated with modernism, he was asked whether he would support the boards and agencies. He replied that he would support them insofar as they were true to the Bible. This answer did not please presbytery, and he was asked if he would support the boards regardless of what they did. When the young man declined to make any such blind promise, the presbytery refused to ordain him.

One of his friends remarked that the difference between modernism and Christianity might be stated thus: in modernism you believe as you please but do what the officials tell you; in true

191

Presbyterianism you do as you please so long as you believe what the Confession says.

The changing majorities of a Council or General Assembly, which push a conjectural translation of the Bible one year and another year issue Sunday School lessons whose conjectures are still worse, may boast that their theology is not static, but dynamic. A different doctrine every decade—while the orthodox blockheads keep on believing the same thing all the time.

But what moral chaos there is, when the law of God is abandoned for the latest style of unbelief. It used to be Ritschl's value-judgments; now it is an encounter with paradox; next it will be—who can guess?

A very good guess is that the larger denominations are heading toward Rome in a great ecumenical union. Well-publicized gatherings of Protestant prelates parade in robes, and the press reports the colorful pageantry. Impressive imitation of popery! And the same eventual results are to be expected.

The twentieth century is a century of dictatorship and totalitarianism. As the United States has deprived its citizens of one right after another (e.g., the confiscation of gold in the thirties, the denial of free speech to management in labor troubles, etc., etc.), so too the ecclesiastical politicians seek unrestricted power. We surmise that the American members of the World Council made no protest against the idea of a state church because such a protest would have hindered the formation of a world-church organization.

So too is the now obvious rapprochement with the Roman church. Leaders who vigorously attacked the infallibility of the Bible, the Virgin Birth, the Atonement and the Resurrection, are curiously silent in the presence of idolatry and medieval superstition. A one-church world is evidently worth a little compromise.

In opposition we reject unwarranted intrusions in formal worship and church government, and in daily life also. The Confession says that God hath left us free from every human commandment that is "beside" his Word in matters of faith. This includes public worship, but it also includes any conscientious action whatever.

Strange to say, evangelicals, fundamentalists, pietists or other devout people, who would be horrified at the sign of the cross or bowing to images, have invented religious requirements and taboos

192

of their own. There is a Bible school which insists that the girls put their hair up in buns, for a looser hair-do would be "worldly." Similarly, a very evangelistic denomination in America strongly opposes lip stick. Then too an acquaintance of mine, a seminary president, staying overnight in a Texas home, suggested that the family play a game of dominoes. They were shocked! Didn't he know that dominoes was a gambling game?

There are also Christian colleges which forbid their students to go to the movies. If the argument were that the students ought to spend twenty hours reading Tolstoi's *War and Peace*, instead of seeing it in three, the prohibition might have a certain literary justification. But I am afraid this regulation did not originate in any alert English department.

Of course, there is a lot of filth in the movies, and a lot of silly nonsense too. But there are also filthy books, yet the reading of books is not prohibited. Such is the inconsistency one falls into when one decides to improve on the Bible.

These people are in general afraid of Christian liberty. They think it leads to sin. Dominoes is supposed to tempt people to gamble. Of course, such is not the case. Many families with their children have played dominoes without giving a thought to gambling. Nor does Christian liberty lead to sin. The activities objected to are not sins—they are not forbidden by Scripture.

Further, the Confession states plainly that Christian liberty must not be used as an excuse for sin, for the purpose of this liberty is "that, being delivered out of the hands of our enemies (who would glory in our flesh) we might serve the Lord without fear, in holiness and righteousness before him, all the days of our life."

CHAPTER XXI.

OF RELIGIOUS WORSHIP AND THE SABBATH-DAY.

Section I.—The light of nature showeth that there is a God, who hath lordship and sovereignty over all; is good, and doeth good unto all; and is, therefore, to be feared, loved, praised, called upon, trusted in, and served, with all the heart, and with all the soul, and with all the might.[1] But the acceptable way of worshipping the true God is instituted by himself, and so limited by his own revealed will, that he may not be worshipped according to the imaginations and devices of men, or the suggestions of Satan, under any visible representation, or any other way not prescribed in the Holy Scriptures.[2]

Section II.—Religious worship is to be given to God, the Father, Son and Holy Ghost; and to him alone:[3] not to angels, saints, or any other creature:[4] and, since the fall, not without a Mediator; nor in the mediation of any other but of Christ alone.[5]

1. Rom. i. 20; Acts xvii. 24; Ps. cxix. 68; Jer. x. 7; Ps. xxxi. 23; xvii. 3; Rom. x. 12; Ps. lxii. 8; Josh. xxiv. 14; Mark xii. 33.—2. Deut. xii. 32; Matt. xv. 9; Acts xvii. 25; Matt. iv. 9,10; Deut. xv. 1-20; Ex. xx. 4-6; Col. ii. 23.—3. Matt. iv. 10; John v. 23; 2 Cor. xiii. 14.—4. Col. ii. 18; Rev. xix. 10; Rom. i. 25.—5. John xiv. 6; 1 Tim. ii. 5; Eph. ii. 18; Col. iii. 17.

Section i says that "the acceptable way of worshiping the true God is instituted by himself, and so limited by his revealed will that he may not be worshiped according to the imaginations and devices of men . . ." This principle ought to be obvious. Who but God himself could tell us how God wants us to worship him? If an author wants a manuscript prepared for publishing, it is the author and not the typist who decides, not only the contents and the subtitles, but also the width of the margins, the precise punctuation, and (in some cases at least) the number of letters on each line.

So it is with the worship of God. It is he alone who can tell us what pleases him. Deuteronomy 12:32 says, "What thing soever I command you, that shall ye observe to do: thou shalt not add thereto nor diminish from it." This verse expresses what in church history has come to be called the Puritan principle. The

194

Puritans were so called because their aim was to purify the church of non-scriptural practices. In 1660 Charles II not only allowed such practices, but made them mandatory.

Let it be clearly understood, not all worship is pleasing to God. Read Isaiah 1:10-17. God upbraids the Israelites for sacrificing to him. He scolds them for attending the temple services. Their observance of holy days displeases him. Now, the liberals have tried to use this passage to prove a deep cleavage between priestly and prophetic religion. On the theory of the destructive critics the priests were representatives of a lower type of religion, one that depended on ritual and sacrifices. The prophets, however, were supposed to have invented a new idea of God and to have called for the abolition of sacrifice. In accord with this theory Christ's death is not to be construed as a sacrifice to propitiate the Father, but as heroism in the face of tragedy. This critical theory is patently wrong. Isaiah not only reproaches the Israelites for their sacrifices, but for their prayers as well. Can the liberals say that prayer is found only in lower forms of religion and should not be practiced in higher types? Isaiah's denunciation is not directed against prayer as such, nor against sacrifice, but against the kind of prayer and sacrifice that the Israelites were offering at that time. His point is that acceptable worship is ordered by God, and deviations from it in one direction or another is not acceptable.

Therefore, to jump the gap of many centuries, Presbyterians do not make the sign of the cross, sprinkle themselves with holy water, bow to the altar, or invent any rite not prescribed in Scripture.

For the same reason "Religious worship is to be given to God . . . alone; not to angels, saints, or any other creature." It is evident therefore how far Roman Catholicism, with its images, its prayers to the saints, and its Mariolatry, has departed from the Christian faith. Roman Catholics try to defend themselves from the charge of idolatry by saying that they do not confuse the image with the person represented and do not worship the image; they merely use the image to help them concentrate on Mary, a saint, or Christ. But if this is what it takes to have idolatry, and if idolatry can exist only when the worshiper confuses the image and the god, then we wonder whether the Ephesians who worshiped Diana were idolators. Those pagans never thought that the silver images were Diana. Diana was in heaven; she had thrown down a wooden image of herself; and the silversmiths were making reasonable facsimiles. The Romanists therefore in defending themselves from the charge of idolatry have also defended the Ephesians. The worship of the two groups is essentially the same; they both do what the Scriptures prohibit. Similarly the Roman exaltation of Mary as immaculately conceived, as Queen of Heaven, and as co-redemptrix is not less than blasphemy. Again they defend themselves by making a scholastic distinction: they worship (*latreuein*) God alone, they give *doulia* to the saints and *hyperdoulia* to Mary. But the Scriptures make no such distinction. *Doulos* is the word Paul most frequently uses to express his relationship to God.

It is lamentable to note that Protestants are beginning to imitate Romish idolatry. One day I visited a Baptist seminary that makes some claim to being conservative and evangelical. In the building was a small prayer room. I saw there a railing, a kneeling pad in front of it, and on the wall behind it a large picture of Christ. The arrangements were such that the students were supposed to kneel facing the picture and pray to it.

One also wonders how many Protestants have accepted St. Christopher medals so that St. Christopher would protect them from accidents as they drive 80 mph over the turnpike.

> *Section III.—Prayer with thanksgiving, being one special part of religious worship,[6] is by God required of all men;[7] and, that it may be accepted, it is to be made in the name of the Son,[8] by the help of his Spirit,[9] according to his will,[10] with understanding, reverence, humility, fervency, faith, love and perseverance;[11] and, if vocal, in a known tongue.[12]*

> *Section IV.—Prayer is to be made for things lawful,[13] and for all sorts of men living, or that shall live hereafter;[14] but not for the dead,[15] nor for those of whom it may be known that they have sinned the sin unto death.[16]*

6. Phil. iv. 6.—7. Ps. lxv. 2.—8. John xiv. 13,14; 1 Pet. ii. 5.—9. Rom. viii. 26.—10. 1 John v. 14.—11. Ps. xlvii. 7; Eccles. v. 1,2; Heb. xii. 28; Gen. xviii. 27; James v. 16; i. 6,7; Mark xi. 24; Matt. vi. 12,14,15; Col. iv. 2; Eph. vi. 18.—12. 1 Cor. xiv. 14.—13. 1 John v. 14.—14. 1 Tim. ii 1,2; John xvii. 20; 2 Sam. vii. 29; Ruth iv. 12.—15. 2 Sam. xii. 21-23; Luke xvi. 25.26; Rev. xiv. 13.—16. 1 John v. 16.

Sections iii and iv speak about prayer. Prayer is a divine requirement, and in church services, session and presbytery meetings the requirement is uniformly observed—at least formally. In the meetings of the smaller denominations which I have attended, these prayers have been utterly sincere. In other places they may be perfunctory. Combined worship services have occurred, in which a Roman priest, a Jewish rabbi, and a Protestant minister have participated, and perhaps a Buddhist or Mohammedan also, and in which something called prayer is spoken, but without a single reference to Christ. To be acceptable to God, however, prayer must be offered in the name of Christ.

Does this mean that every prayer must close with the words, in the name of Christ, Amen? Another question: on the inside face of an imposing gateway to the grounds and buildings of a fraternal organization, so that everyone could see it as he left the grounds, was a large inscription, Allah Be Praised. Do you think the prayers of that place were acceptable to God?

For what may we legitimately pray? For health? For wealth? For a charmed life? For whom may we pray? For the President? For the Communists? For the dead? If the dead person is in heaven, does he need our prayers? If in hell, would our prayers be of any use? And is there a purgatory that is neither heaven nor hell? Where is purgatory mentioned in the Bible?

The Confession also says, in conformity with I John 5:16, that we should not pray for anyone whom we know to have sinned unto death. The writer wishes he knew what the verse means and how to apply it. He does not, and proceeds to the next point.

Section V.—The reading of the Scriptures with godly fear;[17] the sound preaching,[18] and conscionable hearing of the Word, in obedience unto God, with understanding, faith, and reverence;[19] singing of psalms with grace in the heart;[20] as also the due administration and worthy receiving of the sacraments instituted by Christ; are all parts of the ordinary religious worship of God:[21] besides religious oaths,[22] and vows,[23] solemn fastings[24] and thanksgivings upon special occasions,[25] which are, in their several times and seasons, to be used in an holy and religious manner.[26]

Section VI.—Neither prayer, nor any other part of religious worship, is, now under the gospel, either tied

197

*unto, or made more acceptable by, any place in which
it is performed, or toward which it is directed:*[27] *but God
is to be worshipped everywhere,*[28] *in spirit and in
truth;*[29] *as in private families,*[30] *daily,*[31] *and in secret
each one by himself;*[32] *so more solemnly in the public assemblies, which are not carelessly or willfully to be neglected or forsaken, when God, by his word or providence,
calleth thereunto.*[33]

17. Acts. xv. 21; Rev. i. 3.—18. 2 Tim. iv. 2.—19. James i. 22; Acts x.
33; Matt. xiii. 19; Heb. iv. 2; Isa. lxvi. 2.—20. Col. iii. 16; Eph. v. 19;
James v. 13.—21. Matt. xxviii. 19; 1 Cor. xi. 23-29; Acts ii. 42.—22.
Deut. vi. 13; Neh. x. 29.—23. Isa. xix. 21; Eccles. v. 4,5.—24. Joel. ii.
12; Esth. iv. 15; Matt. ix. 15; 1 Cor. vii. 5.—25. Ps. cvii; Esth. ix. 22.
—26. Heb. xii. 28.—27. John iv. 21.—28. Mal. i. 11; 1 Tim. ii. 8.—29.
John iv. 23,24.—30. Jer. x. 25; Deut. xi. 6,7; Job i. 5; 2 Sam. vi. 18-20;
1 Pet. iii. 7; Acts x. 2.—31. Matt. vi. 11.—32. Matt. vi. 6; Eph. vi.
18.—33. Isa. lvi. 6,7; Heb. x. 25; Prov. i. 20,21,24; viii. 34; Acts xiii. 42;
Luke iv. 16; Acts ii. 42.

Although sessions, presbyteries, mission boards and the like
are careful to offer prayer at every meeting, one may ask if they
are equally careful to read the Scriptures. Reading the Scriptures
and the preaching of a sermon are parts of ordinary corporate
worship. In the Synod of our denomination there is always a
sermon. Then the Synod as such recesses and the various boards
meet. In these meetings there is prayer, but no sermon. Obviously there must be a time for business as well as for public
worship. The local congregations, of course, exist chiefly for the
purpose of public worship and at all regular meetings should engage in prayer, praise, reading and preaching the Word, as well
as at stated intervals administering the sacraments. On special
occasions there may be fasting, special vows, or covenants made,
or whatever is required in conformity to the Biblical commands.

Where these elements of worship are performed is immaterial.
It is not necessary to go up to Jerusalem to pay our vows. Nor
need we face the east to repeat the Apostles' Creed. After all, we
are not Mohammedans.

*Section VII.—As it is of the law of nature that,
in general, a due proportion of time be set apart for the
worship of God; so, in his word, by a positive, moral,
and perpetual commandment, binding all men in all ages,
he hath particularly appointed one day in seven for a
Sabbath, to be kept holy unto him;*[34] *which, from the beginning of the world to the resurrection of Christ, was
the last day of the week; and, from the resurrection of
Christ, was changed into the first day of the week,*[35]

198

which in Scripture is called the Lord's day,[36] and is to be continued to the end of the world as the Christian Sabbath.[37]

Section VIII.—This Sabbath is then kept holy unto the Lord, when men, after a due preparing of their hearts, and ordering of their common affairs beforehand, do not only observe an holy rest all the day from their own works, words and thoughts about their worldly employments and recreations;[38] but also are taken up the whole time in the public and private exercises of his worship, and in the duties of necessity and mercy.[39]

34. Ex. xx. 8,10,11; Isa. lvi. 2,4,6,7.—35. Gen. ii. 2,3; 1 Cor. xvi. 1,2; Acts xx. 7.—36. Rev. i. 10.—37. Ex. xx. 8,10; Matt. v. 17,18.—38.Ex. xx. 8; xvi. 23,25,26,29,30; xxxi. 15-17; Isa. lviii. 13; Neh. xiii. 15-19,21,22.—39. Isa. lviii. 13; Matt. xii. 1-13.

Although the place of worship is immaterial, and although worship may be offered to God at any time, God has set apart a special time in which worship is obligatory. From the creation of Adam the calendar has been arranged in seven-day weeks, and God commanded Adam to keep the seventh day holy in commemoration of God's completion of his creative work.

With the resurrection of Christ the day of rest and worship was changed from the seventh to the first day of the week. Who changed it? The Roman church claims to have authorized the change; and the Seventh Day Adventists refuse to worship on the first day because the Roman church had no authority to change God's command.

However, while some imperial edict of the fourth century may be cited as authorizing this change, the change was made not by any emperor or pope, but by the immediate disciples of Christ. I Corinthians 16:2 says, "Upon the first day of the week, let every one of you lay by him in store as God hath prospered him, that there be no gatherings when I come." A Seventh Day Adventist told me that this did not indicate any offering at a service on the first day of the week, but on the contrary meant that on the first day each worshiper was to put aside what he intended to give the next seventh day. But consider: if a man is paid his wages at the end of the working week—Friday night—and then worships on Saturday, it seems strange to admonish him to put aside his offering on the next morning.

From Acts 20:7 we know that the Christian worship service, including communion, took place on the first day of the week.

This day was called the Lord's Day, as we may infer from Revelation 1:10. Thus the New Testament makes it perfectly clear that the Christians did not observe the seventh day for three hundred years to change only upon a fourth century imperial or papal edict.

As to how the first day should be kept holy has been a point of disagreement among professing Christians. The Roman church with its looser morals has prohibited "servile labor" on the Lord's Day, but has generally encouraged all manner of sports. So long as a person attends mass in the early morning, he can treat the rest of the day pretty much as he treats the other days of the week. The Lutherans have not been much stricter. The French Reformed have been more careful, though in Switzerland I observed the young men of a conservative group playing football before the morning worship service. The Director of the Bible School, at which the service was held, explained that the young people needed social contacts.

The English and especially the Scottish Reformed were much stricter. Not only did they object to servile labor, but also to "such worldly employments and recreations as are lawful on other days" (Shorter Catechism, 60).

Irreligious people have heaped a great deal of contempt upon John Knox and the Presbyterian "Sabbatarians." They have in particular been compared with the Pharisees, who added non-scriptural restrictions to the divine law. Unlike the Pharisees, however, John Knox was not a hypocrite. He may have been inconsistently strict, for it is hard to say that shaving desecrates the day any more than washing one's hands or brushing one's teeth does.

But the faults of those who were too strict do not exonerate those who are too lax; and no one can deny that this age errs on the side of laxity. I know one man and wife who could not come to church because that was just the time they had to walk their dog. Again, many fundamentalists who refuse to play dominoes or go to the movies or use lipstick on any day of the week contend that keeping the Sabbath is legalistic and have no compunctions against going on a picnic or studying their high school or college lessons. They have made their own rules without any divine warrant, while at the same time they reject the Ten Commandments. Note well, if keeping the Sabbath holy is legalistic, a ritualistic requirement meant only for the Mosaic dispensation, then not only is the Sabbath before Moses inexplicable, but also the first, second, sixth and other commandments are ritualistic too. These other commandments are obviously not ritualistic, and it is hard to see how with that context the fourth alone could be such.

Another attack on the Christian Sabbath and on Christianity looms on the horizon. The advocates of calendar reform propose to abolish the regular sequence of seven-day weeks. Their recent proposal is to have every week begin on a Monday and to put a Sunday at the end of the week. This is just a nasty way of expressing contempt for the day of Resurrection, but by itself it would cause no religious hardship. The anti-Christian part of the proposal is to insert a day at the end of each year, which would be neither a Sunday, Monday, Tuesday, nor any other week day. The result of such an arrangement would be as follows: the year would end on a Sunday; then comes the No-Day; then comes Monday. Hence the following Sunday would be eight days after the previous Sunday, instead of seven. A Christian then would be required to worship on Saturdays that year, on Fridays the following year, and so on, with all the economic penalty and social hostility an atheistic nation would impose on this obedience to God.

Perhaps a more immediate danger lies in Senator Dirksen's anti-Christian proposal to hold national elections on the Lord's Day. This would be an effective way of disfranchising Christians. Apparently the time of the antichrist is approaching.

CHAPTER XXII.

OF LAWFUL OATHS AND VOWS.

Section I.—*A lawful oath is a part of religious worship,[1] wherein, upon just occasion, the person swearing solemnly calleth God to witness what he asserteth or promiseth; and to judge him according to the truth or falsehood of what he sweareth.[2]*

Section II.—*The name of God only is that by which men ought to swear, and therein it is to be used with all holy fear and reverence:[3] therefore to swear vainly or rashly by that glorious and dreadful name, or to swear at all by any other thing, is sinful, and to be abhorred.[4] Yet as, in matters of weight and moment, an oath is warranted by the word of God under the New Testament as well as under the Old;[5] so a lawful oath being imposed by a lawful authority, in such matters, ought to be taken.[6]*

Section III.—*Whosoever taketh an oath, ought duly to consider the weightiness of so solemn an act, and therein to avouch nothing but what he is fully persuaded is the truth.[7] Neither may any man bind himself by oath to anything but what is good and just, and what he believeth so to be, and what he is able and resolved to perform.[8] Yet it is a sin to refuse an oath touching anything that is good and just, being imposed by lawful authority.[9]*

Section IV.—*An oath is to be taken in the plain and common sense of the words, without equivocation or mental reservation.[10] It cannot oblige to sin; but in anything not sinful, being taken, it binds to performance, although to a man's own hurt;[11] nor is it to be violated, although made to heretics or infidels.[12]*

1. Deut. x. 20.—2. Ex. xx. 7; Lev. xix. 12; 2 Cor. i. 23; 2 Chron. vi. 22,23.—3. Deut. vi. 13.—4. Ex. xx. 7; Jer. v. 7; Matt. v. 34,37; James v. 12.—5. Heb. vi. 16; 2 Cor. i. 23; Isa. lxv. 16.—6. 1 Kings viii. 31; Neh. xiii. 25; Ezra x. 5.—7. Ex. xx. 7; Jer. iv. 2.—8. Gen. xxiv. 2,3,5, 6,8,9.—9. Num. v. 19,21; Neh. v. 12; Ex. xxii. 7-11.—10. Jer. iv. 2; Ps. xxiv. 4.—11.1 Sam. xxv. 22,32-34; Ps. xv. 4.—12. Ezek. xvii. 16,18, 19; Josh. ix. 18,19; 2 Sam. xxi. 1.

In the courts of the United States oaths are frequently administered. The procedure is perfunctory, and many people only calculate whether they can be actually convicted of perjury. Three hundred years ago an oath was so awesome that some people had religious scruples against taking an oath for any reason. So great was their conviction, that governments deferred to their conscientious scruples and provided for solemn affirmations as a substitute for oaths. Governments today are more likely to view such people as anti-social, as fanatics, as divisive, whose scruples should be brutally trod upon.

The Presbyterians did not agree that God prohibits oaths, indeed they held that on certain occasions one is under obligation to take an oath.

It is clear that the Old Testament approves of oaths on proper occasions. Deuteronomy 6:13 reads, "Thou shalt fear Jehovah thy God; him shalt thou serve, and shalt swear by his name." The third commandment does not forbid swearing, but forbids swearing "in vain." This would include trivial, useless oaths, as well as swearing falsely. Swearing is therefore a religious act. The secularists in the United States, who wish to eradicate Christianity, naturally oppose the use of oaths in courts and in the inauguration of officials. But' the fact that oaths have had their place since the founding of the nation shows that the kind of separation of church from state so popularly propounded today is not what the constitution intended.

An oath is not merely an assertion that the person realizes he is speaking in the presence of God. Rather an oath is a specific appeal to God's penal justice against everyone who deliberately lies. In Joshua 22 there is an account of the building of an altar by the children of Reuben. The other Israelites accused the Reubenites of building this altar to a foreign god in order to rebel against the Lord. But the Reubenites answered: "The Lord God of gods, he knoweth—and Israel shall know—if it be in rebellion, or if in transgression against the Lord, save us not this day . . . let the Lord himself require it." Thus the Reubenites invite God's curse upon themselves, if they have spoken or acted falsely.

At this point someone may wonder whether oaths are allowed by the New Testament or whether they are an Old Testament practice only. Such a person may recall the words of Jesus, "Swear not at all" (Matt. 5:35-37). The wording, however, seems to refer to swearing about trivial matters in the day by day routine. There are some people who are constantly swearing—I do not mean cursing or profanity—but constantly swearing that their ordinary statements are true. The Pharisees were such people. Jesus is rebuking this thoughtless habit. But that he did not intend to prohibit all oaths is obvious from his own conduct.

In his trial in court Jesus refused to answer a number of questions. Then "the high priest . . . said unto him, 'I adjure thee by the living God, that thou tell us whether thou be the Christ, the Son of God!' Jesus saith unto him, Thou hast said [i.e., Yes, I am]; nevertheless (but, except that) . . . later on you shall see the Son of man sitting on the right hand of power and coming in the clouds of heaven."

That was quite an oath, wasn't it!

Section iii teaches that a man may not bind himself by an oath to anything evil or unjust; and section iv repeats the idea by saying that an oath cannot oblige us to sin. Sometimes people, in ignorance, perhaps, swear to do something sinful. The taking of such an oath is itself sinful; the breaking of it is not.

For example, the Roman church permits its members to marry Protestants, if the Protestant will promise to bring up the children as Catholics. This promise should be broken, for it is a sin to teach children to be idolators. Of course, the promise should not have been made in the first place. There is where the sin occurred. Unfortunately there are so many ways for teen-agers to ruin their lives before they have enough knowledge and character to understand and solve their problems. It is the business of a faithful church to see that its children are properly instructed.

Section V.—A vow is of the like nature with a promissory oath, and ought to be made with the like religious care, and to be performed with the like faithfulness.[13]

Section VI.—It is not to be made to any creature, but to God alone;[14] and that it may be accepted, it is to be made voluntarily, out of faith and conscience of duty, in way of thankfulness for mercy received, or for the obtaining of what we want; whereby we more strictly bind ourselves to necessary duties or to other things, so far and so long as they may fitly conduce thereunder.[15]

Section VII.—No man may vow to do anything forbidden in the word of God, or what would hinder any

204

duty therein commanded, or which is not in his own power, and for the performance whereof he hath no promise of ability from God.[16] In which respects popish monastical vows of perpetual single life, professed poverty, and regular obedience, are so far from being degrees of higher perfection, that they are superstitious and sinful snares, in which no Christian may entangle himself.[17]

13. Isa. xix. 21; Eccles. v. 4-6; Ps. lxi. 8; lxvi. 13,14.—14. Ps. lxxvi. 11; Jer. xliv. 25,26.—15. Deut. xxiii. 21-23; Ps. l. 14; Gen. xxviii. 20-22; 1 Sam. i. 11; Ps. lxvi. 13,14; cxxxii. 2-5.—16. Acts xxiii. 12,14; Mark vi. 26; Num. xxx. 5,8,12,13.—17. Matt. xix. 11,12; 1 Cor. vii. 2,9; Eph. iv. 28; 1 Pet. iv. 2; 1 Cor. vii. 23.

Religiously a vow is essentially of the same nature of an oath. It differs by being taken with reference to some private matter, instead of being imposed by a public court of justice. As section vii says, no man may vow to disobey God's commands, nor may he vow anything that would hinder obedience to the Biblical precepts. Because the vows of monkery are sinful, Luther was justified in breaking those vows.

The Scripture references attached to these sections will provide interesting detailed information on the taking of vows.

Even vows which are not promises to commit sin may be foolish. For example, one may vow to walk around the block five times for the next five days as an expression of thanksgiving to God for the gift of good health. Such a vow, when taken, should be observed with scrupulous care; but there are better ways to thank God for health. If one forms a habit of making foolish vows, it is more than likely that spiritual decay will set in. The multiplication of self-imposed duties is a form of will-worship, like one's hair in a bun and not using lipstick, which the Apostle condemns. The best procedure would be to follow the example of the Covenanters, who in times of great moment bound themselves by a common vow to discharge duties that God had already imposed on them.

CHAPTER XXIII.

OF THE CIVIL MAGISTRATE.

Section I.—God, the supreme Lord and King of all the world, hath ordained civil magistrates to be under him over the people, for his own glory and the public good; and to this end, hath armed them with the power of the sword, for the defence and encouragement of them that are good, and for the punishment of evil-doers.[1]

Section II.—It is lawful for Christians to accept and execute the office of a magistrate, when called thereunto;[2] in the managing whereof, as they ought especially to maintain piety, justice and peace, according to the wholesome laws of each commonwealth;[3] so, for that end, they may lawfully, now under the New Testament, wage war upon just and necessary occasions.[4]

1. Rom. xiii. 1-4; 1 Pet. ii. 13,14.—2. Prov. viii. 15,16; Rom. xiii. 1,2,4.—3. Ps. ii. 10-12; 1 Tim. ii. 2; Ps. lxxii. 3,4; 2 Sam. xxiii. 3; 1 Pet. ii. 13.—4. Luke iii. 14; Rom. xiii. 4; Matt. viii. 9,10; Acts x. 1,2; Rev. xvii. 14,16.

Godless people outside the Church of Christ, if by chance they should ever read the preceding chapters on the mediator, effectual calling, the perseverance of the saints, and so on, would consider the topics trivial, or even nonsense, and the reading tedious. These people dismiss all spiritual matters as "irrelevant." They mean irrelevant to their low materialistic interests. Politics however, is not irrelevant, even to these people, and especially to these people. Politics touches many points of our daily living: our pocketbook is affected by heavy taxes and restrictions on business; our safety also is affected in matters of war and when criminals roam the city streets.

Politics also affects religion. When dictator Franco and the Roman church attempt to force American military and civilian personnel stationed in Spain to beg permission of a Roman bishop in order to marry one another, a Christian and the secularist too ought to sit up and take notice of what is going on, not just in Spain, but in Washington.

Many non-Christians are also interested in the moral problems of war, pacifism, crime, and capital punishment. On these subjects the Westminster Confession has something to say, and it would not harm the secularist to know what it is.

Any conclusion relative to war, capital punishment, the relation of church and state, and taxes too, depends on some theory of civil government. By what right does a government exist? Does a government have any right to exist? Rousseau wrote, "Man is born free; and everywhere he is in chains. . . . How did this change come about? I do not know. What can make it legitimate? That question I think I can answer." Rousseau then proceeds to defend a theory of government in which Christians can be legitimately banished or executed as anti-social enemies of the state.

John Locke has a somewhat different theory, which on the surface at least seems to be less brutal than Rousseau's. An ancient theory tried to explain the state as a development from the family. The Bible and the Confession base state authority on its divine ordination. This is not to be confused with the divine right of kings, nor does it grant government unlimited or totalitarian powers. But it does establish government on right and not on brute force.

In another volume I have analyzed several of the secular theories of the state and have attempted to make clear that the social contract theory, either in Rousseau's form or in Locke's form, and all other secular theories as well, are in the final analysis simply assertions of brute force. My thesis is that secularism necessarily implies dictatorship and totalitarian rule. For example, Aristotle pointedly objects to Plato's communism; but his own theory defines the state as the partnership or "community" which includes all partnerships, and the good of the state as the good which includes all goods. The result is state control of religion and of all human good, nothing excepted.

It is only the Hebrew-Christian revelation, as exemplified in the condemnation of King Ahab's violation of Naboth's private property, that justifies both the authority of a state and the limitations on that authoriy.

The Confession in section i states that it is God who has ordained civil magistrates. Their authority comes from him; therefore, they cannot rightfully act as dictators; their just powers are only those which God has assigned them. What those powers are and what they are not is indicated here and there throughout the

Bible; and appeals to the Bible must settle such questions as pacifism and capital punishment, as well as the principle of private property.

This chapter of the Confession in its first sentence asserts that God has armed the state with the power of the sword. Such is the Bible's position on war. Even Christian pacifists, whom in spite of their lovely character we believe to have misunderstood the Bible, cannot claim that the Old Testament forbids war. In fact God explicitly commanded war. Has then God given a different commandment in the New Testament? Since he abrogated the food laws, he might have changed his orders on this point too. But as a matter of fact he did not. Christ said, "Render unto Caesar the things that are Caesar's." Of course, the immediate reference was taxes, but Christ knew that Caesar had an army. He did not refuse to pay taxes to Rome on the ground that some of the tribute would be used to support that army. Yet in the United States today some people think it a Christian duty to refuse to follow Christ's teaching and example. They would rather go to jail than to pay one penny to support the military. Of course, in Christ's statement war is not explicitly mentioned—it is an inference, howbeit a justifiable inference, we believe. But the New Testament provides more than an inference. In Romans 13:4 the power of the sword is explicitly assigned to civil government. This disposes of pacifism, and if the relatively juster governments of the West had been willing to wage war against international criminals, the lives of twenty million Chinese, Koreans, and Russians might have been saved. And the United States would have been in a much safer position today.

In addition to the unscriptural agitation in favor of pacifism, there is also a great clamor against capital punishment. Secular humanism propounds the theory that the state has no right to punish anybody for anything. The police, the courts, and the prisons exist only for the purpose of rehabilitation. Secular humanism is devoid of any sense of justice. The criminal is regarded not as a criminal, but as a sick man who needs hospitalization. Since capital punishment obviously does not rehabilitate, life imprisonment must be substituted for it.

Of course by life imprisonment these humanists do not mean life imprisonment. The Indiana Legislature of 1965, as it voted to abolish capital punishment, defeated an amendment that would have kept the murderer in jail for life, and provided that he may be paroled after seven years. So, after seven years the murderer is free to kill again.

Subsidiary to the main theological objection to such a system of penology, there are some practical objections. First and obviously a policy of easy parole soon sets the murderer free to murder again. But what is worse, the abolition of capital punishment may prevent any conviction at all. Whether it be the case of an habitual criminal on parole committing a felony, or whether it be the case of a man committing his first murder, the criminal is encouraged to kill the arresting officer or other witnesses to his crime. He has everything to gain and nothing to lose. The murder of the witnesses precludes their testifying in court. The murder of the officer frees the criminal from arrest. This is all pure gain to the criminal. But if perchance he is caught after these additional murders, he faces no greater penalty than if he had not committed them—just a few more years in jail with a chance of escape or parole. No wonder the wives of policemen ask for the retention of the death penalty.

However, the main objections to substituting seven years rehabilitation for the death penalty are theological and religious rather than practical. The anti-christian humanist has no sense of justice. He does not believe that man was created in the image of God; therefore he sees murder as only an offence against society and not as an offence against God. Without a sense of justice, his sympathies lie with the criminal rather than with his victims. Therefore he wants to do away with all penalties and substitute rehabilitation.

The Scripture is very clear on the subject and very clearly in opposition to this secularistic theory. The general principle is that man was created in the image of God, so that anyone who commits murder loses his right to live. Genesis 9:6 reads, "Whoso sheddeth man's blood, by man shall his blood be shed; for in the image of God made he man."

The New Testament also arms the state with the power of the sword and expressly rules out rehabilitation as the main motive in punishing crime. Read Romans 13:4 very carefully: "If thou do that which is evil, be afraid; for he beareth not the sword in vain;

for he is a minister of God, a revenger (not a rehabilitator) to execute wrath upon him that doeth evil."

The relation of church to state is another lively issue at the present time. Where the Roman church controls the government, Protestants suffer oppression and physical persecution. Our churches are bombed and our ministers are murdered. The Greek church, a part of the World Council, has caused the arrest and is prosecuting Protestants for distributing New Testaments. In our own land the Romanists are constantly attempting to divert public funds to their own purposes. A while back they were advocating an ambassador to the Vatican, and will probably push it again when they see an opportunity. In New Mexico, that is, in the United States, Protestant Indians have been denied by court order the right to hold Protestant prayer meetings even in their own homes. (Cf. *United Evangelical Action*, February 1, 1954, p. 18). And bills have been introduced into Congress to honor the Virgin Mary by issuing commemorative stamps for the Marian year.

Unfortunately there are also Protestants who want a close tie-in of church and state. Some of the large denominations support lobbies for socialist legislation. But what is worse, there are those who want the state to define the articles of religion. For example, the North Rocky Mount Baptist church, in North Carolina, by majority vote, withdrew from the Southern Baptist Convention. As to the issues involved and the wisdom of their withdrawal, I have nothing to say. It is their legal right to withdraw that is the important point. The minority went to court and the court awarded them the property. The judge claimed that he did not rule on religious beliefs. But the court defined what a church is, and held that a Baptist church could not withdraw from the Convention and be independent. Now, certainly, the definition of the church is a religious belief on which denominations differ. The Baptists, contrary to the Presbyterians, have always held to independency and have claimed there is no ecclesiastical authority superior to the local congregation. But the news reports say that the North Carolina supreme court has made it illegal for Baptists to conduct their affairs in accordance with Baptist doctrine. In spite of the fact that the minority has won a legal case in favor of the Southern Baptist Convention, we wonder whether the Convention in good conscience can accept the verdict. Will they insist on retaining the local

210

property at the cost of having their beliefs on the nature of the church settled by the civil government?

It is also interesting to note that the socialistic *Christian Century* hailed the decision of the court. This radical periodical wants uniformity and ecumenicity enforced by civil decree when possible. The ecumenicists generally favor centralization of power; they want to control property; they do not object to state churches, or even to the Greek persecution of evangelicals. These medieval ways may cause the demise of Protestantism and its return to Rome.

Section III.—Civil magistrates may not assume to themselves the administration of the word and sacraments;[5] or, the power of the keys of the kingdom of heaven;[6] or, in the least, interfere in matters of faith.[7] Yet as nursing fathers, it is the duty of civil magistrates to protect the Church of our common Lord, without giving the preference to any denomination of Christians above the rest, in such a manner that all ecclesiastical persons whatever shall enjoy the full, free and unquestioned liberty of discharging every part of their sacred functions, without violence or danger.[8] And, as Jesus Christ hath appointed a regular government and discipline in his Church, no law of any commonwealth should interfere with, let or hinder, the due exercise thereof, among the voluntary members of any denomination of Christians, according to their own profession and belief.[9] It is the duty of civil magistrates to protect the person and good name of all their people, in such an effectual manner as that no person be suffered, either upon pretence of religion or infidelity, to offer any indignity, violence, abuse or injury to any other person whatsoever: and to take order, that all religious and ecclesiastical assemblies be held without molestation or disturbance.[10]

Section IV.—It is the duty of people to pray for magistrates,[11] to honour their persons,[12] to pay them tribute and other dues,[13] to obey their lawful commands, and to be subject to their authority, for conscience' sake.[14] Infidelity, or difference in religion, doth not make void the magistrate's just and legal authority nor free the people from their due obedience to him;[15] from which ecclesiastical persons are not exempted;[16] much less hath the Pope any power or jurisdiction over them in their dominions, or over any of their people; and least

211

of all to deprive them of their dominions or lives, if he shall judge them to be heretics, or upon any other pretence whatsoever.[17]

5. 2 Chron. xxvi. 18.—6. Matt. xvi. 19.—7. John xviii. 36.—8. Isa. xlix. 23.—9. Ps. cv. 15.—10. 2 Sam. xxiii. 3; 1 Tim. ii. 1; Rom. xiii. 4.—11. 1 Tim. ii. 1,2.—12. 1 Pet. ii. 17.—13. Rom. xiii. 6,7.—14. Rom. xiii. 5; Tit. iii 1.—15. 1 Pet. ii. 13,14,16.—16. Rom. xiii. 1; 1 Kings ii. 35; Acts xxv. 9-11; 2 Pet. ii. 1,10,11; Jude 8-11.—17. 2 Thess. ii. 4; Rev. xiii. 15-17.

At the time of the Reformation the state, in Protestant countries, was looked to for protection against Roman persecution. It was natural therefore to assign to the states some prerogatives that later reflection has judged improper. Section iii of this chapter does not appear here as originally written. Its original form said, "The civil magistrate . . . hath authority, and it is his duty to take order, that unity and peace be preserved in the Church, that the truth of God be kept pure and entire, that all blasphemies and heresies be suppressed, all corruptions and abuses in worship and discipline prevented or reformed, and all the ordinances of God duly settled, administered and observed. For the better effecting whereof he hath power to call synods, to be present at them, and to provide that whatsoever is transacted in them be according to the mind of God."

When the Confession was written there was a strong Erastian party in England, which held that the Church was nothing more than a department of the state. The original Confession was not intended in favor of Erastianism, and in fact the Erastians argued against the section as adopted. Yet it seems today that the original section was still too Erastian. It would mean that the President of the United States could call a meeting of the General Assembly, decide what is the mind of God, and approve or veto the acts of the Assembly. If we mention by name some of the recent Presidents, the incongruity of such an arrangement would be apparent.

In England, where the Anglican Church is essentially Erastian, the incongruity is actualized in the fact that the established church cannot alter its Prayer Book except by a vote of Parliament, most of whose members are not Anglicans; and similarly bishops are appointed by a Prime Minister who might be glad if there were no church at all.

In the United States the separation of church and state has been almost universally accepted. Unfortunately this principle is in danger of becoming misunderstood and transformed into something very different. Ever since the time of Emperor Constantine civil governments have intermeddled in ecclesiastical affairs, and the temptation is now reviving. Our Confession states that the civil officials are not to give preference to any denomination of Christians above the others. The Constitution of the United States forbids Congress to enact any law establishing a religion or preventing the free exercise of religion. Well and good. Let us keep it this way. But the secularists wish to alter this principle so as to use the civil government for the purpose of hindering and eventually suppressing Christianity. Public education, grants from certain Foundations, and UNESCO not only eliminate all Christian teaching but actively teach secularism. The state universities are beginning to ban Christian organizations from their campuses. In the elementary schools Christian textbooks are prohibited, but anti-Christian textbooks are adopted and imposed on the children over the protests of local Christians. And William Heard Kilpatrick, who has taught 35,000 public school teachers, declares that it is undemocratic (and therefore should be banned by the government) to allow parents to teach their children the principles of their own religion.

Other instances of governmental interference in religious affairs include the closing of Amish schools, for Amish ideals of life are different from secular ideals; and the confiscation of the horses of Amish farmers because the Amish, being religiously opposed to any form of insurance, refused to pay Social Security. Also, there are cases of courts ordering blood transfusions to be performed on people whose religion is opposed to such an operation.

The Confession states that "no law of any commonwealth should interfere with, let or hinder, the due exercise (of religious freedom) among the voluntary members of any denomination of Christians, according to their own profession and belief." One side of the coin is separation of church and state; the other side is a true freedom, not merely a grudging toleration, of religion.

213

CHAPTER XXIV.

OF DIVORCE AND MARRIAGE.

Section I.—Marriage is to be between one man and one woman: neither is it lawful for any man to have more than one wife, nor for any woman to have more than one husband at the same time.[1]

Section II.—Marriage was ordained for the mutual help of husband and wife,[2] *for the increase of mankind with a legitimate issue and of the Church with an holy seed*[3] *and for preventing of uncleanness.*[4]

Section III.—It is lawful for all sorts of people to marry who are able with judgment to give their consent;[5] *yet it is the duty of Christians to marry only in the Lord.*[6] *And therefore such as profess the true reformed religion should not marry with infidels, Papists or other idolators; neither should such as are godly be unequally yoked, by marrying with such as are notoriously wicked in their life or maintain damnable heresies.*[7]

1. Gen. ii. 24; Matt. xix. 6,7; Prov. ii. 17.—2. Gen. ii. 18.—3. Mal. ii. 15.—4. 1 Cor. vii. 2,9.—5. Heb. xiii. 4; 1 Tim. iv. 3; 1 Cor. vii. 36-38; Gen. xxiv. 57,58.—6. 1 Cor. vii. 30.—7. Gen. xxxiv. 14; Ex. xxiv. 16; Deut. vii. 3,4; 1 Kings xi. 4; Neh. iii. 25-27; Mal. ii. 11-12; 2 Cor. 14.

The forms used in wedding ceremonies usually state that marriage is an honorable estate, instituted by God in the time of man's innocency, which estate Christ adorned with his first miracle, and is commended by the Apostle Paul.

In the case of Adam and Eve it is obvious that marriage was instituted between one man and one woman. Deuteronomy 17:17 gives the command: "Neither shall he | a coming king, and by implication all his people | multiply wives to himself." I Timothy 3:2,12 requires a bishop or pastor and a deacon to be the husband of one wife. In Old Testament times the prohibition of polygamy was not well obeyed; in Old and New Testament times divorce has been an evil that in effect results in polygamy as defined in Scripture.

Instruction on marriage should begin with the most general, most normal, and least complicated circumstances. The Confession states that it is lawful or right for all sorts of people to marry

214

who are able with judgment to give their consent. This applies to the heathen as well as to Christians—for marriage is not a Christian sacrament.

The second instruction deals with Christians: they should marry only in the Lord, that is, a Christian should not marry a heathen. Therefore anyone who professes the true reformed religion should not marry an infidel, a Papist, or any other type of idolater.

Mixed marriages between Protestants and Papists, in which the Roman church requires the Protestant party to bring up the children as Romanists are a recurring source of misery to the Protestants. Sometimes even in the United States, these iniquitous vows after the couple has separated, are enforced by the civil courts, despite the American principle of the separation of state from church.

Parents and ministers should do their best to impress teenagers with the Scriptural principles before they get interested in the wrong sweetheart. In courtship as in various other activities there are so many ways in which a young person can ruin his life before he is aware of what he is getting into.

This advice to parents must also be taught to the young people too, for they will soon be parents; and as one of the purposes of marriage is to provide the church with a holy seed, those contemplating or entering upon marriage must be given the Scriptural injunction to bring up their children in the nurture and admonition of the Lord. Juvenile delinquency starts with careless parents.

> *Section IV.—Marriage ought not to be within the degrees of consanguinity or affinity forbidden in the word;[8] nor can such incestuous marriages ever be made lawful by any law of man or consent of parties, so as those persons may live together as man and wife.[9] The man may not marry any of his wife's kindred nearer in blood than he may of his own,[10] nor the woman of her husband's kindred nearer in blood than of her own.*
>
> *Section V.—Adultery or fornication committed after a contract, being detected before marriage, giveth just occasion to the innocent party to dissolve that contract.[11] In the case of adultery after marriage, it is lawful for the innocent party to sue out a divorce,[12] and after*

the divorce to marry another, as if the offending party were dead.[13]

Section VI.—Although the corruption of man be such as is apt to study arguments unduly to put asunder those whom God hath joined together in marriage, yet nothing but adultery or such wilful desertion as can in no way be remedied by the Church or civil magistrate is cause sufficient of dissolving the bond of marriage;[14] *wherein a public and orderly course of proceeding is to be observed, and the persons concerned in it not left to their own wills and discretion in their own case.*[15]

8. Lev. xviii.; 1 Cor. v. 1; Amos ii. 7.—9. Mark vi. 18; Lev. xviii. 24-28.—10. Lev. xx. 19-21.—11. Matt. i. 18-20.—12. Matt. v. 31,32.—13. xix. 9; Rom. vii 2,3.—14. Matt. xix. 8,9; 1 Cor. vii. 15; Matt. xix. 6.—15. Deut. xxiv. 1-4.

Fortunately in our society incest, that is marriage or sexual relations within the prohibited degrees of consanguinity, causes us very little trouble. The sin may indeed occur, but it is not a national scandal.

The Confession as quoted says that after one spouse dies "The man may not marry any of his wife's kindred nearer in blood than he may of his own," nor the woman similarly. This statement is based on Leviticus 20:19-21. It is quite likely, however, that the Scriptural passage does not refer to a second marriage, but to fornication or adultery while the couple are both living. Leviticus 18:18 does indeed speak of a man marrying his wife's sister, but it explicitly places this marriage within the lifetime of the wife.

If incest is not a national scandal, divorce is. It was so also among the Jews. The Pharisees tempted Christ by asking him whether it was lawful for a man to divorce his wife for just any trivial reason. Some of the Jewish teachers approved of divorce on the grounds that the wife had burnt the dinner. The school of Hillel allowed divorce on any ground at all, even on the ground that the man had found a younger and more beautiful girl (cf. Strack and Billerbeck, *Kommentar zum N.T. aus Talmud and Midrasch*, in Matt. 5:32). A recent governor of the State of New York seems to have agreed with Hillel.

But Jesus Christ, both in Matthew 5:32 and 19:9 insists that "Whosoever shall put away his wife, except it be for fornication, and shall marry another committeth adultery; and whoso marrieth her who is put away doth commit adultery."

216

Divorce is a national scandal; yet in reaction to the widespread immorality in this country, one should not conclude that divorce is never permissible. The Romanists prohibit divorce, and they sometimes quote the verse, "Whom God has joined together, let no many put asunder." This is a good verse; and we wish Romanists would use Scripture on other occasions also, instead of relying on tradition and papal decrees. But the Roman interpretation of the verse is misplaced. The person who breaks a marriage is not the judge who grants the divorce, nor the innocent party who sought it. The person who has torn the marriage asunder is the party who has committed adultery.

Furthermore, the Roman church has been quite liberal in granting annulments. What made Henry VIII so angry was the Pope's refusal to grant him an annulment when so many others were favored. In fact Henry had a better case than most, because his first marriage had itself been based on a papal dispensation from the law.

The Anglican church also prohibits divorce. Some years back the sister of the Queen, if we may believe all the attendant publicity, took under consideration a marriage with a certain Captain Townsend. He had earlier divorced his wife for adultery. There was no doubt of his wife's guilt. Indeed, she was so unfit for decent society that the court awarded the children, not to their mother, but to the Captain. The adulterous wife later married the correspondent. But whether from religious scruples or pressure by the Archbishop, the Princess finally decided against the marriage. The evidence made public indicates that this decision was most reluctant and painful. If so, the tragedy of it could have been avoided, had the young lady been a conscientious member of the Free Church of Scotland.

Much as one may regret such unnecessary tragedies, the scandal of our land still remains the laxity and frequency of divorce. For some strange reason public sentiment objects to the polygamy of old fashioned Mormonism (and recently arrests have been made in the inaccessible counties of southern Utah), while at the same time the successive polygamy and brazen immorality of the movie people is very often accepted as a desirable ideal.

Laxity affects the churches also. It is not only the pagan public who accept easy divorce. A professor in a seminary complained to me that the traditional attitude toward the remarriage of divorced persons was inhuman. The distinction between a guilty party and an innocent party was unreal, for, he claimed, in a divorce both persons are guilty. Therefore both parties should be permitted to marry again. Of course, he did not maintain that both parties, because guilty, should be forbidden to marry again. In reply, I took him literally and remarked that it is not true that both parties are always guilty of adultery. He admitted this, said it was not what he meant, but in any case it was legalistic to prohibit one party from marrying again, while allowing the privilege to the other party.

In keeping with the laxity of the age the Southern Presbyterian church has recently approved remarriage for the guilty party. This church voted that the decision of a minister whether or not to marry an adulterer should depend, not on what he had done, but on what the person by God's grace has now become, and what with God's help he (or she) honestly intends and hopes to do in the future.

This position is remarkable on several counts. First of all it shows contempt of Scripture and of Christ himself who gave the opposite command. Second it shows that the ministers who voted for this alteration in the government of the church have great faith in themselves. They claim to discern the thoughts and intentions of the heart. They say they can see what God's grace has done for the adulterer in question and can reliably predict the success of the second marriage.

Now, Matthew 5:32 says explicitly that anyone who contracts marriage with a person divorced for fornication is guilty of adultery. Matthew 19:9 says that anyone who divorces his wife, except for fornication, and marries again, commits adultery. Hence the second marriage of the guilty party is sin; and the second marriage of a man, who though he is not guilty of adultery himself has yet divorced his wife without proper cause, is also sin. It follows therefore that the Southern Presbyterian church now approves of adultery and makes itself an accessory before the fact.

Chapter XXV.

OF THE CHURCH.

Section I.—The catholic or universal Church, which is invisible, consists of the whole number of the elect that have been, are, or shall be, gathered into one, under Christ the head thereof; and is the spouse, the body, the fulness of Him that filleth all in all.[1]

Section II.—The visible Church, which is also catholic or universal under the Gospel (not confined to one nation, as before, under the law), consists of all those throughout the world that profess the true religion,[2] *together with their children;*[3] *and is the kingdom of the Lord Jesus Christ,*[4] *the house and family of God,*[5] *out of which there is no ordinary possibility of salvation.*[6]

Section III.—Unto this catholic visible Church Christ hath given the ministry, oracles and ordinances of God, for the gathering and perfecting of the saints in this life to the end of the world; and doth by his own presence and Spirit, according to his promise, make them effectual thereunto.[7]

1. Eph. i. 10,22,23; v. 23,27,32; Col. i. 18.—2. 1 Cor. i. 2; xii. 12,13; Ps. ii. 8; Rev. vii. 9; Rom. xv. 9-12.—3. 1 Cor. vii. 14; Acts ii. 39; Ezek. xvi. 20,21; Rom. xi. 16; Gen. iii. 15; xvii. 7.—4. Matt. xiii. 47. Isa. ix. 7.—5. Eph. ii. 19; iii. 15.—6. Acts ii. 47.—7. 1 Cor. xii. 28; Eph. iv. 11-13; Matt. xxviii. 19,20; Isa. lix. 21.

When the Confession speaks of the catholic Church, it does not mean the Roman church. In fact, the Roman church is not catholic. Catholic means universal, and "the catholic or universal Church, which is invisible, consists of the whole number of the elect." It is called invisible because the whole number of the elect are not on earth at any one time. The Waldensians of the Middle Ages and the believers of next century are parts of this one Church. Then too, the universal Church is invisible because it does not coincide with the membership rolls of the several visible churches. Some people whose names are on the rolls are not Christians; and some Christians are not members of any visible church. The word church itself (ecclesia) is derived from the verb to call or to call out. It refers to the called, the chosen, the elect. The catholic Church then is the aggregate of all whom God has predestined to eternal life.

For similar reasons neither the Roman ecumenical council nor the Protestant ecumenical movement is ecumenical. Neither of these includes all visible churches, much less represents all the elect.

The invisible Church, or more accurately a part of it, becomes the visible church as those who confess Christ, together with their children, are organized into congregations. In chapter 23 it was maintained that civil government ought not to coerce Baptist congregations to renounce their independence. Definition of Baptist belief and practice by civil magistrates is to be deplored and opposed. At the same time we believe that the New Testament (e.g., Acts 15) prescribes an ecclesiastical organization wider than the local congregation. Therefore we are Presbyterians. But the Baptists, we gladly admit, are more nearly right than some ultra devout persons who think there should be no ecclesiastical organization whatever. One's blind spot must be of unusual size to miss all the various organizational, disciplinary, judicial, and administrative prescriptions of the Bible.

Although as Presbyterians we believe that there should be an ecclesiastical organization wider than the local congregation, it does not follow that the visible church ought to be formed into a single organization. Every attempt by the proponents of ecumenical union to support their views by exegesis has been a notable failure. And a study of history shows clearly that the scandal of Christendom is not the multiplicity of small denominations, but the corruption of one big denomination. Those persons who value organizational union over doctrinal and moral purity can readily achieve satisfaction. Let them repent of the schism of Luther and Calvin, and return to Rome.

But all who believe that Luther and Calvin effected, not a schism, but a reformation, place greater stress on doctrinal purity than on a political organization. This is in accord with Scripture.

The amazing thing about the Protestant ecumenical leaders is that they quote Scripture, when they above all others are the very ones most opposed to the full truthfulness of the Bible. Why is it that they are so attached to the verse, "I pray . . . that they all may be one," when they bristle at the verse, "Behold a virgin shall be with child"? For that matter, why do they not examine more closely the remainder of the verse they quote: "that they may be one as thou Father art in me and I in thee, that they also may be one in us"?

What sort of unity was Christ praying for? Unity of organization? John 17 says precious little about ecclesiastical organization, in fact, nothing at all. Who can soberly maintain that the unity of the Father and the Son, with or without the unity of believers in the Father and the Son, is a unity of visible church government? Note clearly that Christ prayed that believers should be one *as* the Father and Son are one, and that believers should be be one *in* the Father and the Son. This unity obviously cannot be the trinitarian unity of substance, but it is surely a spiritual and not a political unity.

The New Testament clarifies the nature of unity quite well. Romans 12:5 says, "We, being many, are one body in Christ." I Corinthians 10:17 says the same thing. I Corinthians 12:13 adds the reason: "For by one Spirit are we all baptized into one body." From these few verses one can see that the unity of the New Testament is not something produced by denominational mergers, but by the baptism of the Spirit.

Ephesians 4:4 says, "There is one body, and one Spirit." This unitary body is not something yet to be produced by ecclesiastical politics. It existed in the time of Paul and it exists today.

The unity, of course, is spiritual. Philippians 1:27 reads, "Stand fast in one spirit, with one mind, striving together for the faith of the gospel"; and in the next chapter, "Be likeminded . . . being of one accord, of one mind" (cf. I Pet. 3:8). What could be clearer than I Corinthians 1:10: "I beseech you, brethren, by the name of our Lord Jesus Christ, that ye all speak the same thing, and that there be no divisions among you; but that ye be perfectly joined together in the same mind and in the same judgment." Corinth was plagued with divisions, and their unfortunate, indeed sinful, condition is often made an argument for organizational union. But Paul exhorts them to unity of mind, judgment, and speech. It is a unity of proclamation, a unity of message, a doctrinal unity that is uppermost in Paul's exhortation. When there is doctrinal unity, there may well be organizational unity within a city or other convenient geographical area; but without doctrinal unity, organizational union is not unity. See how little the ecumenical movement agrees upon! They have no

221

great Confession as we do. They don't dare write a creed. They cannot even hold a united communion service. When they do, it will be because even the Lord's Supper has lost all significance to all their groups.

If we wish to develop the unity for which Christ prayed, we must do it by persuading as many people as possible of the truth of the Scriptures. The church membership must think and say the same thing about the Atonement, about Justification and about the Sacraments. Studying the Confession in a textbook such as this is a means of promoting Christ's form of unity. Maybe organizational union is easier to accomplish, for it depends on such things as the distribution of ecclesiastical jobs; but spiritual unity is incomparably more desirable.

> *Section IV.—This catholic Church hath been sometimes more, sometimes less visible.[8] And particular churches, which are members thereof, are more or less pure, according as the doctrine of the gospel is taught and embraced, ordinances administered, and public worship performed more or less purely in them.[9]*
>
> *Section V.—The purest churches under heaven are subject both to mixture and error;[10] and some have so degenerated as to become no churches of Christ, but synagogues of Satan.[11] Nevertheless, there shall be always a Church on earth, to worship God according to his will.[12]*
>
> *Section VI.—There is no other head of the Church but the Lord Jesus Christ:[13] nor can the Pope of Rome in any sense be the head thereof; but is that Antichrist, that man of sin and son of perdition, that exalteth himself in the Church against Christ, and all that is called God.[14]*

8. Rom. xi. 3,4; Rev. xii. 6,14.—9. Rev. ii., iii; 1 Cor. v. 6,7.—10. 1 Cor. xiii. 12; Rev. ii., iii.; Matt. xiii. 24-30,47.—11. Rev. xviii. 2; Rom. xi. 18-22.—12. Matt. xvi. 18; Ps. lxxii. 17; cii. 28; Matt. xxviii. 19,20. 13. Col. i. 18; Eph. i. 22.—14. Matt. xxiii. 8-10; 2 Thess. ii. 3,4,8,9; Rev. xiii. 6.

Although, as was said a few paragraphs above, the unity of the Church is a present fact and not something that awaits a merger with Rome, this unity exists in different degrees. There are devout Christians who, though they conform to the Scriptural teaching on the Atonement, are confused about the election or perseverance. When these Christians form and control an ecclesiastical organization, the latter may doubtless be a true church, but a very impure one, or a slightly impure one.

The smaller denominations are in general purer than the larger denominations, for in these latter the difficulty is not confusion over election or perseverance, but a rejection of the Bible that undermines all doctrine. When the smaller groups try to persuade good Christians to put their time and resources into sound Christian work instead of supporting unbelief, the larger denominations try to blunt the force of the argument by minimizing the idea of purity. All churches are impure, so they say, suggesting the inference that it does not make much difference what church a person attends.

This reaction, if applied to personal conduct, would be to the effect that since all men are sinners, it does not make much difference what sins a person commits. It also implies that one should not try to improve.

Furthermore there is a great difference between a church which, while accepting the Bible, gets some of its doctrines confused, and a church which, rejecting the Bible, enacts regulations that compel a man to sin if he wishes to remain in good standing. For example, if the officials insist that ministers must persuade their people to support the boards and agencies where these are clearly opposing the Bible, then the minister first and the people later must sin in order to remain in good standing. This occurs when the Sunday School material casts doubt on the Bible and places its approval on the theories and literature of destructive critics. It also occurs when support is demanded for seminaries whose professors attack the doctrines of the Confession.

When impurity has reached this degree, one may legitimately ask whether the organization so operating is a church at all. Not every organization that calls itself a church is a church. One of the great flaws in the large Council of Churches is that they have little or no idea of what a church is. The doctrinal requirements for uniting with such a Council are absurdly minimal, and they have no test by which an organization could have its membership revoked. Provision for revocation is essential because some organizations that once were churches "have so degenerated as to become no churches of Christ, but synagogues of Satan."

When this occurs it is a sin to remain in them. The specious argument that since all churches are in some way faulty it is never right to change one's membership, is an argument that did not appeal to Luther and Calvin, or to the Puritans. Remember in 1660 some two thousand ministers left the Anglican church because the licentious Charles II imposed his anti-Christian regulations. This exodus cost them their financial support; in some instances it brought them jail terms; in all instances it led to their harassment by the government. How many ministers are willing to suffer lesser penalties today? How many in the pews have convictions enough to leave apostate bodies, even when no penalties, aside from a little ostracism, can be imposed upon them?

Section vi now speaks of the head of the Church. Henry VIII and succeeding monarchs claimed to be the head of the Church. Before Henry VIII the Pope's claim to this title was virtually undisputed. The Confession here rules out Henry VIII by implication, but refers explicitly only to the Pope.

Of the Pope the Confession says that he cannot in any sense be the head of the Church. The chief reason is that Christ is the head of the Church. The second reason is that the Roman church is not the Church of Christ.

The Confession then goes further and identifies the Pope or the Papacy with the antichrist. In more recent times there have been some objections offered to this identification. One minor objection is that such an identification, since it is not an abstract doctrine like the doctrine of Justification, cannot be considered as essential to the "system of doctrine." Belief in it should not therefore be required for ordination, nor should it have any place in the Confession. This is a weak objection, however, for the Virgin Birth and the Resurrection are singular events, not abstract doctrines, and yet these events—as well as their doctrinal explanations—are quite properly in the Confession.

A more weighty objection is that the Scriptural evidence for identifying the Pope as antichrist is weak, and that, although it is an opinion worthy of discussion, it is not to be made confessional.

We note that the form of the Confession now recognized by the United Presbyterian Church in the U.S.A. reads: "The Lord Jesus Christ is the only head of the Church, and the claim of any man to be the vicar of Christ and the head of the Church, is unscriptural, without warrant in fact, and is a usurpation dishonoring to the Lord Jesus Christ."

The Reformers, however, had some good reasons for thinking that the Papacy was the antichrist. In the first place II Thessalonians 2:3-4 says that the antichrist shall sit in the temple of God. This indicates at least that he is a religious leader. Whatever political power he may wield, he is primarily a religious personage. In the second place, the woman of Revelation 17, who was drunk with the blood of martyrs, sat on seven mountains or hills and is said to be "that great city which reigneth over the Kings of the earth." Obviously this is Rome.

Now, it is to be admitted that the early Christians probably thought that the Roman Empire was the antichrist. The terrible persecution, not only Nero's, but that of the Stoic emperor Marcus Aurelius, and the final effort of Diocletian fit the descriptions well. Yet Scripture does not permit this identification; for the antichrist will be destroyed by the brightness of Christ's coming, and this has not yet occurred, though the Roman Empire is long since gone.

After World War I some people tried to think of a revived empire under Mussolini. One of these dispensationalists told me in 1927 that the national boundaries within Europe, which he had carefully studied, were exactly as they had been in the time of Christ, and that—I remember his words well—no boundary change would now occur until Christ returned. The gentleman was editor of a popular religious periodical, but it now seems that he was mistaken.

Yet if the woman who makes kings drunk with the wine of her fornication is Rome, then for the last thousand years we can hardly suspect anyone but the Pope. This is clearly not a conclusive argument, and for that reason the statement might be dropped from the Confession; but it seems to remain the most plausible opinion.

Chapter XXVI.

OF COMMUNION OF SAINTS.

Section I.—All saints that are united to Jesus Christ, their head, by his Spirit, and by faith, have fellowship with him in his graces, sufferings, death, resurrection, and glory.[1] And being united to one another in love, they have communion in each other's gifts and graces;[2] and are obliged to the performance of such duties, public and private, as do conduce to their mutual good, both in the inward and outward man.[3]

Section II.—Saints, by profession, are bound to maintain an holy fellowship and communion in the worship of God, and in performing such other spiritual services as tend to their mutual edification;[4] as also in relieving each other in outward things, according to their several abilities and necessities. Which communion, as God offereth opportunity, is to be extended unto all those who in every place call upon the name of the Lord Jesus.[5]

Section III.—This communion which the saints have with Christ, doth not make them in any wise partakers of the substance of his Godhead, or to be equal with Christ in any respect: either of which to affirm is impious and blasphemous.[6] Nor doth their communion one with another, as saints, take away or infringe the title or property which each man hath in his goods and possessions.[7]

1. 1 John i. 3; Eph. iii. 16-19; John i. 16; Eph. ii. 5,6; Phil. iii. 10; Rom. vi. 5,6; 2 Tim. ii. 12.—2. Eph. iv. 15,16; 1 Cor. xii. 7; iii. 21-23; Col. ii. 19.—3. 1 Thess. v. 11,14; Rom. i. 11,12,14; 1 John iii. 16-18; Gal. vi. 10.—4. Heb. x. 24,25; Acts ii. 42,46; Isa. ii. 3; 1 Cor. xi. 20.—5. Acts ii. 44,45; 1 John iii. 17; 2 Cor. viii., ix.; Acts xi. 29,30.—6. Col. i. 18,19; 1 Cor. viii. 6; Isa. xlii. 8; 1 Tim. vi. 15,16; Ps. xlv. 7; Heb. i. 8,9.—7. Ex. xx. 15; Eph. iv. 28; Acts v. 4.

In the Apostles' Creed there occurs the phrase, the communion of saints. The word communion, the words community and commune, are related to the word common. Therefore the communion of the saints means that the saints have something in common. The Confession first mentions that they have Jesus Christ in common and in common have fellowship in his graces, sufferings, death, resurrection, and glory. In short, they have salvation in common.

The phases and details of salvation have been gone over rather thoroughly in the previous chapters of the Confession. What may seem a little new here is the relationship of the saints to each other. This relationship is of course based on their relationship to Christ, but some of its particulars ought to be mentioned.

In one church—and there may be others—I have heard the Apostles' Creed recited and explained so as to make the Holy Catholic Church and the communion of saints synonyms. The punctuation would be, "I believe in the Holy Ghost, the Holy Catholic Church—the communion of saints, the forgiveness of sins," etc. It is difficult to believe that in so short a creed two clauses would be identical in meaning; and yet the items in common, as mentioned in the Confession, can without too much straining be all included in the activity of the Church. The private duties of one saint which conduce to the inward and outward good of another saint may not be the official actions of a church organization; but insofar as the life, the activity, and the motivation of a saint come from the Lord, the head of the Church, and the saint is a member of the Lord's body, these private duties also come within the scope of the Church.

The duty of maintaining public worship is an important phase of the communion of saints; but after the previous chapters it need not be further considered. What immediately follows in section ii is the duty of relieving the poverty of fellow Christians. This injunction was greatly needed and conscientiously performed in the first century. It constitutes an important section in the Book of Acts. In modern times relief of poverty is largely in the hands of government agencies. In favor of this non-scriptural procedure it is said that more money is thus distributed and more poverty is thus relieved. It may also be true that the wealthier denominations have been lax in discharging their obligations, with the result that ambitious politicians rushed in where halfhearted saints drew back.

The Amish and the Mennonites are perhaps the groups best known for taking care of their poor. They do not want government doles. During the depression of the thirties the government agents tried to force relief on these people. Why should poor farmers so stubbornly resist the care of a paternalistic state? They should be forced to become wards of the government. Fortunately the government was then defeated. Now the same oppression is continuing by means of Social Security. Here in Indiana the agents have confiscated the horse of an Amish farmer because he (not the horse, nor indeed the agent, but the farmer) trusted in God rather than in insurance. The Amish have religious scruples against insurance; and while I do not agree with them on this point, I maintain that the government should not interfere in religious matters. The State should keep itself separate from the Church.

Those who, unlike the Amish, welcome government support soon look upon the dole as their right. Some families have lived on government aid now for three generations. Whether or not one can with equanimity view successive generations living on government relief, it should be clear that such relief is not philanthropy. Philanthropy is voluntary; it is motivated by love; but taxes for relief are collected by the force of the government.

It must also be said that in spite of these politically motivated programs, Christians are still under obligation to care for their own. No doubt we should care for others also, if we have the resources; but the Book of Acts and other passages make our duty to Christians clear: "Whoso hath this world's good, and seeth his brother have need, and shutteth up his bowels of compassion, how dwelleth the love of God in him?"

At the end of section iii the Confession states, "Nor doth their communion one with another, as saints, take away or infringe the title or property which each man hath in his goods and possessions." The attempt to derive from the duty of relieving the poor or from the example of the earliest Jerusalem Christians some support for communism is completely perverse. In the first place, the communists desire totalitarian power; but the Christians were motivated by compassion. In the second place, the Christian relief in Acts was entirely private; it had nothing to do with government. And, finally, the Apostles stressed the right of private property. The familiar passage, familiar at least to the opponents of socialism, should be repeated. When Ananias held back some of his money, though claiming credit for giving all, Peter said, "Whiles it remained, was it not thine own? And after it was sold, was it not in

228

thine own power?" Ananias' sin therefore was not that of retaining what was not his—it was his—but of lying to the Holy Ghost.

The Old Testament too, though its national laws are not necessarily to be reenacted today, shows that socialism or communism is not God's requirement for men. In addition to flocks and herds, there was a hard money system. When the Israelites, before Saul, wanted a king like the other nations, God declared that their desire was sinful, and the chief warning he gave them was that a king would impose heavy taxes.

It is sometimes said, particularly by people who wish to destroy capitalism, that Christianity is not tied to any one politico-economic system. There is one sense in which this is true; there is another in which it is false. True it is that the New Testament assigns the authority of capital punishment, waging war, and collecting taxes to the government. The New Testament also instructs us to obey whatever government is in power insofar as its laws do not conflict with our duties to God. But only thus far, and no further. So it was in the Old Testament too, as is seen in the disobedience to Pharaoh's order to drown the Jewish baby boys. But obedience to a Roman, Egyptian, or Communist government does not imply that Christians should be indifferent to politics. Christianity may indeed survive under hostile rule; but it is quite another matter to say that Christianity approves of hostile rule. The Bible definitely disapproves of some types of government and approves of others. Scripture approves of private property. Christ asserted the right of an employer to set the wages he will pay; he advised investment for gain in the market place. There is nothing socialistic in New Testament political economy. Indeed Christianity clearly supports a capitalistic, free enterprise system.

There is one other point concerning the communion of the saints—a point quite different from the immediately preceding. This has to do with prayers for the dead. When a Protestant objects to praying for and especially praying to the dead, invoking a departed saint for his intercession, the Romanist and Anglican with some finality declare that they believe in the communion of the saints.

Such a reply is irrelevant. While saints (i.e., the elect, not some subject of canonization) are on earth it is our duty to pray for them. We never pray to them. Oh, yes, we do, say the Romanists: we ask them, that is, we pray them to pray or intercede for us. Then why should we not pray to them after they are dead, especially after they are dead, when their intercession is presumably more effective?

Whether or not it is prayer when I ask someone living to pray for me is not too important a question. The question has to do with the Scriptural teaching as to our relation with the departed.

In *Christianity Today* (IX, 9, p. 46) there is a letter from Bishop Brown of Albany. He says, "Praying for the dead is . . . an expression of the same Christian concern that prompts praying for others while still in this life." No doubt such prayers are motivated by concern, particularly by concern as to whether the departed is in hell or purgatory, instead of in heaven. But is it a Christian concern, and have such prayers any function? Do the dead have any need of prayer, as the living do?

The Bishop's letter continues by describing the Episcopal General Convention of 1928. There had been "a somewhat flamboyant address (which ended with) 'And when I'm dead, I shall be in God's hands and won't need anyone to pray for me.'" This speech was followed by another in which James C. Foley, Professor at the Philadelphia Divinity School, replied, "Brethren I am in the hands of God already and I hope you still pray for me."

The Bishop further notes that because of this debate prayers for the dead were restored to the Prayer Book in 1928. He then concludes, "Prayers for the departed can be neither proved or disproved by Scripture."

There is some confusion and at least one false assumption in this Bishop's letter and in the debate he describes. First, the expression "I shall be in God's hands" unfortunately missed the point and opened the way for an equally irrelevant but witty rejoinder. The main point, which Professor Foley ignored, was, "I . . . won't need anyone to pray for me." We believe that the soul in hell and the soul in heaven are both fixed in their respective states. No change is possible. Only on the unscriptural theory of purgatory could prayers for the dead be justified.

Second, the Bishop in his letter refuses to follow Scripture, which tells him to turn aside neither to the right nor to the left.

God himself has given us directions for worship. We are not to alter them, either by addition or by subtraction. Prayers for the dead are an addition, for they have no Scriptural support.

Then, third, by inserting such prayers into the Prayer Book and making them mandatory (as is done in some other matters too) the Episcopal Convention claims an authority higher than Scripture. In effect, it claims to know better what God wants, than God does. This is a very strange interpretation of the communion of the saints.

CHAPTER XXVII.

OF THE SACRAMENTS.

Section I.—Sacraments are holy signs and seals of the covenant of grace,[1] immediately instituted by God,[2] to represent Christ and his benefits, and to confirm our interest in him;[3] as also to put a visible difference between those that belong unto the Church and the rest of the world,[4] and solemnly to engage them to the service of God in Christ, according to his word.[5]

Section II.—There is in every sacrament a spiritual relation or sacramental union, between the sign and the thing signified; whence it comes to pass that the names and effects of the one are attributed to the other.[6]

1. Rom. iv. 11; Gen. xvii. 7,10.—2. Matt. xxviii. 19; 1 Cor. xi. 23.—3. 1 Cor. x. 16; xi. 25,26; Gal. iii. 27.—4. Rom. xv. 8; Ex. xii. 48; Gen. xxxiv. 14.—5. Rom. vi. 3,4; 1 Cor. x. 16,21.—6. Gen. xvii. 10; Matt. xxvi. 27,28; Tit. iii. 5.

To understand the nature and significance of the sacraments, it is necessary to remember the doctrine of the Covenant. Perhaps it would be well at this point to review Chapter VII. Since in this age we naturally think first of the New Testament sacraments, it is well to recall the differences pointed out previously between the administration of grace in the Old Testament and that in the New. From the time of Abraham onward circumcision was a sign of the Covenant. From the time of Moses a rather elaborate ritual was added. But the similarities as well as the differences between the two Testaments should also be noted. In the New Testament age too God has ordained certain visible signs of the Covenant of grace. These signs, both Old and New, represent, illustrate, or show forth some aspect of the Covenant. They are visible signs, observable not only by the elect, but by the unregenerate onlookers as well.

Some people who very much like to play chess wear a lapel button on which a chess board is etched. The Mennonite women wear a white bonnet, and Amish men do not wear ties. These are signs of the wearer's opinions. They are not signs instituted by God, however. Presbyterians designate as sacraments only those signs which have been imposed by God—and imposed by God to represent Christ and his benefits to the elect.

To make this point clear by way of contrast, we note that marriage is not a sacrament. True, marriage was instituted by God; but it was not instituted as a sign of anything. Of course the New Testament uses marriage as an illustration of a believer's union with Christ. But this does not make it a sacrament, for the sowing of seed by a farmer in the springtime is also used as an illustration of the kingdom of God, and sowing seed is not a sacrament. In the second place, marriage does not distinguish or "put a visible difference between those that belong unto the Church and the rest of the world." Marriage is for the whole human race, Christian or not; therefore it is not a sacrament. The important thing about a sacrament is that it is a divinely appointed sign of the Covenant of grace.

> *Section III.—The grace which is exhibited in or by the sacraments, rightly used, is not conferred by any power in them: neither doth the efficacy of a sacrament depend upon the piety or intention of him that doth administer it,[7] but upon the work of the Spirit,[8] and the word of institution; which contains, together with a precept authorizing the use thereof, a promise of benefit to worthy receivers.[9]*

7. Rom. ii. 28,29 ; 1 Pet. iii. 21.—8. Matt. iii. 11 ; 1 Cor. xii. 13.—9. Matt. xxvi. 27,28 ; xxviii. 19,20.

The relation between the signs or sacraments, the grace which they exhibit, and the believers who receive the sacraments is explained in section iii. The previous illustration of a lapel button or a white bonnet is helpful here too. Wearing the insignia of a chess club in one's lapel does not automatically make one a Grand Master, nor even a chess player at all. The reality lies in the person's ability, not in the sign. So too, merely going through the motions of the sacraments is of no use, unless the person has the reality of which the sacraments are the signs.

The Romanists hold that the performance of the sacraments sort of automatically, *opere operato*, confers the grace they represent. Some Romanists have even discussed whether a mouse who nibbles the bread on the altar is saved by doing so. Among the decadent Puritans in New England there were some who looked upon the Lord's Supper as a converting ordinance.

The Westminster Confession teaches nothing like this. It stresses the warnings which the Apostle Paul gave to those Jews who trusted in their circumcision.

"Circumcision verily profiteth, if thou keep the law; but if thou be a breaker of the law, thy circumcision is made uncircumcision . . . For he is not a Jew who is one outwardly; neither is that circumcision, which is outward in the flesh . . ." (Rom. 2: 25-29). And to the same effect: "Let a man examine himself, and so let him eat . . . for he that eateth and drinketh unworthily, eateth and drinketh damnation to himself . . ." (I Cor. 11:27-31).

Furthermore, in Romanism the proper administration of a sacrament, and therefore its efficacy, depends on the intention of the priest. Unless the priest has the secret intention of doing what the Church intends in the definition of the sacrament, the thing does not work. Now, there was a priest who came to rebel against the whole system of his church. He came to have a hatred of religion. While in this state of mind, according to his later confession, he baptized many infants with the intention, not of doing what the Church defined, but of sending them to hell. Of course the priest is hardly to be commended for such evil intentions, as he himself later came to see; but consider the position of the Roman church which deprived these infants of regeneration by making a valid baptism to depend on the priest. On the Romish view a priest may outwardly pronounce every word and perform every action prescribed by the ritual, and the recipient may fulfill every condition required of him; yet if the priest has the wrong intention, the worshiper goes away destitute of the grace he thinks he has received.

The Roman system assigns the role of a merely passive recipient to the worshiper. His faith, his worthiness to partake of the sacrament, is sacrificed to the intention of the priest. Therefore there is no need to explain the sacrament to the worshiper. It is the performance of the sacrament itself that counts. For this reason there is relatively little preaching in Romish churches. The Word is of little use to the people; the main thing is the mass.

Contrariwise Protestantism will not have a sacrament apart from the Word. It is the faith and understanding of the believer which count. Therefore the sermon is essential. This is true of the Lutheran church, and historically of the Anglican church too,

234

though both these churches, especially the latter, have tendencies toward sacramentarianism.

In opposition to Rome the Presbyterian and Reformed churches without compromise exalt the Word rather than the sacraments. In fact, it may be said that the Word is essential and the sacraments are unessential. Let there be no superficial misunderstanding here: God's commands to baptize and to celebrate the Lord's Supper ought to be obeyed. Any theory that omits the sacraments from the regular observance of the church is not Biblical. And any individual who refuses or neglects to participate in the sacraments is in open rebellion against God. The sacraments are means of grace, instituted by Christ for our spiritual advancement. Only at our own risk and our own loss can we despise them. At the same time, if by reason of necessity, like the thief on the cross, or even if by reason of unjustifiable carelessness, a person is not baptized and does not eat of the Lord's Supper, this omission does not render his sincere faith of none effect. Fortunately God forgives the sin of neglecting the sacraments, as he forgives other sins. But the forgiveness is granted to those whose faith is sincere; and faith can come only by hearing the Word.

Not only is the Word essential to salvation in the sense that the Gospel must be proclaimed before anybody can believe it; the Word is also essential in the celebration of the sacraments. Pouring on water and eating bread are physical actions; and without the Scriptural explanation, they are no more than appears to the eye. Therefore every time a sacrament is administered, its spiritual significance must be explained.

The explanation, even if it is not wholly and completely given at each service, shows that the Word and the sacrament have the same content. The sacrament can confer no benefit which the Word alone could not confer. He who believes, even if he does not participate in the sacraments, has life, is justified, and sanctified. The identity of content depends on the fact that Christ is the content of both. Obviously the Word is the Word of Christ. We preach Christ. So too the sacraments are the signs and seals of grace and of the covenant. Cf. Gen. 9:12 ff and 17:11; I Cor. 11:25. They are the signs and seals of justification. Cf. Rom. 4:11; Matt. 26:28. They are the signs and seals of faith and conversion. Rom. 2:29 and 6:3 ff; Mark 16:16; I Cor. 10:16; Gal. 3:27. The blessings conferred by the Word and those conferred by the sacraments are identical.

Accordingly the connection between the signs and the grace signified is arbitrary, not natural. Water, wine, and bread would not of themselves signify or suggest Christ and the Covenant. These elements became signs only because Christ chose them. This enforces the previous point that the Word of explanation is necessary. Conformably to this, the minister explains the significance; he does not change the nature of the water, wine, and bread.

The worthy receiving of the sacraments depends on faith. To have faith, a person must believe; and to believe, a person must understand. If a minister spoke in Chinese or in Latin, the person in the pew could not believe what the minister said for the simple reason that he would not know what the minister said. Faith depends on understanding. There is nothing automatic or unintelligible about it. Therefore the minister must explain the sacrament in plain English. Mumbling some Latin phrases up in front never extends grace to the rear. It is faith that conditions the efficacy of the sacrament: not a blind or implicit faith, but a clear understanding of what Christ has told us.

> *Section IV.—There be only two sacraments ordained by Christ our Lord in the gospel; that is to say, baptism and the supper of the Lord; neither of which may be dispensed by any but a minister of the Word, lawfully ordained.*[10]
>
> *Section V.—The sacraments of the Old Testament, in regard of the spiritual things thereby signified and exhibited, were, for substance, the same with those of the New.*[11]

10. Matt. xxviii. 19 ; 1 Cor. xi. 20,23 ; iv. 1 ; Heb. v. 4.—11. 1 Cor. x. 1-4.

At the beginning of this chapter reasons were given to show that marriage is not a sacrament. Section iv now considers the question how many sacraments there are, and which they are. The question as to how many sacraments there are was one that agitated the people of the sixteenth century. People were put to death for denying that there are seven sacraments. Baptism and the Lord's Supper are the only two Protestants recognize. In the earlier chapter on Repentance the idea of penance, and therefore the sacrament of Penance, was shown to be contrary to the Bible.

236

Confession, that is confession to a priest, and extreme unction are nowhere taught in the New Testament. Nor can ordination be a sacrament, for it is not to be administered to all believers.

The final section of this chapter repeats the idea that the sacraments of the Old Testament represent the same Covenant of grace represented by the sacraments of the New Testament. Though the ages or dispensations are in certain respects different, there is no such sharp divergence as taught by modern dispensationalism. Ancient Israel was a part of the Church, and the present Church comes under the Abrahamic Covenant. The forms differ: circumcision has been replaced with baptism and the Passover with the Lord's Supper. But the meaning is the same. They were all "instituted by God to represent Christ and his benefits, and to confirm our interest in him."

CHAPTER XXVIII.

OF BAPTISM.

Section I.—Baptism is a sacrament of the New Testament, ordained by Jesus Christ,[1] not only for the solemn admission of the party baptized into the visible Church,[2] but also to be unto him a sign and seal of the covenant of grace,[3] of his ingrafting into Christ,[4] of regeneration,[5] of remission of sins,[6] and of his giving up unto God, through Jesus Christ, to walk in newness of life:[7] which sacrament is by Christ's own appointment to be continued in his Church until the end of the world.[8]

Section II.—The outward element to be used in this sacrament is water, wherewith the party is to be baptized in the name of the Father, and of the Son, and of the Holy Ghost, by a minister of the gospel, lawfully called thereunto.[9]

Section III.—Dipping of the person into the water is not necessary, but baptism is rightly administered by pouring or sprinkling water upon the person.[10]

1. Matt. xxviii. 19 ; Mark xvi. 16.—2. 1 Cor. xii. 13 ; Gal. iii. 27-28.—3. Rom. iv. 11 ; Col. ii. 11,12.—Gal. iii. 27 ; Rom. vi. 5.—5. Tit. iii. 5.—6. Acts ii. 38 ; xxii. 16 ; Mark i. 4.—7. Rom. vi. 3,4.—8. Matt. xxviii. 19,20 —9. Acts viii. 36,38 ; x. 47 ; Matt. xxiii. 19.—10. Acts ii. 41 ; xvi. 33 ; Mark vii. 4 ; Heb. x. 10-21.

Baptism is a doctrine on which there are obvious disagreements among Christians: the meaning of baptism is disputed; the subjects to be baptized are not agreed upon; the method of baptism among the churches is different; and, if we consider some of the small eddies of Christian thought, it is even denied that Christ commanded baptism.

First, let us consider the significance of baptism. Although the difference between Baptists and the other Christian denominations is commonly supposed to be the Baptist's peculiar insistence on immersion, the root of the difference lies deeper in the significance assigned to the rite. Section i of the present chapter explains baptism as a sign of the Covenant, of one's ingrafting into Christ, of one's decision to walk in newness of life. Included among these items is the remission of sins. Why, we may ask, is the use of water connected with the remission of sins? It was, of course, so connected in the baptism of John, a pre-Christian Jewish baptism.

John 3:22-25 throws light on this matter. The practice of baptism by John's disciples and also by Jesus' disciples gave rise to a discussion on purification. Baptism suggested purification. It must have symbolized the washing away of sin. Similarly the baptism of cups and pots in Mark 7:4, following the washing of hands in the preceding verse, shows that baptism is a washing or purification. Then too, Hebrews 9:10 speaks of divers baptisms, and verses 13, 19, and 21 show that these baptisms are sprinklings for purification. Finally, Acts 22:16 says, "Be baptized and wash away thy sins." From these verses we conclude that baptism is a symbol of cleansing from sin.

The Baptists do not so understand baptism. They hold that baptism symbolizes the death, burial, and resurrection of the believer with Christ. They quote Romans 6:3,4 ". . . were baptized into his death. Therefore we are buried with him by baptism into death."

Presbyterians and the other denominations do not deny that baptism refers to Christ and his death; but they insist that this is not the whole story. Different passages in the New Testament usually refer to only a part of the doctrine. For example, Galatians 3:27 speaks of being baptized into Christ, but does not mention his death. Then obviously neither this passage nor Romans 6 mentions the Father and the Holy Ghost; but Christ's command is to baptize into the name of the Father, the Son, and the Holy Ghost. Clearly then restricting baptism to a symbol of Christ's death is entirely inadequate. Naturally therefore if a theory omits two thirds of the relevant material, a number of errors can be expected.

Baptism can be regarded as exclusively a symbol of burial with Christ only by ignoring most of what the New Testament says about its significance. If burial were to be particularly symbolized, it would have been more appropriate to dig a grave and use earth instead of water for baptism. Water is appropriate to symbolize cleansing; and this is indeed the New Testament teaching.

Section iii mentions the mode of baptism: whether by immersion or by sprinkling. More important, however, is the question concerning the subjects to be baptized. Are adults alone to be baptized, or infants also? We shall therefore proceed to section iv, and return later to section iii.

>   *Section IV.—Not only those that do actually profess faith in and obedience unto Christ,[11] but also the infants of one or both believing parents, are to be baptized.[12]*
>   *Section V.—Although it be a great sin to contemn or neglect this ordinance,[13] yet grace and salvation are not so inseparably annexed unto it as that no person can be regenerated or saved without it,[14] or that all that are baptized are undoubtedly regenerated.[15]*
>   *Section VI.—The efficacy of baptism is not tied to that moment of time wherein it is administered;[16] yet notwithstanding, by the right use of this ordinance, the grace promised is not only offered, but really exhibited and conferred by the Holy Ghost to such (whether of age or infants) as that grace belongeth unto, according to the counsel of God's own will, in his appointed time.[17]*
>   *Section VII.—The sacrament of baptism is but once to be administered to any person.[18]*

11. **Mark** xvi. 15,16; Acts. viii. 37,38.—12. Gen. xvii. 7,9; Gal. iii. 9,14; Col. ii. 11,12; Acts ii. 38,39; Rom. iv. 11,12; 1 Cor. vii. 14; Matt. xxviii. 19; **Mark** x. 13-16; Luke xviii. 15.—13. Luke vii. 30; Ex. iv. 24-26.— 14. Rom. iv. 11; Acts x. 2,4,22,31,45,47.—15. Acts viii. 13,23.—16. John iii. 5,8.—17. Gal. iii. 27; Tit. iii. 5; Eph. v. 25,26; Acts ii. 38,41.—18. Tit. iii. 5.

The second question therefore concerns the persons who are to be baptized. Baptists baptize adults only; the other churches baptize infants also. Some of our good Baptist friends (and we are by no means questioning their devotion to our Lord) may maintain that an explicit authorization of infant baptism would be the only justification for the common Christian procedure. But if all the details of a rite had to be explicitly authorized in the New Testament then it would follow that women ought not to be admitted to the Lord's Supper. But not everything is explicitly set down in Scripture. God has given us the divine gift of logical reasoning, so that as the very first chapter of the Confession says (section vi), certain things may be deduced from Scripture by good and necessary consequence.

Part of the material from which infant baptism is deduced was referred to in the chapters on the covenant and on the Church.

240

First, the covenant has always included the children of believers. Cf. Gen. 9:1,9,13; Gen 12:2,3 and 17:7; Ex. 20:5; Deut. 29:10, 11; and Acts 2:38,39. And it hardly needs pointing out that the sign of the covenant was administered to male infants in the Old Testament. Second, the Old Testament church and the New Testament church are the same church. Not only was the Gospel preached to Abraham so that those in Christ are Abraham's seed (Gal. 3:8,29), but Romans 11:18-24 teaches that the Jewish branch was cut off from the tree that a Gentile branch could be grafted into this same tree, and that the Jewish branch will again be grafted back into the same tree. Note that it is all one tree from one root. The Jews will be restored, not to a new and different Church, but to their own olive tree into which the Gentiles have been grafted (Cf. Eph. 2:11-22). Accordingly, if children received the sign of the covenant in the time of Abraham, far from requiring an explicit authorization to continue their inclusion in the Church, it would require an explicit authorization in the New Testament to deny them the privilege now.

This line of reasoning is more than completed by pointing out that, as the Lord's Supper replaces the Passover, so baptism has been substituted for circumcision. If it is not sufficient to point out that baptism is the initiatory rite in the New Testament, that circumcision was the initiatory rite in the Old, and that therefore baptism takes the place of circumcision; it should be sufficient to read Colossians 2:11,12. Indeed we have here the favorite Baptist phrase, "buried with him in baptism," but this is the phrase used to explain "the circumcision of Christ." Verse 11 is speaking of a circumcision made without hands; it consists of putting off the body of sins; these sins are put off by the circumcision of Christ; and what does this phrase mean? It means being buried with him in baptism. The verse might possibly be misinterpreted in favor of baptismal regeneration; but the connection between circumcision and baptism can hardly be mistaken. Infants therefore are to be baptized.

The third question, not the most important but doubtless the one that elicits the greatest public interest, has to do with the mode of baptism. Should baptism be performed by sprinkling or immersion? The Baptists insist on immersion.

In reply to the Baptist contention, the first point is that the Greek verbs, contrary to the usual Baptist claim, do not mean to immerse. This is simply a matter of Greek usage, and it can be easily checked. For example, in the Greek translation of the Old Testament, in Daniel 4:33 (LXX. Dan. 4:30) Nebuchadnezzar is said to have been baptized with the dew of heaven. He may have been very wet; perhaps one could not say scientifically that he had been sprinkled; but surely he was not immersed.

Since the point at issue is merely Greek usage, appeal can be made to books outside the Bible. Now, in the *Apocrypha*, Ecclesiasticus 34:25 (LXX. 34:30) connects the verb baptize with purification. One must wash or baptize oneself after touching a dead body. Numbers 19:13,20 shows that purification from contact with dead bodies was performed by sprinkling. Hence the verb baptize in the *Apocrypha* designates sprinkling.

In the New Testament the verb for baptize and another verb for washing are interchangeable. For example, Luke 11:38 uses baptize for washing the hands before meals, while Matthew 15:2,20 and Mark 7:3 use the other verb for the same thing.

Mark 7:4 ff. says that cups, pots, and couches were baptized. It may be that the word couches is the insertion of a copyist and should not be regarded as a part of Scripture. But the point here is merely Greek usage. The copyist knew Greek and he wrote that couches were baptized. Now, a cup would very likely be immersed; a brazen vessel would be more difficult to immerse; but it can hardly be credited that couches, on which several people reclined at dinner, had to be immersed. Their baptism was simply a washing.

Hebrews 9:10,13,19,21 is exceptionally clear. Although I have read several Baptist works on baptism, I have not found a satisfactory explanation of these verses in them. Alexander Carson is one of the best Baptist defenders of immersion; yet his discussion of these verses is lamentably weak. On one occasion I asked a very good Baptist friend of mine, and a fine Biblical student, how he interpreted these verses; but he changed the subject and did not reply. Of course, Carson's poor attempt, and my failure to find a better Baptist attempt are not conclusive. But I believe the verses in Hebrews are conclusive.

In Greek the divers washings of Hebrews 9:10 are divers baptisms. Let everyone check for himself. Even if one cannot read Greek, he can see that the word begins with B, and the third letter is the algebraic sign for Pi. There is a T and an I easily recognizable. The whole word therefore is baptisms. These washings were of course purifications. Now, all the purifications mentioned in this chapter of Hebrews were performed by sprinkling. Some of these sprinklings were sprinklings of blood. Others were with water, as in verse 19. No doubt one of the Old Testament passages alluded to is Leviticus 14:50-52, where both blood and water were sprinkled. The passage in Hebrews then concludes with references to purging and purification. It follows therefore that the action of sprinkling can be referred to as a baptism.

After so much heavy argument, the discussion on the mode of baptism will have to be concluded with a bit of humor; though I trust it will not offend my good Baptist friends. In I Corinthians 10:1,2 the Israelites are said to have been baptized in the cloud and in the sea. In I Peter 3:20 the flood is said to represent baptism. Now, while the Israelites and Noah may have been sprinkled a little, it was the others who were immersed.

The ideas in sections v and vi have briefly been touched on in passing. Section vii needs no explanation at all. But an unfortunate story may be told to illustrate its denial.

A devout friend of mine attended one of those Bible Schools in which a knowledge of the Bible was neither too profound nor too extensive. There he was persuaded to be immersed; and he became a Baptist minister. A small church wanted his part time services; but they insisted that he permit them to immerse him, for there was no telling whether the Bible school had done a good job or not. So my friend, easy going and desirous of ministering to a neglected congregation, was immersed a second time. Some years later the preaching arrangement terminated, and a Baptist congregation was formed in a village much nearer my friend's home. He had other religious work and was not available to act as pastor; but the people and the pastor they called wanted him to join as a member. He was glad to do so, for this would help another Baptist congregation to get started. But before they would receive him as a communicant member, they insisted that they should immerse him, since there was no telling how good his previous

243

immersions were. At this point my friend decided that two immersions were really enough. He would help the congregation; he would attend; but he would not join. The Westminster Confession states that baptism is to be administered but once to any person.

Chapter XXIX.

OF THE LORD'S SUPPER.

Section I.—Our Lord Jesus, in the night wherein he was betrayed, instituted the sacrament of his body and blood, called the Lord's Supper, to be observed in his Church unto the end of the world, for the perpetual remembrance of the sacrifice of himself in his death, the sealing all benefits thereof unto true believers, their spiritual nourishment and growth in him, their further engagement in and to all duties which they owe unto him, and to be a bond and pledge of their communion with him and with each other, as members of his mystical body.[1]

Section i briefly describes the institution of the Lord's Supper. The last Passover meal had just been eaten. It typified the sacrifice that was to occur the next day. In these circumstances Christ replaced the Passover with a simpler ceremony, which he enjoined us to repeat until he comes again. Do this in remembrance of me, he said, and as often as ye eat of this bread and drink of this cup, ye do show forth the Lord's death till he come. But this simple service has been grossly misunderstood and superstitiously perverted.

Section II.—In this sacrament Christ is not offered up to his Father, nor any real sacrifice made at all for remission of sins of the quick or dead;[2] but only a commemoration of that one offering up of himself by himself, upon the cross, once for all, and a spiritual oblation of all possible praise unto God for the same;[3] so that the popish sacrifice of the mass, as they call it, is most abominably injurious to Christ's one only sacrifice, the alone propitiation for all the sins of the elect.[4]

Section III.—The Lord Jesus hath, in this ordinance, appointed his ministers to declare his word of institution to the people, to pray, and bless the elements of bread and wine, and thereby to set them apart from a common to a holy use; and to take and break the bread, to take the cup, and (they communicating also themselves) to give both to the communicants;[5] but to none who are not then present in the congregation.[6]

245

Section IV.—Private masses, or receiving this sacrament by a priest, or any other alone;[7] as likewise the denial of the cup to the people;[8] worshipping the elements, the lifting them up, or carrying them about for adoration, and the reserving them for any pretended religious use; are all contrary to the nature of this sacrament, and to the institution of Christ.[9]

Section V.—The outward elements in this sacrament, duly set apart to the uses ordained by Christ, have such a relation to him crucified, as that truly, yet sacramentally only, they are sometimes called by the name of the things they represent, to wit: the body and the blood of Christ;[10] albeit in substance and nature they still remain truly and only bread and wine, as they were before.[11]

Section VI.—That doctrine which maintains a change of the substance of bread and wine into the substance of Christ's body and blood (commonly called transubstantiation), by consecration of a priest, or by any other way, is repugnant not to Scripture alone, but even to common sense and reason; overthroweth the nature of the sacrament; and hath been, and is, the cause of manifold superstitions, yea, of gross idolatries.[12]

2. Heb. ix. 22,25,26,28.—3. 1 Cor. xi. 24-26 ; Matt. xxvi. 26,27.—4. Heb. vii. 23,24,27 ; x. 11,12,14,18.—5. Matt. xxvi. 26-28 ; Mark xiv. 22-24 ; Luke xxii. 19,20 ; 1 Cor. xi. 23-26.—6. Acts xx. 7 ; 1 Cor. xi. 20.—7. 1 Cor. x. 6.—8. Mark. xiv. 23 ; 1 Cor. xi. 25-29.—9. Matt. xv. 9.—10. Matt. xxvi. 26-28.—11. 1 Cor. xi. 26-28 ; Matt. xxvi. 29.—12. Acts iii. 21 ; 1 Cor. xi. 24-26 ; Luke xxiv. 6-39.

On one occasion a friend and I visited some Lutheran professors. Perhaps they had not received many Calvinistic visitors, or perhaps they merely wanted to get the conversation started; but at any rate one of them asked what were some of the differences between Calvinists and Lutherans. Since we were not on a polemic mission, it did not seem wise to mention any major topic of contention, such as predestination or perseverance; so I sought for some obscure technicality and remarked that Calvinists do not accept the theory of the *communicatio idiomatum.* (This is the theory that the qualities of Christ's divine nature can be attributed to his human nature.) But instantly, one of the gentlemen, a professor neither of philosophy nor of theology, but of history, replied that a denial on this point would undermine the whole Lutheran view of the sacraments. At such immediate penetration, my esteem of Lutheran scholarship, already high, soared still higher. But it struck me as a great tragedy of history that

Lutheranism has tenaciously held to the one point at which Luther differed from the Calvinists, while at the same time it has departed from Luther on the many points of agreement.

In attributing to Christ's human nature, particularly to his body, the divine attribute of omnipresence, the Lutherans maintain a view of the Lord's Supper that is not far removed from the very objectionable Romish view.

As one might expect, the Westminster Confession in explaining the Lord's Supper emphasizes the distinction between the evangelical and the Romish views. The two most important points at which Romanism has departed from Scriptural teaching are its theory of transubstantiation and the derivative doctrine that the mass is actually an expiatory sacrifice.

Transubstantiation is the theory that the bread and wine, by the magic pronouncement of the priest, become in substance the very body and blood of Christ. Inasmuch as the sensible qualities (i.e., the color, taste, consistency, etc.) of the elements remain unchanged, Rome supports the theory of transubstantiation by an appeal to the philosophy of Aristotle in which a particular relationship between substance and accident is elaborated. Aristotle's philosophy is too subtle to be discussed here, and the Bible-centered thinker can hardly make Aristotle his guide for the Lord's Supper. As a Scriptural basis for transubstantiation the Romanists teach that Christ's words, "This is my body," changed the bread into his body. And even the Lutherans, though they repudiate transubstantiation, take these words literally and insist that the verb *is* can have only one meaning. It requires no profound scholarship to see that this is not so. The verb *to be* in Scripture can and does take on figurative as well as literal meanings. When Christ said "I am the door," he surely did not mean he was an oak panel three inches thick. Again, "I am the resurrection," does not mean literally that Jesus was Lazarus walking out of the tomb. In the book of Revelation the verb *to be* is frequently used in the sense of *to represent*. For example, "The seven stars are the angels of the seven churches, and the seven candlesticks . . . are the seven churches" (Rev. 1:20; "these are the two olive trees" (Rev. 11:14); and "the seven heads are seven mountains" (Rev. 17:9).

If our opponents wish to descend into trivialities and argue that the examples given use the verb *to be* in the plural, whereas

247

it is the singular which can have only one meaning, and cannot mean *to represent*, we refer them to Revelation 17:18, "The woman which thou sawest is that great city, which reigneth over the kings of the earth." See also Matthew 13:37, "He that soweth the good seed is the Son of Man"; that is, the farmer of the story represents the Son of Man. "The field is the world . . . and the enemy that sowed them—the tares—is the devil; the harvest is the end of the world." This should be sufficient to show that the singular *is* can and often does mean to represent. Similarly the bread is a figure of Christ's body.

What further makes transubstantiation abhorrent to those who abide by the Scriptures is the inference drawn from it. If the bread is literally Christ's body, and if the priest breaks the bread, then Christ's body is broken again and the sacrifice of the cross is repeated every time the mass is said. The Council of Trent (Twenty-second Session, chapter 2) asserted that "this sacrament is truly propitiatory . . ., for the Lord, appeased by the oblation thereof, . . . forgives even heinous crimes and sins. For the victim is one and the same." Against this view the Scriptures are particularly explicit. Hebrews 9:22-28 can hardly be misunderstood: "Nor yet that he should offer himself often . . . but now once in the end of the world . . . So Christ was [just] once [once for all] offered to bear the sins of many."

From these unscriptural theories imposed by the arbitrary authority of the Roman church, a number of subsidiary objectionable practices follow, for once the rule of Scripture is bypassed, there is no restraining man's fertile imagination. Hence the Roman church "reserves" some of the body and blood of Christ and carries them around in processions. Instead of celebrating the Lord's Supper as a common meal, it serves private masses. Contrary to the express command of Christ, it denies the cup to the laity; and it has even done away with the bread in favor of a glucose wafer. Then too, whereas Christ instituted the Lord's Supper after the regular Passover meal, the Roman church, again by an arbitrary act of authority, requires its people to fast from midnight until they receive the wafer in the morning. Why must a supper be eaten before breakfast?

But if the Roman church is so obviously unchristian, what shall be said of modernistic churches? When ministers reject the sole authority of the Bible, where can they find the rules and practices of the Lord's Supper—or any part of ecclesiastical administration—except in their own arbitrary imaginations? If it seems aesthetic to them they will push the pulpit and its Bible over to one side, abolish the communion table, and put up an altar against the back wall. Now, it is easy to understand why they wish to remove the Bible from its place of central importance; but what do they put in its place? What are they asking the congregation to center attention upon? That piece of furniture they call an altar—what do they sacrifice upon it? Surely they do not hold to transubstantiation. Unfortunately they do not believe even that Christ's sacrifice on Calvary was satisfactory to his Father's justice. In fact, we might ask why such churches go through the motions of celebrating the Lord's Supper at all. What do they mean by it? Such a question, I fear, cannot be answered clearly because these churches have no infallible rule of faith to direct them how they should glorify God.

On the contrary, a confessional church, if it believes its Confession, knows what the significance of the sacraments is, understands why it administers them, and instead of relying on vague answers, unguided imagination, or aesthetic taste, can give clear-cut, above-board explanations from the Word of God.

Although the orderly administration of the Lord's Supper requires an ordained minister to officiate, the necessity of apostolic succession or its limitation to one or two denominations has no Scriptural foundation.

In Philadelphia some years ago the Episcopal church wanted to sponsor an interdenominational communion service. The details were put before the ministers of the other denominations: the Presbyterian minister would read the Scripture; the Baptist minister would preach the sermon, the Methodist would pronounce the benediction. The Episcopal priest—of course since his church was sponsoring the service, he should take some part—wanted only a very short part in the service: he would offer the prayer preceding the distribution of the elements. So modest. So unassuming.

Among the ministers present was a Reformed Episcopalian. He said he could approve the arrangements if one small change was made. Let the Episcopal priest take any other part of the service, but give the Baptist minister the prayer of institution.

This suggestion broke up the meeting. Why, exclaimed the Episcopalian, you want the whole thing! What the Reformed Episcopalian knew, having broken away from the older denomination, and what the other ministers did not seem to know, was that in Anglican theory, there is no communion service unless an Episcopal or Romish priest pronounces the words of institution. If a Baptist or a Presbyterian made this prayer, the service would not be valid, would not convey grace.

Now, a truly interdenominational service is one in which any of the cooperating ministers could perform any part. An Episcopal communion service does not become interdenominational just because members of other denominations attend.

For all the boasted oneness of ecumenicity, the inability of the World Council to hold a communion service shows that the constituent churches do not regard one another as churches of Christ. The unity is not there. Then why make believe that it is? Why not honestly and openly say, as the Westminster Confession says of the Romish church, that such and such organizations are synagogues of Satan, antichrists, and sons of perdition?

This language may not be polite according to modern standards; but it is honest and Biblical.

> *Section VII.—Worthy receivers, outwardly partaking of the visible elements in this sacrament,[13] do then also inwardly by faith, really and indeed, yet not carnally and corporally, but spiritually receive and feed upon Christ crucified, and all benefits of his death; the body and blood of Christ being then not corporally or carnally in, with or under the bread and wine; yet as really, but spiritually present to the faith of believers in that ordinance as the elements themselves are to their outward senses.[14]*
>
> *Section VIII.—Although ignorant and wicked men receive the outward elements in this sacrament, yet they receive not the thing signified thereby, but by their unworthy coming thereunto are guilty of the body and blood of the Lord to their own damnation. Wherefore all ignorant and ungodly persons, as they are unfit to enjoy communion with him, so are they unworthy of the Lord's table, and cannot, without great sin against Christ,*

250

while they remain such, partake of these holy mysteries,[15]
or be admitted thereunto.[16]

13. 1 Cor. xi. 28.—14. 1 Cor. x. 16.—15. 1 Cor. xi. 27-29 ; 2 Cor. vi.
14-16.—16. 1 Cor. v. 6,7,13 ; 2 Thess. iii. 6,14,15 ; Matt. vii. 6.

In the previous chapter on Baptism notice was taken of the
Romish position that the validity of a sacrament depends on the
intention of the priest and not on the faith of the worshiper. With
respect to the Lord's Supper also Protestantism stresses the faith
and understanding of the recipient. He must discern the Lord's
body. He must understand the significance. Otherwise he eats and
drinks unworthily. People who participate in a communion service
without a sufficient understanding are guilty of the body and blood
of the Lord. Instead of the service being a means of grace to
them, they eat and drink damnation to themselves.

Therefore the minister who officiates should not only preach
the Word in a general way, but particularly warn those present
to examine themselves before they participate. On the one hand
we want no superstitious additions to the Lord's Supper; on the
other hand we want no carelessness and misunderstanding in its
celebration. We simply want a reverent, intelligent, and Scriptural
observance.

251

Chapter XXX.

OF CHURCH CENSURES.

Section I.—The Lord Jesus, as King and Head of his Church, hath therein appointed a government in the hand of church officers, distinct from the civil magistrate.[1]

Section II.—To these officers the keys of the kingdom of heaven are committed; by virtue whereof they have power respectively to retain and remit sins, to shut that kingdom against the impenitent, both by the Word and censures; and to open it unto penitent sinners by the ministry of the gospel and by absolution from censures, as occasion shall require.[2]

Section III.—Church censures are necessary for the reclaiming and gaining of offending brethren; for deterring of others from the like offences; for purging out of that leaven which might infect the whole lump; for vindicating the honour of Christ and the holy profession of the gospel, and for preventing the wrath of God, which might justly fall upon the Church if they should suffer his covenant and the seals thereof to be profaned by notorious and obstinate offenders.[3]

Section IV.—For the better attaining of these ends, the officers of the Church are to proceed by admonition, suspension from the sacrament of the Lord's Supper for a season, and by excommunication from the Church, according to the nature of the crime and demerit of the person.[4]

1. Isa. ix. 6,7; 1 Tim. v. 17; 1 Thess. v. 12; Acts xx. 17,18; Heb. xiii. 7,17,24; 1 Cor. xii. 28; Matt. xxviii. 18-20.—2. Matt. xvi. 19; xviii. 17,18; John xx. 21-23; 2 Cor. ii. 6-8.—3. 1 Cor. v.; 1 Tim. v. 20; Matt. vii. 6; 1 Tim. i. 20; 1 Cor. xi. 27; Jude 23.—4. 1 Thess. v. 12; 2 Thess. iii. 6,14,15; 1 Cor. v. 4,5,13; Matt. xviii. 17; Tit. iii. 10.

"The Lord Jesus, as king and head of his Church, hath therein appointed a government in the hand of church officers, distinct from the civil magistrate." In the United States, perhaps better than anywhere else in the world, the separation of church and state has been maintained. Whenever, as in the Middle Ages, and wherever, as in Spain and other Roman countries today, the church controls the state, the church has been corrupt; and why Anglicans and Scandinavian Lutherans want politicians to control the church is beyond the understanding of an American Calvinist. If we know

252

what is good for us, both civilly and ecclesiastically, we shall resist the socialistic extension of governmental authority that has already, in one or two instances, infringed on our inalienable religious liberty.

To the officers whom Christ has appointed for his Church, he has given authority to impose censures. Censures or heavier penalties are to be imposed when anyone, especially a minister, is adjudged guilty of a public sin. It may be an infraction of the moral law, or it may be the preaching of heresy. In either case, those who know of the commission of such a sin, if they are persuaded that further personal remonstrance will not correct the situation, should file judicial charges before Presbytery.

Church discipline today has become virtually a dead letter in most of the denominations, and the results it was designed to prevent have overtaken us. An occasional scandal may be rebuked. Disobedience to an ecclesiastical prelate is promptly punished. But discipline for preaching and publishing doctrines contrary to the Confession is not held in high esteem. How could it be otherwise in later life, when the original ordination vows are taken in insincerity?

These remarks more or less cover sections i, iii, and iv. Section ii has to do with the keys of the kingdom of heaven and requires a special mention.

In this connection Matthew 16:19 is an interesting verse, for the power of the keys given to Peter is used as a basis for Rome's tyranny over the souls of men. A quick reading of the verse, without regard for the context, makes Rome's claims almost plausible.

The verse, however, does not at any rate establish the primacy of Peter as a pope, for whatever the power of the keys may be, Jesus later gave the same authority to all the other apostles (Matt. 18:18). This power is supposedly referred to again in John 20: 22,23, where it seems that the apostles are authorized to remit or retain sins.

The Roman interpretation is that these passages imply the sacrament of penance, upon which the priest forgives a man's sins, and the priest's act is ratified in heaven.

Of this Roman claim several things must be said here; and many others left unsaid for lack of space. But in the first place, there is no Scriptural basis for penance and confession; there is no basis for asserting that a man's eternal destiny depends on a priest's opening or shutting the gates of heaven. At least, there is no hint of this aside from these verses; and if these verses do not mean this, Rome's claims are entirely without foundation.

Protestants can use and have used several arguments to the contrary. First, it is barely possible that the apostles could forgive sins. They were directly inspired, infallible in their writings, and enjoyed spiritual prerogatives unknown to us. But if they indeed could open and shut heaven in something like a Roman sense of the words, it by no means follows that their followers could do so. To remit or retain sins would require infallibility in judging the hearts of men. It is unthinkable that the eternal destiny of all men should depend on priests who could be mistaken. Rome to be sure claims infallibility; but several previous chapters show the falsity of such a claim.

In the next place, the apostles did not remit and retain sins in the Roman sense. There is not the least whisper that they heard confession and gave absolution. But, obviously, the verses must mean something, and one must ask what is the power of the keys? What does the metaphor of keys stand for? To answer this, one may ask simply, what according to Scripture opens and closes the gates of heaven?

The answer has a number of subsidiary parts, but the main thing that the apostles did to open the gates of heaven to sinners was to preach the Gospel. Their followers today do the same thing: they ministerially declare God's conditions of pardon. And God ratifies the faithful declaration.

Note the words of Calvin. "This command respecting the remission and retention of sins, and the promise made to Peter respecting binding and loosing, ought to be wholly referred to the ministry of the word, which when our Lord committed to the apostles, he at the same time invested them with the power of binding and loosing. For what is the sum of the Gospel, but that, being all slaves of sin and death, we are loosed and delivered by the redemption which is in Christ Jesus, and that those who never receive or acknowledge Christ as their Deliverer and Redeemer, are condemned and sentenced to eternal chains" (*Institutes*, Bk. IV, xi, 1)?

254

To answer more in detail it is necessary to see what powers the Scripture confers on the officers or elders of the Church. The Westminster Confession lists, in addition to the ordinary preaching, the imposition of censures and excommunication upon the impenitent. The Confession expressly makes penitence or impenitence the prerequisite of loosing or binding. The binding and loosing are ratified in heaven only if they accord with the Word.

On the question of the keys and the judicial authority of the Church a great deal has been written. In addition to the works of George Gillespie a serious student must read *Discussions on Church Principles*, by William Cunningham; and everybody ought to read Calvin's *Institutes*, Book IV, chapters i-xii.

CHAPTER XXXI.

OF SYNODS AND COUNCILS.

Section 1.—For the better government and further edification of the Church, there ought to be such assemblies as are commonly called synods or councils;[1] and it belongeth to the overseers and other rulers of the particular churches, by virtue of their office and the power which Christ hath given them for edification, and not for destruction, to appoint such assemblies,[2] and to convene together in them as often as they shall judge it expedient for the good of the Church.[3]

1. Acts xv. 2,4,6.—2 Acts xv.—3. Acts xv. 22,23,25.

Some Christians do not believe in synods or councils and have therefore insisted on a strictly congregational form of government. The congregation admits new members, inflicts censures (if it wishes), and ordains men to the ministry—all without supervision by or appeal to a higher court. Perhaps it is not surprising that congregationalists overlook or reinterpret I Timothy 4:14, which indicates that ordination should occur by the laying on of the hands of the presbytery; but what goes quite beyond my Presbyterian comprehension is the total repudiation of synods and councils in the light of Acts 15. This chapter makes it quite certain that the local congregations could not settle the terms of church membership. To decide the issues, and to decide them authoritatively, it was necessary to convene a general council.

Naturally the message of the Atonement bulks large in the New Testament. Yet this is no excuse for overlooking the several Scriptural injunctions concerning church government. One of the ordination questions in the Reformed Presbyterian Church is, "Do you acknowledge that the Lord Jesus Christ, the only Redeemer and Head of his Church, has appointed one permanent form of ecclesiastical government, and that this form is, according to Scripture, Presbyterian?"

The New Testament does not leave the churches free to adopt just any form of government as they may think expedient. Very definite instructions are given. Some of these instructions are given by implication in Acts 15, particularly the principle that a local congregation cannot discharge all the functions divinely assigned to the Church. In other words, there must be Synods or Councils. Otherwise there would never have been a Jerusalem Council; each local group would have settled the question of terms of membership by itself in its own way.

There is more in the New Testament than the example of the Jerusalem Council. Note that in the city of Jerusalem the Church, since it consisted of thousands of people (Acts 2:41; 4:4; 5:14; 6:1,7), obviously formed more than one congregation, for they met in several places (Acts 2:46). This is still clearer after persecution had scattered them (Acts 9:31; 21:20). Since there were many apostles and other preachers in Jerusalem, each man could have preached only occasionally, if there had been but one congregation. But Acts 6:2 shows that the apostles were burdened with frequent preaching. Then too the diversity of languages mentioned in Acts 2 and Acts 6, if not conclusive by itself, confirms the other evidences of many congregations.

Yet all these congregations were under a single presbyterial government. That was how the diaconate came into existence. Further confirmation of this city-wide government is found in Acts 11:30; 15:4,6,22; 21:17,18; for all these elders are elders of one church, but hardly of one congregation.

Similarly more than one congregation existed in Ephesus. Cf. Acts 19:10,17,18,19,20; I Cor. 16:8,19; Acts 18:19-26. These congregations were one church ruled by elders, as is clear from Acts 20:17,28.

And finally the Scriptures authorize a synod or general council. The Jerusalem Council was not a popular inspirational convention. Its resolutions were not adopted as merely pious advice which the congregations could take or leave as they saw fit. The decision was binding and authoritative. Consider particularly Acts 15:28.

There are other details about church government in the New Testament. An interested student can search them out for himself. And once again he is referred to the writings of George Gillespie.

*Section II.—It belongeth to synods and councils
ministerially to determine controversies of faith and cases*

257

of conscience; to set down rules and directions for the better ordering of the public worship of God and government of his Church; to receive complaints in cases of maladministration, and authoritatively to determine the same; which decrees and determinations, if consonant to the word of God, are to be received with reverence and submission not only for their agreement with the Word, but also for the power whereby they are made, as being an ordinance of God, appointed thereunto in his word.[4]

Section III.—All synods or councils since the apostles' times, whether general or particular, may err, and many have erred; therefore they are not to be made the rule of faith or practice, but to be used as a help in both.[5]

Section IV.—Synods and councils are to handle nothing but that which is ecclesiastical; and are not to intermeddle with civil affairs which concern the commonwealth, unless by way of humble petition in cases extraordinary; or by way of advice for satisfaction of conscience, if they be thereunto required by the civil magistrate.[6]

4. Acts xv. 15,19,24,27-31 ; xvi. 4 ; Matt. xviii. 17-20.—5. Acts xvii. 11 ; 1 Cor. ii. 5 ; 2 Cor. i. 24 ; Eph. ii. 20.—6. Luke xii. 13,14 ; John xviii. 36.

Section ii outlines the duties of these assemblies. Their decisions in the cases enumerated are to be received if they are consonant with the Word of God. One hopes that this is usually the case. In denominations recently formed and in those which take special care to preserve Scriptural purity this would probably be true. But after corruption goes on for a time, the mistakes that have occurred involuntarily become ingrained, the officials succumb to the temptation of amassing power, with the result that the majority of the decisions may be unscriptural. Concerning such circumstances A. A. Hodge writes, "If their judgments are unwise, but not directly opposed to the will of God, the private member should submit for peace' sake. If their decisions are opposed plainly to the Word of God, the private member should disregard them and take the penalty."

The penalty is sometimes excommunication. The General Assembly of the Presbyterian Church in the U.S.A. ordered J. Gresham Machen to resign from the Independent Board for Presbyterian Foreign Missions, and at the same time placed support

258

of its own modernistic Boards on a level with participating in the Lord's Supper. Dr. Machen's refusal to obey this sinful edict led to his expulsion and the founding of the Presbyterian Church of America, now the Orthodox Presbyterian Church.

Section iv states that Synods are to handle ecclesiastical business only and are not to intermeddle with civil affairs. It seems the part of wisdom for a church not to concern itself with the thousand and one political controversies that naturally arise in any nation. There is neither time nor the requisite knowledge in Synod to arrive at sound decisions on financial regulations, anti-trust procedures, or the diversion of water from the Colorado River.

In France before the advent of de Gaulle I questioned one of the most theologically conservative pastors of the Reformed Church about the politics of his congregation. He told me that every party was represented except the communists. Clearly unanimity in theology produced no agreement as to what Christian principles implied with respect to civil affairs. In such a case it is not cowardice but wisdom, the wisdom of recognizing one's limitations, for a church to avoid dabbling in politics.

The Confession, however, permits Synod to petition the government in cases extraordinary; but it does not state what sort of case is extraordinary. In one sense a declaration of war is extraordinary, for it has occurred only half a dozen times in the history of the United States. But probably the authors of this Confession would not have put this subject up for debate in a Synod.

Surely one could not object to a Synod's taking cognizance of some governmental infringement of the church's liberty. In Wisconsin a court upheld the right of a labor union to fine a member because she attended church instead of the union meeting on Sunday morning. Should not the church speak loudly on such issues?

It is hard, however, to know what a Synod can and what it cannot properly discuss. In 1958 a commission of the National Council of Churches publicly advocated the recognition of Red China and its admission to the United Nations, condemned hostility to communism, urged the creation of a United Nations army, and the abolition of the draft. It would seem that actions concerning the draft and the establishment of a United Nations army are improper for a church to take. Conservatives, especially in the

259

South, deplored this unwarranted intrusion into national and international politics. Yet, because of the atheistic nature of communism, it might well be proper for an ecclesiastical body to make a public stand. If criticism is to be directed against the National Council, it is not so much that they spoke out on these matters, but that their speech was evil. In general it may be said that the National Council has taken the wrong side of nearly every moral and religious question. Today the churches should speak loudly and speak Scripturally.

CHAPTER XXXII.

OF THE STATE OF MEN AFTER DEATH, AND OF THE RESURRECTION OF THE DEAD.

Section I.—The bodies of men after death return to dust, and see corruption,[1] but their souls (which neither die nor sleep), having an immortal subsistence, immediately return to God who gave them.[2] The souls of the righteous, being then made perfect in holiness, are received into the highest heavens, where they behold the face of God in light and glory, waiting for the full redemption of their bodies;[3] and the souls of the wicked are cast into hell, where they remain in torments and utter darkness, reserved for the judgment of the great day.[4] Besides these two places for souls separated from their bodies the Scripture acknowledgeth none.

Gen. iii. 19; Acts xiii. 36.—2. Luke xxiii. 43; Eccles. xii. 7.—3. Heb. xii. 23; 2 Cor. v. 1,6,8; Phil. i. 23; Acts iii. 21; Eph. iv. 10.—4. Luke xvi. 23,24; Acts i. 25; Jude 6,7; 1 Pet. iii. 19.

Otherworldliness is a reproach frequently brought against Christianity. Belief in heaven is crudely ridiculed as "pie in the sky." Distinguished leaders of American education use more dignified language. For example, one professor writes that the humanism which he advocates "means that the comforting faith in some guarantee of human values is replaced by a resolute readiness to face the tragedies and crises of life in terms of our knowledge of their naturalness and probability, finding in the sense of friendly comradeship with our fellows a more than satisfying compensation for the loss of the cozy but illusory feeling that underneath are the everlasting arms of a divine protector." Another humanist is more forthright in stating that theistic religion is "the most active and pervasive menace to civilization which confronts us today."

Over a hundred years ago Jeremy Bentham founded the school of Utilitarianism and sponsored the Reform Bill of 1832. No doubt many of those reforms were needed in Great Britain; but the theory on which Bentham recommended his reforms had no place for a future life and divine rewards and punishments. The sanctions of morality were basically physical, inflicted either by human physiology itself, by the police power of the nation, or by social pressure. Religious sanctions were a form of social pressure, exerted physically, in this life, without any basis in a life to come.

Bentham's theory does not imply the desirability of the reforms Bentham sponsored. Since a calculation of earthly rewards and punishments determines right and wrong, Stalin's calculation and conduct must be judged outstandingly moral because he obtained many rewards and very few punishments.

Whether in Britain, in Russia, or in the United States, left wing religious liberals today fill their periodicals and sermons with socialistic politics and confine their hopes to this world. No otherworldliness for them. Insofar as this type of accusation against historic Christianity is made to imply that the orthodox are "socially irresponsible" and have no interest in present human ills, it is a propaganda device to conceal the fact that theological conservatives are very much concerned with present human misery and are concerned not to increase it by subjecting the nation to secularistic socialism; but insofar as it reproaches us for having our citizenship in heaven, it should not so much be borne in silence as proclaimed proudly, publicly, and with vigor.

Those who deny the life beyond the grave should be forced, by insistent challenge, to face the implications of their thought. Although they have a program of socialization, which no doubt they sincerely believe will improve the conditions of humanity, they should be made to explain how their philosophic naturalism can logically support any particular program, no matter what. They should be questioned pointedly how secularism can furnish a basis for morality. Frequently they speak of morality as a social code; sometimes they speak of it as an individual emotional reaction. In any case there is no "cosmic guarantee" that the effort expended in advancing their program will be rewarded and that opposition to it will be punished. Nor do history and observable facts show that devotion to the good (whatever anyone thinks the good is) is worth the trouble. On naturalistic assumptions, therefore, no reason can be given for choosing a life of honesty and truth rather than a life devoted to becoming a communistic dictator. Honor and truth may offer lesser risks with mediocre rewards; Stalin's choice brought immense rewards even though the risk was great. Because secularism and left wing politics provide no logical ground for choosing a life of honesty and truth, the theological conservatives are justified in suspecting that totalitarianism will be the actual result.

For that matter, can humanism give a reason for not committing suicide? Of course, when things go well with us and we are enjoying ourselves, we may prefer to live a little while longer. But this is only a personal preference; it is not a moral duty binding all men. Humanism can motivate neither morality nor life itself.

Not so with a consistent Christian theism. Not so with the Biblical view that includes heaven and hell. Although observable history shows that good people have endured pain and persecution, although it cannot be proved by this life that honesty is invariably the best policy, a future life with rewards and punishments meted out by an omnipotent and omniscient Sovereign clearly provides logical justification for choosing a life of righteousness at whatever temporal cost.

How selfish! the secularists deride; we always have said that Christianity is egoistic.

At this point the secularist must be brought back forcefully to his own position. How is it that he uses egoism as an accusation of moral inferiority? On humanist principles what is wrong with egoism? Since a naturalistic world view cannot justify any type of life, or even life itself, except as an expression of irrational personal preference, it has no more ground for objecting to Christianity than to communism.

We turn now to God's revelation to learn the truth about what happens after death. The body is buried and returns to dust, but a man's soul—we might even say the man himself—appears before God to receive his final destiny.

Some religious groups which call themselves Christians teach that the soul does not immediately return to God but falls asleep until the resurrection. This is not what the Bible says. The best known verse on the subject is Luke 23:43 in which Christ says to the thief, "Today thou shalt be with me in paradise." In II Corinthians 5:8 Paul equates being absent from the body with being present with the Lord. He expresses a similar idea in Philippians 1:23. To depart this life, he says, is to be with Christ. Likewise the parable of the rich man in hell makes sense only if that man between death and the resurrection knew cf his brethren's hardness of heart.

One argument humanists have used against a future life is that the annoyances of our present life make the thought of continued existence uninviting. Perhaps these gentlemen are influenced by Gulliver's account of the Struldbrugs—the people who could not die and passed endless years in senility. At any rate the gentlemen in question have not derived their notions of a future state from the Bible.

Life after death will not be a repetition of the annoyances, the tragedies, the sin of this life. The elect will be made perfect in holiness, there will be no more sorrow and crying, and all tears shall forever be wiped away. It is amazing that Corliss Lamont in his chapter "This Life Is All and Enough," with his praise of communism and atheism, with his materialism and behaviorism, with his antagonism against Christianity and his ridicule, feels compelled to confess, "Even I, disbeliever that I am, would frankly be more than glad to awaken some day to a worth-while eternal life" (*Humanism as a Philosophy*, p. 124). Does this not reveal how utterly sad a humanist must be?

Section II.—At the last day, such as are found alive shall not die, but be changed;[5] and all the dead shall be raised up with the selfsame bodies, and none other, although with different qualities, which shall be united again to their souls for ever.[6]
Section III.—The bodies of the unjust shall, by the power of Christ, be raised to dishonour; the bodies of the just, by his Spirit, unto honour, and be made conformable to his own glorious body.[7]

5. 1 Thess. iv. 17; 1 Cor. xv. 51,52.—6. Job xix. 26,27; 1 Cor. xv. 42-44. —7. Acts xxiv. 15; John v. 28,29; 1 Cor. xv. 43; Phil. iii. 21.

At various times through church history Plato's arguments for the immortality of the soul have seemed to be a noble pagan anticipation of Christian doctrine. Augustine is called a Christian Platonist, and the introduction of Aristotle by Thomas Aquinas is viewed as a serious regression from the faith. In the nineteenth century a scholarly volume was written with the title, *The Christian Element in Plato*.

To those who are sympathetically familiar with these sentiments it may come as a surprise to learn that Tertulian was converted to Christianity by discovering that the arguments for the immortality of the soul are fallacious. There are two reasons for this paradox. The first and philosophical reason is that Plato's arguments, if valid, prove that the soul is eternal and has therefore never been created. The second reason, a Scriptural reason, is that while Christianity does indeed teach that the soul lives forever, the emphasis falls on the resurrection of the body; and this is something Plato would have abominated, had he known of it.

Furthermore our belief in the resurrection does not depend on philosophic arguments based on observation of nature. Our belief in our own resurrection is based on the historical occurrence of Christ's resurrection, plus the divine promise to raise us from the dead.

Here is a stumbling block to humanists. They cannot account for Christ's resurrection. Of course, they try to deny it happened. But whatever theory they may use to establish the existence of Alexander the Great or Julius Caesar will equally well establish Christ's resurrection. The event is recorded in several different sources and was attested to by hundreds of witnesses. How strange it is then that men like Bultmann insist that we can know nothing of Jesus, nothing that he said, nothing that he did; all we can know is what the early Christians said about him. But if there is a theory of historiography that allows us to know the events of the apostolic church, the same methods give us Jesus' words and deeds.

How sad a humanistic mind must be! These materialists have no hope. To them our sixteenth century theology (which is of course first century theology) is "irrelevant." Irrelevant perhaps it is to twentieth century politics, the diminishing gold supply, and our nation's retreat before communism. But when cancer strikes, or when a man drops dead, then nothing else except our theology is relevant. Confrontation with death needs the resurrection.

As this message conquered the Roman Empire, so let us din it into modern ears.

CHAPTER XXXIII.

OF THE LAST JUDGMENT.

Section I.—God hath appointed a day wherein he will judge the world in righteousness by Jesus Christ,[1] to whom all power and judgment is given of the Father.[2] In which day not only the apostate angels shall be judged,[3] but likewise all persons that have lived upon earth shall appear before the tribunal of Christ, to give an account of their thoughts, words and deeds, and to receive according to what they have done in the body, whether good or evil.[4]

Section II.—The end of God's appointing this day is for the manifestation of the glory of his mercy in the eternal salvation of the elect, and of his justice in the damnation of the reprobate, who are wicked and disobedient. For then shall the righteous go into everlasting life, and receive that fulness of joy and refreshing which shall come from the presence of the Lord; but the wicked, who know not God, and obey not the gospel of Jesus Christ, shall be cast into eternal torments, and be punished with everlasting destruction from the presence of the Lord, and from the glory of his power.[5]

1. Acts xvii. 31.—2. John v. 22,27.—3. 1 Cor. vi. 3 ; Jude 6 ; 2 Pet. ii. 4.—
4. 2 Cor. v. 10 ; Eccles. xii. 14 ; Rom. ii. 16 ; xiv. 10,12 ; Matt. xii. 36,37.
—5. Matt. xxv. 31-46 ; Rom. ii. 5,6 ; ix. 22,23 ; Matt. xxv. 21 ; Acts iii.
19 ; 2 Thess. i. 7-10.

In the previous chapter mention was made of Jeremy Bentham's very secular utilitarianism. The objection to this system of ethics is not that it is egoistic. Christianity too offers the egoistic inducement of individual salvation. Nor is the objection based on the idea of sanctions. Morality without sanctions is a morality without obligations. Utilitarianism and similar forms of ethics are futile—aside from the fact that calculation and prediction are impossible—because secular sanctions do not work. Morality needs the divine sanction of a judgment day.

Furthermore secular philosophy cannot make sense of history. Without a divine judgment history is sound and fury, signifying nothing. Several scholars in this century have tried to understand history. One of the more popular is Arnold Toynbee. In spite of the unbelievable mess the United States has allowed the world to sink into, Toynbee is optimistic. He does not believe that the collapse of our civilization is inevitable. He offers a hope of escape. But his hope is slim, for all the evidence he has gathered points in the opposite direction. The best he can say is that the evidence is not enough: the fact that all other civilizations have collapsed, he insists, does not absolutely prove that ours must. Pitirim Sorokin also tries to avoid the word inevitable. But his theory implies that our collapse is in fact inevitable, and he pictures us as a piece of wood on the brink of Niagara. Oswald Spengler says bluntly that the collapse of western civilization is inevitable. Arthur A. Ekirch also has published a book, *The Decline of American Liberalism*. His conclusions are pessimistic.

Why then should not intelligent secularists commit suicide and avoid the pain, brutality, and suffering that is upon us? Do they think they can predict the hour at which the bombs will fall and safely delay suicide until a minute in advance? Perhaps they do not think. They attend to a rising stock market and superficial prosperity; they divert themselves with trivial amusements; they worry about petty inconveniences, and resolutely shut their eyes to the course of history.

In these unstable times of onrushing destruction, when American foreign affairs have been conducted for twenty years with incredible stupidity, when satanic totalitarianism sweeps from victory to victory, a degree of sanity and equilibrium can be maintained and a rational view of history can be held only on the ground that Christ will return to culminate the course of history and to visit destruction upon his enemies.

This justification of history returns us to the chapter on the eternal decree. God works all things according to the good pleasure of his will. He established a plan or schedule that embraces every event. And he drives the plan through to completion. The completion will be the day of judgment.

> *Section III.—As Christ would have us to be certainly persuaded that there shall be a day of judgment, both to deter all men from sin, and for the greater consolation of the godly in their adversity;[6] so will he have that day unknown to men, that they may shake off all carnal security, and be always watchful, because they*

*know not at what hour the Lord will come; and may be
ever prepared to say, Come, Lord Jesus, come quickly.
Amen.*[7]

6. 2 Pet. iii. 11,14; 2 Cor. v. 10,11; 2 Thess. i. 5-7; Luke xxi. 27,28;
Rom. viii. 23-25.—7. Matt. xxiv. 36,42-44; Mark xiii, 35-37; Luke xii. 35,
36; Rev. xxii. 20.

No one knows the date of the day of judgment nor that of
Christ's return. Yet some people have foolishly attempted to set
the date. What is more possible, though it has given rise to diver-
gent views, is the attempt to list in chronological order the various
events that immediately precede, accompany, and follow Christ's
return.

The Confession has very little to say on Christ's return. Its
last chapter gives a relatively full account of the judgment, but
only in the last few phrases of section iii is Christ's return mentioned at all. Yet it would seem that there is more material in the
New Testament on this subject than on the identification of the
Pope as the antichrist. Historically this lack of balance is understandable; but theologically it is unfortunate. Because the struggle
with Rome centered on justification by faith and the sole authority
of the Bible, the order of events concomitant with the second
advent was not a matter of discussion. Calvin, for example,
though he wrote commentaries, wrote none on Revelation.

For the last hundred years, however, the details of eschatology
have evoked a great deal of interest. Before World War I there
was a theory widespread that the Gospel would permeate the world,
that nearly everyone would accept Christ, that therefore a millennium of righteousness would be introduced, after which epoch
Christ would return to earth. This is the theory called postmillennialism. David Brown, last century, wrote *The Second Advent* in its defense. This seems to have been the view of St.
Augustine also, as may be seen in the *City of God*, Book 22, last
chapter, where he speaks of an age of rest following the present
age but preceding the resurrection and the eternal state.

In this century postmillennialism is not so popular. One
reason for its decline in popularity is the disillusionment caused
by two World Wars. The Christian missionary enterprise in Asia
seems to have been a failure; Africa may go communist; and the
moral collapse in the United States is no harbinger of a righteous
society. If the Bible really predicts a rule of righteousness ushered

in by the ordinary preaching of the Gospel before Christ returns, such an epoch must be located in the far distant future, contrary to devout hopes for an early advent. Of course, too, Scriptural material is used to convince us that there will be little or no faith on earth when Christ returns.

Premillennialism is a second view of the Lord's return. It is simply that the course of history continues with its wars and rumors of wars, getting no better and very likely worse, until Christ comes in flaming fire to take vengeance on them that obey not the Gospel, and to set up a millennial kingdom of righteousness. This view was held by such scholars and exegetes as Alford and Zahn.

Dispensationalism is a species of premillennialism that has attracted more attention than the scholarly views of Alford and Zahn. In addition to the idea that Christ comes to initiate the millennium, dispensationalism teaches that Christ comes again twice rather than once: he comes secretly and then seven years later he comes publicly. It also denies the doctrine of the covenant and holds that some men have been saved and other men will be saved apart from the sacrifice of Christ. Further, dispensationalism teaches that the Reformation, instead of being the greatest spiritual awakening since the apostles, is represented by the church at Sardis in Revelation 3:1 and was an epoch of deadness and works that are not perfect. Obviously the present writer is a little less than enthusiastic about such a view; but what is particularly peculiar is this: even if some of the dispensational details should be true, how can people that honor the Bible put such tremendous emphasis on these details, while at the same time they pay little or no attention to some of the much more important doctrines? For a critical analysis of dispensationalism we suggest O. T. Allis' *Prophecy and the Church.*

Because dispensationalism has brought premillennialism into disrepute in some quarters, there is renewed interest in a third view, amillennialism. This is the simple view that there is no millennium at all. Christ just comes and heaven ensues. The amillennialists claim that the Westminster Confession favors them, though one researcher asserts that the Westminster divines were postmillenarians. The Confession itself asserts neither the postmillennial or premillennial view. Nor does it assert amillennialism.

In the Larger Catechism there are phrases about a general resurrection that do not favor premillennialism. But whether the authors of the Confession individually accepted one view or another, they refrained in the Confession from either asserting or denying a future millennium.

The Reformers were in general opposed to premillennialism. Just as in the early church some people interpreted Christ's death as the payment of a ransom to the devil, and so, illogically, brought the idea of ransom itself into disfavor with later liberal theologians; so too the extravagances of the chiliasts or millenarians in early Protestant times brought the premillennial idea into disfavor. The Westminster divines, however, were wise in avoiding a choice among these views: the subject was not ready, nor is it yet ready, for creedal determination. Loraine Boettner, whose book *The Millennium* is one fourth a defense of postmillenarianism and two thirds an attack against premillenarianism, makes a notable statement on page one, which ought to be reaffirmed by advocates of all three views: "Each of the systems is therefore consistently evangelical, and each has been held by many able and sincere men. The differences arise, not because of any conscious or intended disloyalty to Scripture," but, may I add, because there are disagreements in exegesis.

Because there is much interest in and study of the subject at present, a few considerations and a little exegesis will be here appended. Of the three views the denial of a millennium seems least tenable. The Bible in four consecutive verses explicitly mentions a period of a thousand years. Further, the passage refers to conditions on earth rather than in heaven because during the period Satan cannot deceive the nations as he formerly did, and after the period he deceives them again. This period of time may come before or after Christ's return, and the accompanying events may be in one order or another, but the Bible definitely predicts such a period in history.

Nor is it true that the idea of a millennium is found only in Revelation 20. The designation *a thousand years* is found only there, but predictions of a future rule of righteousness are frequent. For example, Psalm 72 says, "He shall have dominion also from sea to sea . . . his enemies shall lick the dust . . . Yea, all kings shall fall down before him, all nations shall serve him."

Another familiar example is Isaiah's prophecy about a time when the nations shall beat their swords into ploughshares and learn war no more. Such passages as these ill accord with the denial of a millennium of righteousness.

If, now, the Scripture predicts a millennium, obviously Christ must return either before it or afterward. Of these a reason or two may be mentioned for preferring premillennialism. First, to return to the Book of Revelation, if this book allows any place at all for Christ's return, it is chapter nineteen. An amillenarian interpretation that would deny any reference to Christ's return, other than Revelation 22:7,20, would be an incredible interpretation. It is impossible to believe that the Apocalypse never refers to the greatest of all apocalyptic events. The dispensational view that Christ returns between chapters three and four is a wild, unsupported speculation. Accordingly, if Christ's return is mentioned in chapter nineteen, it comes before the thousand years of chapter twenty.

It is often objected that the book of Revelation is highly figurative and that therefore we must be guided by the literal passages in the other books. This is a sound principle. But regardless of how figurative it is, and how doubtful many of its identifications may be, the points mentioned are as clear as any literal language could make them.

After these positive considerations it may also be noted that objections to premillennialism often sound peculiar to the ears of its advocates. Without extending the discussion unmeasurably, overlapping objections by four gentlemen may be offered as samples.

The Lutheran theologian I. A. Dorner argues that premillennialism disparages the Gospel in that the victory of Christianity is not secured by what God has already given, but depends on events other than preaching. If this objection were sound, it would rule out Christ's return altogether, and the resurrection of the saints as well, for these events are not the effects of preaching. Dorner, fortunately, is not consistent and does not use his objection to deny these events.

The Baptist theologian A. H. Strong, who explicitly puts the millennium before Christ's coming, argues that the premillennial

271

interpretation of Revelation 20 requires a literal, physical resurrection of the saints, whereas I Corinthians 15:44,50 "are inconsistent with the view that the resurrection is a physical resurrection . . ." This is a strange argument, for Strong himself says, "The nature of Christ's resurrection, as literal and physical, determines the nature of the resurrection in the case of believers" (*Systematic Theology*, Vol. III, pp. 1008, 1011, 1012, 1018).

Charles Hodge also uses the same odd argument and contends that there cannot be a literal resurrection when Christ returns, after which the saints dwell on earth and share the glories of Christ's reign here, because "flesh and blood cannot inherit the Kingdom of God" (*Systematic Theology*, Vol. III, p. 843). But Christ in his glorified body walked on earth.

A. A. Hodge insists that the view is Jewish in origin and judaizing in tendency. But, we recall, the idea of the Covenant is also Jewish in origin, and the Confession does not disguise its dependence on the Old Testament along with the New. In fact, so far as an alleged judaizing tendency is concerned, the fault of many premillenarians, which fault we do not condone by any means, is rather an antinomianism that sharply contrasts with the legalism of the judaizers.

It is no doubt true that the dispensationalists deny the present kingship of Christ and contradict the teaching of Ephesians on the unity of Jews and Gentiles in the Church, the body of Christ. But arguments against a heretical sect are irrelevant when applied to a view that is free from these unscriptural positions.

Now, finally, much is made of the Scriptural scheduling of many events *at* the return of Christ, and the conclusion is then drawn that all these events are simultaneous. But the Scripture does not speak of the coming of Christ in the ordinary English sense of an arrival. The Greek word is *parousia*, and it means presence, rather than coming. It is used in pagan literature to denote a king's tour of inspection. During the tour many things can happen at different times, and yet all are "at" his presence. Hence it cannot be insisted upon that all that occurs at Christ's Parousia must be simultaneous. Various events can be placed at various times during the span of the millennium.

There is one advantage, however, that so-called amillennialism has over the nineteenth century form of postmillennialism.

By the assertion that there is no reign of righteousness in the far distant future, only after which Christ can return, amillennialism allows us to hope that Christ will return soon.

This blessed hope, as the first few paragraphs of this chapter indicated, sustains one's equilibrium and equanimity under the intolerable moral and political conditions of this century.

Peoples that have not emerged from savagery have a vote in the United Nations and help in their irresponsible way to control our lives. Communistic Russia was granted several votes in that unfortunate organization, but the United States has only one. Delivering China from the terror of Chiang Kai Chek to the beneficent rule of the Reds can be explained only as insanity sent by God to punish a disobedient people. Within the United States, republican government is breaking down under the impact of mob demonstrations. And the college population wallows in liquor and lewdness.

The world is very evil; the times are waxing late.

Be sober and keep vigil; the Judge is at the gate:

The Judge that comes in mercy, the Judge that comes in might,

To terminate the evil, to diadem the right.

We look forward to and hope for the appearance of our Lord Jesus Christ, when he shall have dominion from sea to sea, when his enemies shall lick the dust, when all kings shall fall down before him and all nations serve him. Even so come, Lord Jesus.

THE REFORMED FAITH AND THE WESTMINSTER CONFESSION[1]

By the invitation of *The Southern Presbyterian Journal* I have the privilege of addressing this distinguished and consecrated audience on the subject of the Reformed Faith and the Westminster Confession. This title is not to be interpreted as introducing an exposition of the Confession's thirty-three chapters with their several articles. Nor does it announce an historical account of the Westminster Assembly and the later role of its great creed. On the contrary, I propose to speak of the significance of the Westminster Confession as an existing document, a document to which ministers and churches subscribe as defining their policy and stating their reason for existence, a document that distinguishes Biblical Christianity from all other forms of thought and belief. Moreover I hope to indicate, all too briefly, its significance with reference to contemporary circumstances. For this purpose it seems best to divide the document into two parts, Chapter I and all the rest.

Chapter I of the Westminster Confession asserts that the Scriptures of the Old and New Testaments are the Word of God written. Its sixty-six books are all given by inspiration of God. The authority for which Holy Scripture ought to be believed and obeyed dependeth wholly upon God, the author thereof. In these books the whole counsel of God for man's salvation is either expressly set down or by good and necessary consequence may be deduced from its statements. Therefore, concludes Chapter I, the Supreme Judge, by whom all decrees of councils and doctrines of men are to be examined, and in whose sentence we are to rest, can be no other but the Holy Spirit speaking in the Scripture.

One day I stood beside a small lake in the Rocky Mountains of Wyoming. Water flowed out of the lake from both ends. The water that flowed out one end descended into the stifling canyons and blistering deserts of Utah and Arizona; the water that flowed

---

1. An address given at Weaverville, N. C., August 17, 1955.

out the other end of this lake went through the fertile fields of the Midwest. I was standing on the great continental divide.

Metaphorically the first chapter of the Westminster Confession is a continental divide. Although the written Word of God has been the touchstone of pure doctrine in all ages, the twentieth century shows still more clearly that this chapter forms the great divide between two types of religion, or to make it of broader application, between two types of philosophy. Perhaps it would be plainer to say that the acceptance of the Bible as God's written revelation separates true Christianity from all other types of thought. In order to be specific and in order to face our immediate responsibilities, let us select two contemporary schools of philosophy, each of which in its own way contrasts sharply with the first chapter of our Confession.

The first of these two and the more obviously anti-Christian movement is variously called naturalism, secularism, or humanism. These names are simply more complimentary titles for what formerly was bluntly called atheism. The purpose of this meeting may not seem to call for a discussion of atheism; with its denial of God and therefore of revelation, naturalism may appear to be a philosophical development that the Church can afford to ignore. But a church that ignores secular humanism is simply shutting its eyes to the situation around about and failing to maintain the first chapter of the Confession against all opponents. Unfortunately brevity is required, and therefore without any reference to communism, the most blatant form of atheism, mention will be made only of certain political and certain educational events on the American scene.

In recent civil and public life there has developed an opposition to the practice of Christianity. According to reports by the National Association of Evangelicals an adoption agency stamped "Psychologically Unfit" on the application papers of a wide-awake minister and his wife. A navy chaplain tells of attempts, successful attempts, to discharge active Christian young men as psychotic. In another public field, the city of Indianapolis refuses the use of its parks to Christian groups if they so much as intend to ask a blessing at mealtime or sing a hymn. Other groups may hold their programs, but Christian groups are discriminated against. Then again the released time program for religious instruction is an object of attack. The strategy of the humanist is to occupy the time and the attention of children to such an extent that they will have no opportunity to hear the Gospel. The public schools with their compulsory attendance are to be used for the inculcation of secularism. And those who oppose secularism and who want to give their children Christian instruction are branded as anti-social, undemocratic, and divisive. Such events are straws in the wind, which show how the humanists are using government agencies to curtail religious liberty.

Behind these particular events stands the naturalistic philosophy that is taught, I mean, that is inculcated, in a number of American colleges and universities. Let it not be thought that professors are uniformly objective and indifferently teach all views alike. Secularism is actively forced upon the students. For example, consider the statement of Millard S. Everett, a professor in Roosevelt College, Chicago, quoted in *Philosophy in the Classroom,* page 27, by J. H. Melzer: "Our course is built and conducted along liberal lines. Moreover, we have not confused liberalism with indifferentism or neutrality on basic issues, but we have organized the course definitely for the purpose of increasing the student's acceptance of the scientific attitude, liberal and secular morality, and the democratic goal of liberty and equality. We . . . leave no doubt in the student's mind by the end of the term that we stand with the forces of democracy, science, and modern culture." With this espousal of secularism in black and white, one can more easily give credence to the rumor that there are universities which will not knowingly graduate a student who is a fundamentalist.

From our benighted Christian viewpoint these humanists do not seem to have much understanding of the laws of logic. They take the principle of the separation of church and state and consider it reprehensible to use public school facilities for released time education. The American Civil Liberties Union will go to court against released time, but I have never heard of their opposing the use of tax money for anti-Christian instruction. They have never sued a university for teaching secularism. They will defend communists; they will defend the publishers of obscene comic books; but when have they ever defended religious liberty or protested against the inculcation of humanism in tax-supported institutions? Consistency does not seem to be one of their virtues.

Christian opposition to humanism has ordinarily been ineffective politically and has often been worthless philosophically. In attacking a materialistic or mechanistic world view, Christians have sometimes pontificated that no one can believe the universe to be the result of chance. Unfortunately this is not true. There are many people who do so believe; and until Christian thinkers face the realities of the situation, improvement cannot reasonably be expected.

Not every minister, not every church, has a profitable occasion of combatting the sources of humanism. Only in exceptional cases can a minister come face to face with naturalistic professors and authors. Only rarely can a minister answer these men in print. There are some churches, situated in university towns, that have opportunities of working with students. It is to be hoped that they also have the equipment to be effective. Each of us should examine his own situation to see what his possibilities are. Most unfortunately shortsightedness or selfishness sometimes produces a tragedy. There was one church in a university city, whose minister wanted to work with the students. There was also a group of students willing to help him. The situation was ideal—but for one thing: the congregation could not see the university as a mission field, complained that their minister was neglecting them, and forced his resignation.

All the more honor to those congregations and pastors who take this part of their responsibilities seriously. And all honor to the few colleges that are Christian, not in name only, but in actual instruction. And all honor to those who are founding Christian primary schools where God is not ignored, treated as unimportant or non-existent. The opportunity and responsibility of establishing Christian grade schools is one that I should like to urge upon you, but time and my subject forbid.

At the beginning of this paper I stated that the first chapter of the Confession, on divine revelation, is the great divide between two types of thought. On the one side of this divide stands naturalism, secularism, or humanism. But it does not stand alone. Also on the same side of the great divide is another system of thought. This system asserts, even vigorously asserts, the existence of God, at least some kind of God, and goes so far as to speak of revelation; but what it says about God and revelation is so opposed to the first chapter of the Confession that Christianity, far from welcoming its support, must regard it as a most subtle and deceptive enemy. I refer to what is often called neo-orthodoxy.

The originator of neo-orthodoxy was the Danish thinker Soren Kierkegaard. With his penetrating mind he saw that the Hegelian Absolute was not the God of Abraham, Isaac, and Jacob. With his passionate nature he revolted against the stolid ecclesiastical formalism of his day. The Lutheran church was dead. Some might describe the situation as dead orthodoxy. But Ludwig Feuerbach, Kierkegaard's contemporary, diagnosed the situation, not as dead orthodoxy, but as lively hypocrisy. The people went to church on Sunday and paid lip service to what they did not believe. They were not orthodox but pagan at heart. Yet the empty form remained. Against this deadly disease, Kierkegaard stressed passionate appropriation and personal decision. With biting sarcasm he flayed hypocrisy, contrasted the despised Christians of the first century with the respectable sham of nineteenth century Europe, and urged more emotion, less intellect, more suffering, less complacency, more subjectivity, less objectivity.

No doubt Kierkegaard was substantially correct in viewing the church as too formal, too Hegelian, too pagan. And no devout person can quarrel with the need of personal decision and appropriation. But, and this is the important point, if a person is to appropriate, there must be something to be appropriated. Kierkegaard and his present day followers, for all their talk about God and revelation, offer us little or nothing to appropriate. Kierkegaard himself said, "Christ did not propose any doctrine; he acted. He did not teach that there is redemption for men; he redeemed them." Now, it is true that Christ redeemed his elect; it is true that he acted; it is even true that his chief mission was not to teach; but it is untrue that Christ proposed no doctrines. Kierkegaard wrote a book called *Either-Or*, and he too often practiced such a principle. A better principle is Both-And. Christ both acted and he taught. Moreover he especially commissioned his disciples to teach, to teach a great many doctrines, found in Romans, Corinthians, and the rest of the New Testament.

Because Kierkegaard offers us nothing to appropriate and puts all his stress on the subjective feeling of appropriation, it makes no difference whether we worship God or idols. In his engaging literary style Kierkegaard describes two men: one is in a Lutheran church and entertains a true conception of God, but because he prays in a false spirit, he is in truth praying to an idol. The other man is in a heathen temple praying to idols; but since he prays with an infinite passion he is in truth praying to God. Once again Kierkegaard acts on the principle of Either-Or instead of Both-And. Both the Lutheran who prays in a false spirit and the heathen who prays to idols are displeasing to God. Just because a heathen has some intense passionate experiences, it does not follow that he is worshiping the true God. But for Kierkegaard the truth is found in the inward How, not in the external What. What a man worships makes no difference. It is his passion that counts. "An objective uncertainty," says Kierkegaard, "held fast in an appropriation process of the most passionate inwardness is the truth, the highest truth attainable for an existing individual . . . If only the How of this relation is in truth, then the individual is in truth, even though he is thus related to untruth."

However peculiar this type of philosophy may be, contemporary Protestantism is largely dominated by it. The neo-orthodox ministers may talk about God and revelation, but they do not have in mind the objective God and the objective revelation of the Westminster Confession. They do not believe that the Bible tells the truth. For example, Emil Brunner, who through his books and through his one-time position in Princeton Theological Seminary has become popular in the United States, is so far removed from the Confession that he holds neither the words of Scripture nor the thoughts of Scripture to be the truth. To quote: "All words have merely an instrumental significance. Not only the linguistic expressions but even the conceptual content is not the thing itself, but just its framework, its receptacle, and medium." A few pages later he continues, "God can . . . speak his word to a man even through false doctrine." God then reveals himself in falsehood and untruth. What a revelation!

This type of theology is to be explained partly as a reaction to the immanentism of Hegel, for whom God or the Absolute is nothing other than the unity of the total universe. For Hegel, without the world there could be no God. Kierkegaard, Brunner, and their disciples want a transcendent God. Either immanence,

279

or transcendence; not both-and. By insisting on the transcendence of God they are able to cloak themselves with the pseudo-piety of their infinite passion and to deceive many Christians who know little about German theology. They can quote Scripture: of course it may be false, but it still is a revelation. For example, in exalting God above all human limitations they remind us that God's thoughts are not our thoughts. Therefore, they say, the divine Mind is so far above our finite minds that there is not a single point of coincidence between his knowledge and ours. When a Calvinist attempts to reason with them logically, they disparagingly contrast human logic with divine paradox. God is totally other. He is never an object of our thought. In one ecclesiastical meeting I heard a minister say, the human mind possesses no truth at all. And last year in Europe I visited a certain professor who asserted that we can have no absolute truth whatever. When he said that, I took a piece of paper and wrote on it, We can have no absolute truth whatever; I showed him the writing, the sentence— We can have no absolute truth whatever; then I asked, Is that sentence absolute truth? Do you not see that if the human mind can have no truth, it could not have the truth that it has no truth. If we know nothing, we could not know we know nothing. And if there is no point of coincidence between God's knowledge and ours, it rigorously follows, since God knows everything, that we know absolutely nothing.

With such skepticism it is not surprising that their religion consists in a passionate inwardness that appropriates nothing objective. Unfortunately skepticism, particularly when discussed in such an academic tone as this address, does not provoke as passionate a reaction among the evangelically minded as it ought. But one ought to realize that even the most gentle and innocuous skepticism is sufficient to defeat the Gospel. To speed the dissolution of Christianity it is not necessary to say that we know a contrary philosophy is true; it is equally effective to say that we do not know anything is true. The Gospel is a message of positive content, and whether it is dogmatically denied or merely silenced makes little difference.

What is more unfortunate is that the skepticism of neo-orthodoxy is especially insidious. Men who adopt the position of Kierkegaard and Brunner not only make use of terms such as God and revelation, but they also talk of sin and justification. Some of them might even preach a tolerably good 'sermon on imputed right-eousness. This deceives simple-minded believers. When people hear the familiar words they naturally assume that the familiar ideas are meant. They fail to see that the neo-orthodox consider neither the words nor even the intellectual content to be the truth. Although the sermon may be on Adam and the fall, the neo-orthodox minister understands the words in a mythological sense. Adam is the myth by which we are stimulated to an infinite passion.

Although it is to be expected, it is still discouraging to see rightminded people deceived by this sort of talk. At the meeting of the World Council at Evanston, the European theologians supported the notion of an apocalyptic return of Christ. In contrast with the American theologians who place their hope in a future socialistic government, the talk of an apocalypse sounded refreshing; and the poorly informed, those who had not studied the history of German thought in the last century, congratulated themselves on signs of a return to Biblical thinking. In this vain imagination the evangelicals are completely deceived. They need to be alerted to the wiles of the devil.

But if it is unfortunate to be deceived, what can be said about the deceivers? Ever since Arius twisted Scriptural language to avoid the crushing arguments of Athanasius, unbelievers in the church have used Scriptural phraseology to disguise their underlying meaning. What a contrast with the policy of the Westminster divines. They spared no effort to make their statements clear, unambiguous, and completely honest. Their purpose was not to deceive or conceal, but to explain and clarify. And so carefully did they define their terms that it is almost impossible for a normal intelligence to mistake the meaning. Not only was the intellectual content plainly put forward, but it was made plain and intelligible by a careful attention to the words they chose.

The Reformers and their successors in the following century were honest; many of the ecclesiastical leaders of the present century are not. They take solemn ordination vows, subscribing to the Westminster Confession; but they do not believe it is the truth. Perjurers in the pulpit! What a tragedy for the people in the pews! And what a tragedy also for those ministers!

The late J. Gresham Machen was an honest man and a brilliant scholar. In 1925 he published a salutary volume entitled, *What Is Faith?* Although he was not particularly concerned with neo-orthodoxy at that time, his first chapter is an incisive attack on skepticism and anti-intellectualism. He stressed the truth, the objective truth of the Bible and the primacy of the intellect. Today, thirty years later, the book should be re-read, for neo-orthodoxy is even more anti-intellectual than the old modernism. And if skepticism prevails, if there is no truth, no gospel that the human mind can grasp, we might as well worship idols in a heathen temple.

On the other side of the continental divide the water flows in the opposite direction. Instead of the stifling deserts of Arizona, the Mississippi Valley with its wheat and corn come into view. Here we have life and the fruits of the soil. However, not all the soil, not all the rivers on the east of the divide are equally fruitful. Had there been time today, it would have been possible to give an ample description of two rivers, but as it is, only an indication can be attempted. There is one stream which, accepting the Scripture as the only and infallible rule of faith and practice, does not accept all the other thirty-two chapters of the Confession. Though it may accept several, and be called broadly evangelical, it rejects chapter three and other chapters which are definitely Calvinistic. The waters of this stream flow in the same general direction, and we rejoice that they eventually reach the same heavenly ocean; but they flow through stony ground with sparse vegetation, or sometimes they ooze through swamps where the vegetation is dense enough but unhealthful and useless. This stream in its rocky course babbles about faith and repentance being the cause instead of the result of regeneration; and it claims that its swampy free will can either block or render effective the almighty power of God. All there is time to say of this stream of thought is that its inconsistencies make it an easy prey to the attacks of humanism. It cannot defend the principle of revelation because it has misunderstood the contents of revelation.

On the other hand that blest river of salvation, flowing through the land of tall corn and sturdy cattle, is to be identified with the doctrines of the great Reformers. These men and their disciples in the following century studied out and wrote down the system of doctrine which the Presbyterian and Reformed churches

282

still profess. The Westminster Confession is no abbreviated creed written by men of abbreviated faith. On the contrary it is the nearest approach men have yet made to a full statement of the whole counsel of God which Paul did not fail to declare. The Westminster divines were the best Biblical scholars of their time and as a group have not been surpassed since. For a full five years or more they labored unremittingly to formulate their summary of what the Bible teaches. And so successful were they that their document is justly the basis of many denominations. The factual existence of the Westminster Confession testifies to several of these convictions of our spiritual forebears; and three of these convictions may serve as a conclusion to this talk.

First, our forefathers were convinced, the Westminster Confession asserts, and the Bible teaches that God has given us a written revelation. This revelation is the truth. As Christ himself said, Thy word is truth. It is not a myth, it is not an allegory, it is no mere pointer to the truth, it is not an analogy of the truth; but it is literally and absolutely true.

Second, our forefathers were convinced and the Reformed Faith asserts that this truth can be known. God has created us in his image with the intellectual and logical powers of understanding. He has addressed to men an intelligible revelation and he expects us to read it, to grasp its meaning, and to believe it. God is not totally other, nor is logic a human invention that distorts God's statements. If this were so, as the neo-orthodox say, then it would follow, as the neo-orthodox admit, that falsity would be as useful as truth in producing a passionate emotion. But the Bible expects us to appropriate a definite message.

Third, the Reformers believed that God's revelation can be formulated accurately. They were not enamored of ambiguity; they did not identify piety with a confused mind. They wanted to proclaim the truth with the greatest possible clarity. And so ought we.

Dare we allow our Biblical heritage to be lost in a nebulous ecumenicity where belief has been reduced to the shortest possible doctrinal statement, in which peace is preserved by an all-embracing ambiguity? Or should we ponder the fact that when the Reformers preached the complete Biblical message in all its detail and with the greatest possible clarity, God granted the world its greatest spiritual awakening since the days of the apostles. May we not similarly expect astonishing blessings if we return with enthusiasm to all the doctrines of the Westminster Confession?

to swift physical action to counter any errors of judgement.

Dracula enjoys an exaggerated gymnastic animal repertoire. He can climb face-foremost down a castle wall, gripping the vertical surface with toes and fingers — though of course he does not fear death should he fall, being immune to the natural laws of mortality. These wall-descending activities are described as 'lizard-like' (*D* 3:47). Later, Dracula's agility is expressed as 'panther-like'; he has a 'snarl' on his face; and shows 'lion-like disdain' (*D* 23:364). His general empathy with the animal world is demonstrated by his control over the lower forms of life: rats, bats, and wolves.

In many other of his attributes and propensities Dracula is a classical example of the vampire spoken of in European folklore. Being undead, his flesh is icy to the touch; he casts no reflection in the mirror, and when standing in front of flames does not obstruct a view of them. He is unable to impose his presence on a victim at the time of first contact, unless the target shows complicity in some form. This is evident in Harker's stepping over the threshold at Castle Dracula (*D* 2:26), and in the Count's later visits to Lucy and Renfield (*D* 21:332). Dracula possesses enormous physical strength and speed of movement; his eyes can induce hypnotic effects; and with selective victims he is capable of psychic transfer.

Dracula can direct the elements around him, such as creating a puff of wind. He can see in the dark and vaporize himself at will. He is able to change into a dog, wolf, or bat; he can dematerialize to be transported as mist; and he can take shape from phosphorescent specks riding on moonbeams — which can themselves weaken powers of resistance. He is restricted by the presence of running water, being unable to cross it except at the slack or flood of the tide, unless with manual assistance. He sleeps and wakes with the precision of clockwork — dawn and dusk being calculated to the second. While sleeping, Dracula appears to be dead, eyes open with no pulse or respiratory motion. All the while he is 'conscious' of activity around him, although searching hands cannot 'wake' him (*D* 4:67).

Crucially, although Dracula can be repelled by garlic and other pagan safeguards, he is essentially a vampire of the Christian mould. In other words he is a representative/client/manifestation of the devil (in London he aptly assumes the alias 'Count *de Ville*' [*D* 20:326]) and must therefore be shown to be vulnerable to Christian icons and imagery. The crucifix — arch-symbol of the Christian faith — makes him recoil and cower, and the application of a Holy

Wafer can sterilize his place of rest.[5]

But Stoker was not content to restrict his vampire-king within the parameters prescribed by folklore. Dracula would have to be special, both in his attributes and in his manner of becoming a vampire. In particular, there are several qualities about Dracula which differentiate him from more common varieties of his ilk. The first concerns Stoker's insistence that Dracula can sleep only in consecrated earth: 'in soil barren of holy memories [he] cannot rest' (D 18:288). This requirement would seem to possess neither folkloric nor historic antecedent.[6] According to the superstition of Orthodox lands, the undead, if excommunicated, were reputedly *unable* to rest in hallowed soil. Stoker probably intends Dracula's sacrilege to heighten the reader's sense of outrage and blasphemy: it also makes the Count's lairs harder to locate, 'sleeping' deceitfully as he is among God's true dead. And, of course, Vlad Tepes himself was buried in consecrated earth.

Another example of Dracula's uniqueness as a vampire is his immunity to the rays of the sun. The vampire of superstition is the quintessential apparition of night; it being assumed that sunlight could pass through, or harm, sensitive tissue. Dracula, however, cannot be destroyed by direct sunlight as film versions would have us believe. That would make him too vulnerable. Once he is strong and vigorous from the consumption of fresh blood, he is permitted in the book to wander the streets of London quite naturally. The only handicap is that his vampire powers become neutralized during the hours of daylight, when he reverts, to all intents, to being a mere mortal. He must therefore take care that at the moment of sunrise he is in the place and form that he wishes to be for the coming day. Otherwise he must await the precise moment of noon or sunset to effect the desired transference (D 22:347-8).

Most important of all, Stoker could not allow his arch-fiend to have become a vampire originally by any of the numerous qualifying procedures, for they all imply falling victim in some manner. Count Dracula can be a victim of nobody and nothing. As he has become a vampire it must be because he *wanted* to be one. He was neither bitten whilst alive by another undead, nor was he sentenced to a vampiric punishment for any of the appropriate transgressions. In his human life, Count Dracula was an alchemist and magician. He had studied the secrets of the black arts and other aspects of devilry through being a student at the Scholomance (D 18:288; 23:360) — a mythical academy situated high in the Carpathian Mountains overlooking the town of Sibiu